ANITA LESLIE
has also written

Train to Nowhere
Love in a Nutshell

LEONARD JEROME

THE FABULOUS
LEONARD JEROME

ANITA LESLIE

With 37 Illustrations

HUTCHINSON
STRATFORD PLACE, LONDON

Hutchinson & Co. (Publishers) Ltd.
London   Melbourne   Sydney   Auckland
Bombay   Cape Town   New York   Toronto

First published November 1954
Reprinted . . January 1955

Set in eleven point Monotype Bembo
one point leaded

Printed in Great Britain
by The Anchor Press, Ltd.,
Tiptree, Essex

"To Bill, my husband, who helped,
and to my children Richard Tarka
and little Leonie, who did not."

"I too lived—Brooklyn of ample hills, was mine;
I too walked the streets of Manhattan Island, and
    bathed in the waters around it;
I too felt the abrupt questionings stir within me."

WALT WHITMAN.

ACKNOWLEDGEMENTS

I wish to express my gratitude to:

My father Shane Leslie who handed over his notebooks, scrap albums and many anecdotes concerning Leonard Jerome; Clare Sheridan who lent the letters written to her mother by King Milan of Serbia and descriptions of life at the Tuileries and at Compiègne; Seymour Leslie who ransacked his tin trunks and entertained me with many reminiscences pertinent to this book; Hugh Frewen of Sydney, Australia; Captain Oswald Frewen and Roger Frewen of Brede Place, Sussex; and to my brothers John I. Leslie and Desmond Leslie who assisted me to collect material.

I am also indebted to:

W. de Witt Manning of Rochester.

Dr. Blake McKelvey, City Historian of Rochester.

The Board of Union College.

The Board of Princeton College.

Professor Wertenbaker of Princeton.

The New York Historical Society.

The New York Public Library.

The Metropolitan Opera Guild.

My thanks are due to Sir Winston Churchill and Odhams Press Ltd. for permission to quote from *My Early Life* and *Lord Randolph Churchill*; and to Lloyd Morris and Random House Inc. for permission to quote from *Incredible New York*.

I would also like to express gratitude to the late Mr. Rudolph Bernauer for the trouble he took in discovering how Leonard Jerome lived when in Trieste in the eighteen fifties.

JEROME FAMILY TREE

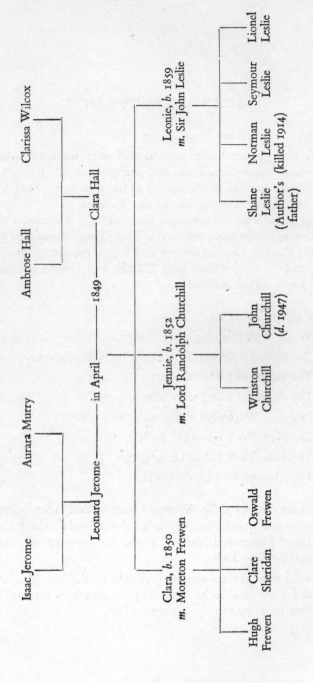

LIST OF ILLUSTRATIONS

PROLOGUE

Soft rain pattered on the attic roof. From the dormer window we looked out over hillsides of slate roofing and could hardly see the lake with its rush-lined shore where wild duck had rested since days when the Great Irish Elk came from the forests to drink, or to slip and die, leaving their bones fos-silized in the mud. An entire long corridor in one of the wings of our straggling house had been lined with glass cases containing pre-historic remnants dug from the bog; bronze swords and petrified butter lightening a somewhat tedious collection of bones and massive antlers.

When it was wet, we used to be turned loose to play among these oddities, a diversion which kept us quiet in the sense that our screams could not be heard in the rest of the house. Tutors and governesses, groaning at their incarceration in the depths of Ireland could, for a time, ignore their charges who had, they complained, "too much American blood".

But today we were, surprisingly as it always seemed in this house of our childhood, for good or for bad, grown up. The forbidden upstairs rooms had become ours by inheritance; we turned keys as we willed, opened monster cupboards built to contain the wired skirts of former ages, and rummaged through boxes of useless trinkets. Enamelled lorgnettes with gold initials tumbled out of voluminous nightdresses of hand-embroidered lawn and beneath layers of fine petticoats we found hats all decked with roses and ostrich plumes. One we knew well and carefully replaced. Grandmother had worn it "the day he proposed". Sentimentally she had carried it around for years in the brass-handled trunk, nearly four feet square, needing two men to lift, known as a 'hat box'. In the end it rested here, in the rambling musty-smelling top storey, where, as she often sighed, "there seems room for all the junk in the world". Camphor, lavender and dust filled the air and made our eyes tingle but we toiled on obsessed by this occupation, so perfectly in keeping with the drip of rain-drops.

Trunk after trunk could be dragged out and our fingers turned back layers of thick satin, and rotting fragile lace. We found the 18th-century brocade suit worn by a great-great-grandfather, Charles Leslie, one of the many Irish gentlemen who refused a Peerage and voted against the Union of Ireland to England. Evidently his best suit, he had worn it when being painted by Gilbert Stuart. The portrait hung in the dining-room, but it did not reveal the quality of this brocade which sprang alive in our fingers. The years seemed to have been rolled up in tissue paper and locked here into cedar-wood chests.

From one vast Victorian trunk with a padded interior we drew out the ball-gown of heavy rose-coloured satin embossed with flowers which our grandmother had worn at Dublin's Viceregal Lodge in the eighties. Then, gasping and laughing, we tried on the brilliant orange dress of thick corded silk made by Worth for Lady Randolph Churchill. Silken stitches inside the nineteen-inch waist band dated it 1876 and a ticket read: "Jennie's smartest day dress. Keep." And in the dark recess of a high alcove made presumably for the storage of countless riding boots was an old-fashioned side-saddle, marked "Count Kinsky had this saddle made for Jennie after he won the Grand National on Zoedone in 1883 no one thought an Austrian could." (She meant, of course, win the race.)

In a tin box we found three parasols; small labels telling the story of each had been affixed to their handles. A delicate cane of carved ivory, bearing a white silk dome trimmed with a ruffle of black lace, bore the inscription: "Mrs. Jerome's parasol in the fifties. Her husband's first extravagance." I pressed down the catch and opened it carefully, half expecting the silk to crack, but the hundred-year-old material took the strain as if new.

The next parasol, drawn from its little linen bag, appeared to be made of ruched black lace, fancy and fluffy like a dark cobweb, spread on its tiny stem of carved wood. This had belonged to Leonie, our grandmother, the youngest daughter of Mr. Leonard Jerome: and the third, a work of art, bore the legend: "Given to Jennie Jerome for her wedding to Randolph Churchill April 14, 1874, and in her hand when she drove away." Her dark eyes must have flashed against the white Alençon lace, and the long exquisite handle of tortoiseshell ringed with gold been clasped tight with excitement. For Jennie was a very inflammable person, we all knew that. And as we folded away those treasures in their black paper, the 'best' dresses, the precious gifts that had been kept for a hundred years, we remembered little scenes, unwritten but recounted to us in our childhood, chiefly by that grandmother Leonie, who had been the youngest of the three astonishing Jerome sisters.

From the attic we wandered downstairs to the glass-fronted cabinet where, beside Queen Catherine Parr's needle-case, and old Bishop Leslie's 1640 'silver pen for writing on horseback', lay a tangle of family heirlooms. There was a bracelet woven of hair from the heads of Christina Leslie's "nine lovely children", and a silver medal with a bullet attached reminded us of the role played in the 1854 Crimean War by the third son of this brood. Tom Leslie had been the A.D.C. Lord Raglan sent galloping off with that famous order which started the Charge of the Light Brigade. Major

Nolan, a superior officer, snatched it from Tom's hand, and delivered the message with a wrong insinuation to Lord Lucan. As the 'noble six hundred' charged, Nolan had his head blown off, which saved him a court martial. Meanwhile Lord Raglan picked this Russian bullet from Tom's leg and posted it off with a line of praise to his mother. "Someone had blundered. . . ." But for once it was not a Leslie!

A large glass box contained the Duke of Wellington's bridle and bit used at Waterloo; he had sent it to the Charles Leslie of the day with a note of thanks for paying for his education as a boy at Trim School, near Dargan Castle. (Mrs. Charles Leslie was a sister of the Duke's mother, Lady Mornington.)

Around these knick-knacks a few later souvenirs had been stacked and forgotten. Leonard Jerome's consular sword, decorated with a medallion of Emperor Francis Joseph and purchased in Trieste in 1852, lay entangled with his horseshoe-shaped gold racing badge, on which his name had been engraved. And folded around them was a thin shirt of white and blue stripes, the racing colours which gallant Kentucky had often carried past the winning-post. Mr. Jerome's feelings for his greatest horse had been clearly epitomized in a coloured print which hung in the hall. Kentucky, fine-necked and with rolling eye, occupied the entire foreground, while Leonard waved from a six-horsed coach in the back of the picture. Enlarging lens could reveal his friend James Gordon Bennett sitting beside him, while two ladies in bonnets, identifiable as Mrs. Jerome and the beautiful Mrs. Ronalds, peeped at Jerome Park Club house.

That was almost all we knew. Mr. Jerome had raced horses and sailed yachts, and was an American. "Rather a rare thing to be," a great-aunt had once told us; "nowadays quite usual but then considered strange and original." The badge lured me on to the chest of letters. Here when I delved amidst packets of envelopes, which my grandmother's unmistakable pencil had marked "family twaddle", a medley of forgotten incidents could be deciphered dimly illuminating a background for the brocade gowns and the three parasols.

I began to wonder what he had really been like, that Mr. Jerome of New York who created a fine stir in the sixties, and whose daughters had swept the board of London society for the next forty years. Faded sepia photographs filled several albums but comments were scarce. One might start making a few enquiries, scribble down memories handed by word of mouth, and perhaps tack the fragments into a pattern.

The first book mentioning old Jerome which I happened to pick up was *Clipperships*, by Frank Griswold. The author had never interested me before although I had heard of him as a well-known sportsman. The bundles of letters revealed that he had tried to marry our grandmother. So had Freddie Gebhart, and after she refused him he "made a perfect fool of himself over Lily Langtry". Leonard wrote cryptically, "tell Leonie it is well she escaped that match". One letter written to her years later fell from the package in my hand. It was from Griswold and commented in restrospect:

"You are quite right about Freddie Gebhart, he was a lovable boy that never grew up, and his weakness which was so attractive was his undoing. We often talk of him still. You were lucky not to marry him, or me either, for I was too much of a butterfly in those days to have made a good husband. It was the hunt after foxes and petticoats that occupied my mind."

Griswold admired the father as well as the daughter.

"When I was a boy," reveals his book, "Mr. Jerome took me out in his sledge, built like a yacht to commemorate *Henrietta's* victory across the Atlantic. The thing that struck me most was that he drove the horses ten miles through the snow without putting on gloves."

This at least gave a clue to great-grandfather Jerome's blood-stream!

My father had done a good deal of family research. Every drawer and chest and cupboard of the old house contained notes in his neat script and whereas it had been grandmother's habit to tantalize the future by tucking away some pin-cushion in an envelope saying "given to A——, by Z——, 1880, so in love, all letters burnt", her eldest son, the scholar of a sporting family, showed no such tact. When he rummaged through the family documents the dots were sure to be placed on the i's. He had jotted down a few vivid impressions of that gaunt old American who died in a Brighton boarding-house in 1891. No little family distress occurred when old Mr. Jerome refused to be comforted by religion. Carriages had drawn up at his London house daily, with flowers and jelly and Bibles. But after beginning with Genesis my great-grandpapa soon laid the Old Testament aside, remarking "What *horrible* people," and refused to read another word. He did not want condolence either. What he did desire was the sight of romping grand-children and this his doctor frowned at.

As the fogs descended cold and thick over the city, Mr. Jerome was ordered to Brighton for better air. His wife chose Lyon Mansions near the sea. She had stayed on this front with her girls when in flight from the Franco-Prussian war in 1870. Three rooms sufficed. Most of Leonard's fortunes were dispersed, and he had the simplest of tastes.

During the last days he lay quietly, watching the firelight flicker over his bedroom wall, flaring into sudden patterns before they faded into twilight. Soon he knew the coals must cease to glow. Soon it would be night and very quiet. But he liked the darkness as well as the day, for there had been enough of light and brilliance and violent pace. It made no difference to him where he died, an English boarding-house with the sea-rain beating against the window pane would suffice for this brief back cloth. Having wrung so much out of life he must have been ready to go.

But firelight awakens the memory of old loves and for him there had been many. With intensity he had cared if not with single mind. Music had been his quest, but not his goal. Women learnt they must share his heart with gallant horses and with great schooners straining under storm-canvas in Atlantic gales. . . .

A packet of newspaper cuttings fell at my feet, yellowed obituaries which called Leonard Jerome millionaire and sportsman. Wall Street quoted him as a legend, citing fortunes lost as well as made; the Racing Clubs he founded named him Father of the American Turf; and crews he had sailed with spoke of a 'staunch comrade'. We knew more than this. Many a woman must have paused, wistfully thinking for a moment, "So he is gone, dear Leonard; there was never another like him and surely he loved me the best."

All of his acquaintances struggled to record his intense aliveness. Many of the notices used the word 'gentleman', throwing him into clear-cut perspective against a vital ungentlemanly background. One New Yorker wrote: "I have known Leonard Jerome going on for thirty years now, and I've got just one thing to say about him. He was a white man and a gentleman if ever there was one;" and another: "One rode better, sailed better, banquetted better when Mr. Jerome was of the company."

There must have been more to his story. My father, a little boy of six, had been among the solemn grand-children brought to wave from behind a screen when the old man lay dying, and Cousin Clare Sheridan remembered her shoulder ribbons being tied into bows by grandmother Jerome for the occasion.

His three daughters—Clara, Jennie and Leonie—had stood sombre by the bedside. In vain he tried to make them smile: "I've given you all I have," he said. "Pass it on."

He meant strength and joy of life not the debris of his fortunes, and with gratitude he looked towards the screen beyond which his grand-children were not allowed to venture. Yet there was not an American among them, and to one born and bred as he, and with no son of his own, this rankled.

Frequently he mentioned the eldest, Winston Leonard Spencer-Churchill, his sixteen-year-old namesake. When this boy had been born to Jennie and her English husband Lord Randolph Churchill, Mrs. Jerome had been shocked by a racing friend who wrote, "Interesting breeding, stamina goes through the dam, and pace through the sire." What might this first grand-child grow into? Would he unite Jennie's vital force and Randolph's nervous brilliance? Or continue his present determination to prove himself a dunce at Harrow? Might America hear of him? Old Mr. Jerome hoped so, but the boy belonged to that very aristocracy whose influence America had repudiated, in the War of Independence, and again in the Civil War when the southern landowners saw their way of life destroyed for ever.

Leonard belonged to the hard core of new America. His grandson belonged to old England.

Could the double heritage enable any man to understand and serve both?

I

TURNING back the pages I found a few clues. Leonard Jerome had been born in 1818 in a straggling white farmhouse near Syracuse in western New York. He came of well-to-do pioneer stock and was the fifth of eight brothers. There was also one sister, Mary. A lanky boy with dark grey eyes, black hair and long sinewy limbs, Leonard apparently "crashed around indoors". His mother's complaints were accompanied by the statement that he was "good on the farm and very musical". All the Jerome boys were strong and worked hard from early youth. Their animal vitality seems to have slightly distressed their diligent, God-fearing parents. Among the nine youngsters Leonard was the most restless and rebellious. Trouble continually came his way.

Isaac Jerome, father of this large animated brood, thought it wicked to care about enjoyment. When he perceived a frivolous, happy-go-lucky turn of mind in one of his boys he thought they were on the road to hell. The Jeromes came of a line of French Protestants who had left La Rochelle for religious reasons and always taken life seriously.[1] Isaac tried to beat the Puritan code into his sons but neither scoldings nor switchings lessened the smile on Leonard's wide mouth.

Leonard's earliest memories were of a bustling kichen where children were discouraged from falling under people's feet, and sent off on farm

---

[1] The Jeromes were proud of their Huguenot blood. Timothy Jerome, the first to become an American, had sailed from the Isle of Wight in 1710, and founded a home in Meriden, Connecticut. His son, Samuel, moved to Massachusetts, and built a house about two miles from Stockbridge (still standing and owned by Mr. Rodney Proctor). Samuel's son, Aaron, married Betsy Ball (a cousin of George Washington's mother), and settled in the Berkshire hills. He experimented with wheat, specialized in breeding cattle, and raised crops to feed the local expanding villages. The eldest of his sons, born in 1786, was Leonard's father Isaac, who in 1812 had bought land near his grandfather's Stockbridge home. The 1812–15 war against England broke out soon after he had married a young Scots woman Aurora Murray, and all through this period military activities kept him away soldiering. When the snows of 1815 melted, Isaac Jerome, now a Captain, returned home with his troops, and asked his wife to move west. In 1816 Isaac and Aurora Jerome and their small children moved westward by stage coach and wagon to Syracuse, where they purchased a large tract of land. The Indians had retreated into their own settlements and life was safe and pleasant in the beautiful wooded valleys that lay east of the Genesee. The Jerome house, built of wood and painted white, lay on a hillside with a wide view, and here Leonard, the fifth son, had been born.

errands. The young Jeromes could milk cows, feed cattle and manage horses, There was no time for complexes.

Aurora Jerome rustled around the house locking cupboards and sending everyone about their work. She scented linen, indexed jars of preserves and checked cider casks. When her long day ended, when the potatoes, apples, crackers and cheeses had been stored, and the butter set in a cool place, when the smallest child had been plucked from her swirling skirts and laid in its cot, she would sit down untired to make decorations for the house. Leonard remembered his mother thus, working red berries into patterned mats, and making dolls from wool and straw. She found time to re-decorate the house annually as well as having to supervise the feeding of farmworkers and family. Servant girls were scarce and continually being lured away to matrimony by the stream of settlers passing westward.

"That will teach her," Aurora would mutter, as one girl after another married and left.

The Jerome children grew up in a countryside lately carved from the wilds. As far as recollection stretched, Leonard had known the glittering fantasia of ice in winter, and spring carpets of flowers that slid from the departing snow. He learned to hunt deer or maundering bears, to kill rattle-snakes and fish trout, to canoe and sleep out in the sweet-smelling woods. All through his boyhood he gathered vegetables and fruits, and enjoyed the drama of harvesting. When snow fell he tobogganed and romped with the other boys who were growing up in the painted wooden houses, which were replacing log shacks throughout the countryside. In the village school they all learned mathematics and Latin, while in their homes they were taught to be 'God-fearing'. Most of these boys yearned to escape from parental discipline and planned to 'save up for college' or dreamed of adventure in the undiscovered realms to the west.

As one of eight brothers, Leonard could not expect a long-drawn-out expensive education. At the age of fourteen he still lived at home in the white wood house with its green Venetian shutters, but he was expected to contribute to the family exchequer.

The four eldest brothers—Allen, Thomas, Addison and Aaron—went to Princeton. Allen took a degree in theology; the others worked their way through two years, but as their father could provide only very small allowances they found the going hard. Addison set off to New York City, without a penny but confident he would soon be rich enough to help his younger brothers.

Meanwhile, Leonard obtained employment in his village store at a salary of one dollar a week. It was fun to debate the merits of scythes, axes, guns, fishing rods and ploughs, barrels of whiskey and cider. Almost all purchases had to be made through exchange instead of using ready money, and it sharpened a boy's wits to deal with the shrewd farmers who came to 'dicker' and the transients making their way westward.

After working hours, Leonard fled to his books, curled before a roaring log-fire in winter, or stretched on the porch during warm summer evenings.

Old Isaac watched his sons' efforts without comment. Life would teach them he thought; life later, and the birch now. It was quite simple.

And then one evening Leonard walked back to the white house on the hillside to find a plan being made for him. Isaac's elder brother, Hiram Jerome, become a Judge in the town of Palmyra sixty miles westward, had offered to take Leonard into his home and supervise his schooling. Leonard had long considered himself a man and eagerly accepted the change. His store career had proved successful, his salary having been increased to $2 a week, but even so, it did not look as if this would enable him to cut a swath at college. He took his money-box and felt its weight. Temptation assailed.

He never forgot the pride of purchasing his first pair of long trousers. Throughout his sixty miles journey along the Erie Canal Leonard hoped that the other passengers on the tugboat would notice the grown-up coverings on his long, coltish legs.

Casually he could then remark: "I paid for them myself."

2

JUDGE HIRAM believed in austerity and hard work. He disapproved when his nephew Aaron, while studying divine law at Princeton, wrote he had staked his every penny in the famous Mulberry Tree Speculation, but as the rage for silk-worms swept America and Aaron reaped $40,000 profit the Judge could not but express a cautious admiration. Aaron organized a hostel for destitute fellow students, and wrote jubilantly to his younger brothers that he would finance their way through college.

Overwhelmed by the sense of family riches, Leonard spent most of his own savings on a violin. Such treasures were rare in western New York and Leonard, who could play any instrument by ear, practised ceaselessly. Uncle Hiram wrote to Isaac crossly, stating that the boy was working out melodies half through the night and amusing young folk at parties.

On his next visit home Leonard took the violin with him, and pleasure in his own prowess outweighed discretion. Isaac Jerome had always ruled his household with the iron touch of the Puritan male. The Sabbath had to be fanatically observed. (Once on a late Saturday night when a deer had been driven into the farm stockades along with his cattle he forbade anyone to shoot the frightened animal for twenty-four hours, because Sunday had crept in.) It was incautious of Leonard to sneak off with his fiddle on the Lord's Day, but, unable to resist the temptation, he found a barn and played away in secret.

Disaster was inevitable. One Sunday afternoon Isaac caught the sound of far-off music. Unable to believe his ears, he strode forth to be greeted by the stark realization that melodies were issuing from the remoter cow-stall. Tracing the sounds to a wooden door, he burst in and smashed the precious violin to pieces.

For a week thunderclouds hung over the Jerome house. Aurora wept, and Leonard, simmering in silent fury, renounced God—or rather, as he put it later, "that God of father's".

At eighteen Leonard was ready for college. Aaron sent sufficient funds to cover one year at Princeton, and Addison wrote encouragingly from New

York where, according to a contemporary, he had arrived "with nothing save a brave heart and keen brain". While tramping the streets in search of a job, the first advertisement which caught Addison's eye was that of a dry-goods merchant, John Stewart. Stepping inside he asked to speak to the head of the firm; then, catching the eye of this hard-bitten personage, he held forth with such ardour that he was given a job. "You *must* try me," were the exact words he used; "give me anything however slight, and I'll write my name in your cheque book before I'm through."

Three years later he had become a partner in this firm, and could promise all the younger brothers he would see them through college.

According to the *Princeton Alumni*:

"It was upon a November day in 1836 that a stage coach drew up before the Mansion House at Princeton and a group of youths clambered out. Among them was a tall, erect, handsome boy who had come all the way from Palmyra, named Leonard Jerome. The young men stared up and down the broad street which was lined on one side with shops opposite which lay the College of New Jersey flanked by 18th century residences."

Leonard, country-bred, carried himself bravely and his efforts at earning a living had given him a certain sureness, if not quite the sophistication he wished for.

Trying to quell their apprehension, the new students crossed the street to the president's house where they handed in letters of introduction and took their entrance examinations. "When the college professors had questioned and passed him, young Jerome hastened out with a light heart to secure a room and bring over his chest." Fortunately, he was assigned to the new dormitory, East College, where he was to share No. 36 with a senior, Samuel G. Reeves of Philadelphia. When he had unpacked and arranged his few belongings, Leonard wandered out on the campus to stare at the Georgian college buildings.

"I was fluttering with nervous apprehension and the excitement of finding Nassau Hall, its white cupola half hidden in a grove of trees. Except in books I had never seen a beautiful building before. The beauties of nature had always been around me but not those of man."

Evidently Leonard had powers of concentration. According to the *Princeton Alumni*:

"At the end of his first freshman term he stood well ahead in his class with an average grade of 83·6. After the spring vacation he made a daring venture by leap-frogging an entire year to join the Sophomore class. In this advance group his grades remained high until he became a junior, when he found himself in deep water. Mathematics were never Leonard Jerome's strong point and the junior session was known at Princeton as the 'mathematical year'. He floundered with difficulty through the quagmires of analytical geometry, descriptive geometry and differential calculus but ended the summer term with a grade of 69."

Soon after coming to college Leonard applied to join the American Whig Society. Escorted to the library building he climbed to the top floor with a group of other excited entrants. They stood waiting on the landing until the door swung open to let them advance towards a red curtain hung across the east end of the room. To build up an atmosphere of drama this was suddenly drawn aside and they found themselves in a large blue hall with concave bookcases in the corners. At the far end of the room sat the society officers. As the initiates walked forward, the members rose and the moderator solemnly accepted the new initiates.

The American Whig Society was pre-eminently a literary club. They made and enforced their own discipline and fined those who "lay down on a bench or forgot themselves sufficiently to yell or tussle in public". During July and August 1837 Leonard was appointed society treasurer and kept account of the fines which ranged from 20 to 40 cents. The book includes those listed against himself.

On the fourth of July the boys were up before dawn to see the Stars and Stripes hoisted at sunrise amidst the ringing of bells and firing of cannon. After this came a string of orations, moving to a generation of young Americans, whose fathers or grandfathers had nearly all fought for their country's independence. Fireworks filled much of Leonard's letters home, and Isaac began to wonder if the young men at Princeton did not perhaps see too many 'splendid illuminations'.

Among the great teachers of this time was the scientist Joseph Henry, who was contributing to the invention of telegraph. His lectures on electro-dynamics and the decomposition of light were added to the basic formula for education, which rested almost entirely on Latin, Greek and mathematics. In a popular demonstration he would lift a group of "sneezing coughing students weighing approximately 3,500 lbs. with an enormous magnet".

The outstanding figure at Princeton was 'Johnny', Vice-President Maclean, an old scholar with white hair in a long bob, who maintained college discipline and took the Latin classes. A list of college pranks instigated by Leonard Jerome is on record. Practical jokes age worse than witticisms. We read of raids on the village for sign posts, gates, henhouses and fences, mules led upstairs to the third floor of Nassau Hall, test tubes sabotaged before chemistry class so poor Professor Torrey's experiments exploded, and tar on the seats in the prayer hall. The humour of such escapades cannot survive a hundred years. A more original effort and one which has gone down with satisfaction in Princeton history was the 1838 'Raid of the Cannon'.

During the American Revolution two cannon of different sizes were abandoned in Princeton village. The larger had been sent to New Brunswick in the War of 1812 to be added to the town's defences against expected attack. There it stood for over twenty years until in 1835 sixteen members of the Princeton Blues attempted to bring it back. But when their wagon collapsed under the weight they had to abandon the great trophy in the suburb of Queenston, east of Princeton. Three years later Leonard chose a warm summer night to rally his own troop after a meeting in Whig Hall. He made an inflamed speech laying out the strategy necessary to get the gun back to Princeton. The cheering students elected him commander-in-chief and a big band marched straight off. An unfortunate Mr. Julick, owner of a heavy wagon with strong axles, was roused from bed and his conveyance hired for the night. Leonard's own words describe the incident:

"We started a tug-of-war to raise the gun on to the truck; we had at least two hours hard work doing it. At last all being ready, the word of command was given and we marched direct for the campus. The body guard was about 100 strong. We marched in military order, silently, but treading firmly, ready to do battle to the death with anyone who dared dispute our way. Arriving at the centre of the campus, as silently as possible, the coupling of the truck was loosed, the four horses made a vigorous pull, out went the fore wheels and down went the butt end of the great gun.

At this moment a whisper of 'Johnny' echoed through the crowd. In an instant every mother's son disappeared from the gun as though it was about to burst. Poor Mr. Julick!

Vice-President Maclean (Johnny) rushed across the campus in dressing gown and slippers.

'What means this?' said he to Julick.

'All I know about it is that I was hired to bring this 'ere gun up here and dump it!'

'Very well, sir,' said the doctor, 'I command you instantly to take it away again.'

Said Julick: 'As it has taken a hundred men two hours to load it, I don't see how I am to load it up again all by myself.'

It ended by Julick drawing away his wheels and going home while the good doctor returned to bed—if not to sleep."

The cannon lay on the front campus until it was taken to Nassau Hall quadrangle to be sunk muzzle down in cement and become an object of veneration for the future.

Leonard's frolics ended when Addison started his own firm and wrote he would be unable to provide future funds. Princeton was more expensive than most colleges and Leonard had been hard pressed to make ends meet. He had given up his room in East College, and moved to a lodging, but tuition fees were $40 a year, while room rents stood at $12 and board was charged at $77. Leonard could not make ends meet. Having jumped an entire year, he found extra cramming necessary, and the earnings to be made out of study hours were small. He wore his clothes until they were transparent, and tried to eat "very little and very cheap", but to no avail. In August 1838 he withdrew from Princeton and entered his name in Union College, Schenectady, where living expenses were lower.

After a holiday at home he travelled along the Old Erie Canal to Schenectady, on the Mohawk River, and entered 'with advanced standing', for the final year. Union College, which lay in a park on the town's outskirts, had taken its name in 1797 to signalize "that the whole movement had welled up from the desire of a great number of people, of all social grades, and racial stocks, and of all religious persuasions, with provision against control by any".

During its first fifty years, Union had developed exceedingly liberal tendencies,[1] and the introduction of French into the curriculum revealed an almost revolutionary spirit. Students were at least enabled to translate their college motto: "*Sous les lois de Minerve nous devonons tous frères.*"

The President of Union when Leonard arrived in 1839 was Dr. Eliphatet Nott, a person of inflammable ideas, who had already held this post for thirty-five years.

Apart from reforming the college, and introducing such innovations as an engineering course, the Doctor found sufficient spare time to win patents on thirty different kinds of stove. His design for an anthracite-burning boiler for steamboats virtually ended their horrid casualty record. Happily the college buildings pre-dated Dr. Nott's boilers and had been finished before taste turned Victorian-Gothic.

[1] James Roosevelt, father of President Franklin Roosevelt, transferred from Amhurst to Union just eight years after Leonard Jerome left.

Leonard had been brought up to revel in the dictum of his country's constitution that *artificial* distinctions among men were to be abolished, but strong class feeling certainly existed among Americans. Here among students from other states whose background was utterly different from his own, he formed his own opinions concerning individuals.

"I then began to perceive the difference between artificial and natural distinctions the former being a kind of garment laid on by accident, and the latter a real measure of the human beneath that cloak."

The young gentlemen from the Southern states had other views. Laughingly they talked about their slaves and coloured mistresses and Leonard, half shocked, half enchanted, began to imagine the amoral charm of those plantation homes, where a code had evolved unbelievably different from that prevailing in his own Puritan setting.

The world began to open for him. Within twenty miles of Schenectady lay the towns of Albany and Troy, all on the Mohawk River, but curiously different in atmosphere. On holidays, Leonard ventured into a dreamy Dutch civilization. Here in the Mohawk Valley the leisurely traditions of the 18th century lingered on. This trim continental world was Leonard's first glimpse of a facet of Old Europe. He wandered the wide tree-lined streets watching the life of these wooden colonial houses and noting that, unlike New England only a mountain range away, here the Sundays were frivolously enjoyed as in far-off Holland.

On hot summer evenings with the frogs croaking, crickets singing and fireflies ablaze the honest burghers all with Dutch names and manners would sit out fanning themselves in rocking-chairs on what they called 'stoeps' and Leonard called 'piazzas' and the English travellers called 'verandahs'.

There were townsfolk still living in Schenectady who could remember seeing General Washington and later La Fayette riding down the old post road from Albany, and these old ones liked to reminisce. Leonard was invited to a few quiet entertainments in Dutch homes. The rooms were dark yet gleaming. He carried away an impression of wide colonial fireplaces, tiled wood stoves, copper lustre, eagle mirrors, tall-boys, and mahogany davenports. Heavy old silver graced the sideboards and every object shone from constant polishing. It was quite different from western New York where his parents had pushed as far as they dared towards the retreating frontier and then had to struggle with their farm lands while the hard years knocked their culture off in flakes.

An arduous happy year rolled by. Leonard swam in the Mohawk and lay in the sun with other students talking of vanished Indian tribes. In full

27

summer there were flirtatious haymaking parties, with young people piled on to the buckboard farm carts singing through the twilight. Occasionally he visited Albany and Troy, the other river towns, in each of which a different world had arisen. Schenectady had shown him old Holland; Albany, shrill with early steamboats, opened up a river road with the swift-moving civilization of the Atlantic seaboard; and in Troy, only fifteen miles from Union, he found a city of musical taste which was becoming a usual stopping place for touring artists.

Here Leonard first heard musicians of note. The concert hall with its padded red boxes and huge gas chandelier opened a kind of heaven to him. He could always scrape up enough for a cheap ticket and there, high up on the balcony, where plush gave way to plain wood, and gilt to black paint, Leonard sat with pricked ears and shining eyes, learning there were new wonders in the world.

He had abandoned the violin but there were many musical evenings in the college, and then his clear tenor would ring out above the other voices. Leonard also learned to dance. His partners were young ladies, anxious to get up small parties in their own homes. From these amiable tutors he learnt not only the cotillion and waltz, but Spanish dances. "I will teach them all to you," he wrote his sister. And Isaac lifted an eyebrow . . . it might be fashionable, but was it *good*?

In July 1839 Leonard graduated. He was twenty-one. All life lay ahead, and he felt not ill-equipped.

3

FROM Union Leonard Jerome travelled along the Mohawk River to Albany, the bustling state capital, where he hoped to win renown. After being admitted to the bar and having obtained a first employment in the office of John C. Beach, he saw that the town overflowed with ambitious young lawyers, and work seemed hard to come by.

In 1840 Leonard ruefully decided to return to western New York, where the young expanding towns might offer more opportunity.

The journey home by way of "the longest canal on earth" was not devoid of pleasure. The packet boats which were pulled along the waterway by two or three trotting horses had become increasingly comfortable and elegant. A hundred passengers travelled on each boat, and canal travel was advertised as an excellent method of finding a spouse. "One comes into contact with new people and there is time to dally," exclaimed a contemporary letter. Each boat now possessed a "decorated cabin for ladies, with real beds", and in the dining-rooms, where the sexes sat at opposite ends of a long table, conversation blossomed with ease. The crews were guaranteed "sober and orderly", and one boat boasted that even the workmen who built her had done without "the stimulant of ardent spirits or liquid poison". The voyagers themselves however were not expected to abstain from wine; virtuous, well fed and in amusing mixed company they glided along the ribbon of water for hundreds of miles, and the cost of such travel including board and flirtations was only four cents a mile!

Disembarking at Palmyra, Leonard reported to his uncle who had just been appointed first judge of the Wayne County Court. Hiram Jerome had always wished his nephews to become lawyers. He immediately employed Leonard, and suggested that Lawrence, the next brother, should follow on from Princeton.

Then came two years' hard grind in the Judge's office. Leonard, restive and burning with energy, fretted. He had begun to contemplate trekking westward towards the ever-moving frontier, when Hiram decided to remove to Rochester. This at least was a change. When a small boy, Leonard had seen Rochester as a village of white houses sprawling across the Genesee River Falls. He found the town unrecognizable, the population having increased from a few hundred to twenty-three thousand. Leonard stepped blithely into America's first boom town. The original respectable milling families were busy legislating against billiard halls, ninepin alleys and disorderly newcomers. They welcomed judges and bright young lawyers.

The new Jerome office was established on the corner of Exchange and Main Streets. As principal of the firm, Leonard enjoyed considerable independence.

At eight every morning he left his lodging house after a breakfast of hot corn-bread, and walked briskly through the streets crowded with creaking farm wagons bringing in milk and wheat, apples, potatoes and cheese. At twelve, work ceased throughout the town, and fashionable ladies would appear to promenade. The afternoon was filled with "noise and confusion, bustle and business". At five, the farmers started to drive their wagons home, and by six "everyone was hastening home to supper".

Leonard would drag through the last of his legal work, and then rush off with young friends. Pretty girls were growing up all along the flowering Genesee River, and in Rochester the "refined female academies" had become as numerous as the taverns. Leonard's singing voice and gift of quick repartee kept him in demand for musical evenings and dancing parties, and many an eye lit up when young Mr. Jerome's footstep was heard on the garden parth.

"Rochester's social élite still functioned much as an enlarged family circle, with its hospitality checked only by the facilities of the larger mansions. The young folk kept a succession of gay parties running through each January and February in the numerous big houses, and no doubt the lists of guests, if combined, would supply a tentative social register. The old custom of gathering at four in the afternoon was giving way to the evening party, which sometimes continued until midnight, but the guests still attended as family delegations rather than in couples."

In the following year Lawrence joined the Jerome office as junior clerk. Whatever Uncle Hiram thought of his staff the two brothers won a reputation of being "very popular with the young ladies, owing to the dashing manner in which they rode high-spirited horses".

An old lady writes in her early memories of Rochester:

"My father (Samuel Wilder), when a bachelor, kept house with several of his like-minded brothers in pretty old Ravine Place, off Lake

Avenue. There they were visited by all kinds of witty out-of-towners, as well as home friends. A simple life it must have been in those days, with lots of young fun and warm companionship. Among the visitors were the Jeromes from Pompey Hill and Palmyra. Lawrence and Leonard were constant visitors, and very inclined to borrow the Wilder brother's smart waistcoats and cravates. But they were always screamingly funny boys, and could act a part as easily as breathing."

Two years passed during which the brothers, "screamingly funny" to contemporaries, perhaps less so to their elders, grew into well-known figures at Rochester supper parties and charades. Leonard won a reputation as an able lawyer but Lawrence showed little desire to serve a full apprenticeship in the Judge's office, and could often be observed searching with knitted brows for some more profitable, or at least more spectacular, pursuit.

Suddenly, in August 1844, Lawrence married Miss Catherine Hall, a dark-eyed girl of twenty-one who had been orphaned as a child and brought up by a band of old aunts in Palmyra. She and her two sisters were heiresses to a small fortune, and Lawrence fretted that he could not equal her income with his legal earnings. Soon he and Leonard decided they might earn more money in a publishing business just offered for sale. They obtained a half-share, and arranged to take over entirely in the following year.

It was the very middle of a century in which America's newspapers would leap from 150 in 1800 to 30,000 in 1900. Leonard could not resist the lure of running his own paper. He invested all his savings and reckoned that an immediate profit could be made out of the printing office on side lines.

After much disagreement with the Judge, his nephews abandoned their legal careers and by 1846 they were joint owners of the *Daily American*.

"Politics absorbed a fair portion, but by no means all of the energies of Rochester editors. New publications were frequently launched, occasionally with non-political objectives, but it required more than the income from a few hundred subscribers to put a paper on its feet, and many of these ventures proved ephemeral. The *American* established in the mid-forties, enjoyed greater success and, under the energetic management of the Jerome brothers, and the editor Alexander Mann, a staunch Clay supporter, soon challenged the Democratic leadership of local Whigs."[1]

The financial side of the *American* was run entirely by Leonard. The circulation crept up to 1,000, then to 2,000, and eventually, they said, to

[1] *The Water-Power City*, by Dr. Blake McKelvey.

nearly 3,000. These tiny figures were tremendous for the time. When the paper was running on a sound business basis, Leonard opened fire politically. "What we suffer from that Know-Nothing paper, the local *American*!" raged one of the town's prominent citizens. The *American* became known as a hard-hitting organ, expressly devised to flag the Democrats (who upheld the rights of individual states, as opposed to strong centralized government). Leonard did not lay out the editorials himself, but he organized the talents of his writers clearly.

Through the impact of their paper, the brothers found themselves rich and famous, "big frogs though in so small a pond". When a son arrived for the Lawrence Jeromes they rented a spacious house in Fitzhugh Street, and asked Leonard and the seventh brother Isaac to move in with them.

Now that they had time and money the Jeromes frequented the numerous balls given by the older families, who were 'intent on keeping out brash newcomers'. A fine sense of snobbism was growing up. The brothers let themselves be swept to the top of the tiny social tree. Now that Rochester's more violent period was over, many of the toughs who had found fortune were turning respectable and 'trying to get into Society'. At all costs they must be kept out! The tiny core of early settlers resolved to resist the deluge of *nouveaux riches*, however pure or prim, pretty or well-read the second generation might be. As life grew less hard people had time to cultivate snobbisms, and how they enjoyed them. In January 1847:

> "the younger members of the leading families made one dramatic effort to re-establish their social ascendancy by a costume party at the home of Mrs. William Greenough, where the élite gathered to the number of seventy-six. The gala affair prompted two new young and dashing newcomers in Rochester, Leonard and Lawrence Jerome to bring out an amusing account in prose and verse."

Meanwhile Miss Lillie Greenough, the young daughter of the house, who possessed a pretty singing voice, fell in love with Leonard. Their duets, started breezily enough among "the best people", were to have dire results over a period of many years.

The City Directory now reveals Fitzhugh Street in the "smart Third Ward" as liberally studded with Jerome homesteads. It was a wide street of solid brick houses. The most-refined-of-all female academy had opened at one end, and the Episcopalian and Presbyterian churches glared jealously at each other's stone towers at the other. Lawrence and his wife Catherine with their children lived at number 77, with Leonard and young Isaac as boarders. Their father, the aging Captain Jerome, had left his farm and moved to a house across the street, with his youngest sons Chauncey and Charles; while Uncle Hiram (on speaking terms with hardly anyone) lived next door. The Jerome boys worked eagerly for the *American*. The eight brothers had always been friends, but amidst the boisterous company, Leonard and Lawrence were most in tune with each other. They shared a special sense of humour not always appreciated by others, and had the same taste in young ladies, "hunting well in couples". Happily there were two oval-faced Miss Halls, with black-sloe eyes and sulky mouths.

Catherine had a younger sister Clara, a slightly unmanageable belle who would flirt judiciously in the parlour and then "fall into moods". Leonard had watched her for a long time, and often took the twenty-four-hour canal boat journey down to Palmyra. At that time convention allowed a gentleman wishing to pay court to accompany his lady "to mid-week prayer service without offence, or they might join the family in an apple-paring match, or in a song-fest around the piano, in the sitting-room". Leonard soon tired of the company of the aunts.

"If only the financial success of our paper were assured," he told her, "I might ask you a question. I wonder what you would answer to it? . . . No, don't tell me. I haven't put it yet. . . ."

And Clara, who was inclined to be offish and disdainful with admirers, had to bite her lip. For supposing he hadn't meant *that*?

The aunts soon became weary of the journey to and from Rochester, which took two days by stage coach, or a day and night (of perpetual un-winking chaperonage) by canal boat. Clara *thought* she knew what he meant, that, unlike the impetuous Lawrence, he refused to marry until his income equalled that of his bride, but she could not be sure. She could but take a feverish interest in the sales sheet of the *American*. With beating heart, Miss Hall watched the little paper's spectacular rise and at last, one April day, when the woods were whitening with blossom, Leonard Jerome came to Palmyra, and led her up the aisle of the Presbyterian church.

4

CLARA HALL possessed a curious dark brooding beauty. Portraits show the melancholy oval face fashionable at the period, hair parted in the centre, looped low over the forehead, and black mournful eyes. She had none of Leonard's surface-fire; being secretive and rather shy. The aunts found her detachment irksome.

A strange, unhappy childhood may have left its mark. Clara could hardly remember her parents, who had both died when she was two years old. Only the stories of grown-ups gave her a shadowy picture of that father who lay in Palmyra churchyard beside his mysterious beautiful wife. Relations assiduously compiled a family history. They traced coats-of-arms back to 16th-century England, and produced a detailed 'pedigree book' for the delectation of future Halls. Ambrose, Clara's father, emerged from this research as "a tall man of striking personality". Clara listened with awe while his writings and speeches were read to her; the droning voices evoked a person for ever watching from the habitations of the dead, ready to 'strike'. Her mother she thought of differently, with longing and curiosity, for she had heard a half-hushed rumour, concerning her Indian blood. The old aunts could not resist whispering, and long before she understood the importance of a coat-of-arms, Clara knew herself to be a quarter Iroquois, a descendant of the haughty tribe which had for centuries ruled the wooded hills around her home. Sometimes her mind grew confused at the tales she overheard, stories which always ended abruptly with "Go away and play now, dear." She would creep to a looking-glass to peer at the reflection of a little sharp-pointed face and wonder "Will I grow up to live in the woods?" And a shiver would run up her spine. She wanted to escape, she wanted a way out of this safe, comfortable house which would some day belong to her and her sisters. "You are lucky girls," intoned the adult voices. "Why?" asked Clara innocently. But there would be no answer because it was considered vulgar to speak of money.

As they grew older the girls learnt the facts concerning their parents. Ambrose their father had been born in 1774 to old Mr. Hall and his wife Mehitabel Beach. His birth was recorded in the church register of the little village of Lanesborough, New York. The aunts revelled in ancestry so Clara and her sisters were taken to see the page. As a young man Ambrose Hall set up practice as a lawyer in Williamstown, where he became the town banker and then entered into politics representing Berkshire County in the legislature of Massachusetts in 1812, 1813 and 1817. He inherited a fortune from his maternal grandfather the "haughty John Beach" who "always appeared in public arrayed in velvet knee breeches, ruffled shirt, silken hose and silver shoe buckles with his coloured body servant walking at the proper distance behind him". A great cattle breeder Mr. Beach also owned a sloop which he kept plying between Bridgeport and New York. Mr. Beach was exceedingly rich and when he went to New York City he could be seen "making the journey thither on horseback with one or more slaves (of which he had many) behind him".

When Ambrose Hall inherited this grandfather's fortune he built a white Colonial type house[1] in South Williamstown, choosing as its site a "knoll over-looking a wide valley which reached forth to the green hills of the Taghkania range. . . ." He built it for a certain lady, however, and when the elegant rooms and well-proportioned staircase failed to lure her, Ambrose settled down sulky and alone, swearing never to marry at all. In 1816 he ventured off with a friend on a hunting expedition in the western part of New York State which, at that time, was virgin forest. While riding through the wilds, they came to a cabin in the region where Palmyra now stands. Being weary, the hunters dismounted to ask for a drink. Their knockings brought a girl of unusual beauty to the door. She introduced herself as Clarissa, a daughter of the house, and ran off to call her father David Wilcox, who had been one of the early settlers in this part.

The men stepped inside to sit at the rough wood table. When Clarissa returned, Ambrose Hall did not try to conceal his admiration, but Wilcox, having offered beer and bread, seemed eager to set the hunters on their way. Clarissa, brown and lithe, ran beside them through the woods telling them she had Indian blood, and could "run that way for miles". Ambrose leaned from his saddle to say: "I shall come back soon. Wait for me." Then he rode off with the flash of her black eyes in his mind.

A month or so later, 'spoilt young Mr. Hall' announced he was off on another hunting expedition, alone this time. Within a few weeks he brought back to Williamstown as trophy of the chase a sixteen-year-old bride to be his lady in the large white house. A child of nature, she did not flourish indoors amidst luxury. Used to walls of plain logs she stared unmoved at the plaster-work ceilings and delicate furniture. Babies arrived in quick succession and her health began to fail. Searching for a better climate for his adored

[1] It still stands in a good state of preservation.

35

'wild bird', Ambrose exchanged Massachusetts for the beautiful valley of the Genesee River. On the outskirts of Rochester, still a straggling village, he built another house, but the locality proving malarious, he hurried his wife back to the high land around Palmyra, where her childhood had been spent. They found the woods were giving way to pasture and the log cabins to trim white houses. Since her departure the village had grown into a town. Once again Ambrose Hall built a large house with porticos and colonnades. Re-entering political life, he served for the Assembly of New York State for Wayne County in 1826. But in the following June Clarissa bore her sixth daughter, and within a month her slim body lay buried in the new cemetery. She died leaving only a bunch of tumbling babies, and the legend of her feline grace and strange beauty.[1] Ambrose Hall, the last male of his branch, succumbed three months later. The daughters inherited his ample fortune, and were brought up in stiff Puritan tradition by their mother's Wilcox relations.

Three of the orphans reached maturity. These were twins Catherine and Caroline who had been born in 1823, and Clara born in 1825. They were all self-willed, with a tendency to frown and say the unusual, which disturbed their prim relations. Clara was criticized for "roving the house", and not knowing what she wanted (until she met Leonard Jerome). In her character, beneath the airs and graces inevitable in a small-town belle, there seems to have lurked a restlessness which maddened the aunties. Although told she must never mention her Indian blood, Clara could not forget that it burnt her veins. People might not consider the Iroquois strain 'genteel' but there it was, pounding through her heart with its attendant shadows of physical race memory. The Wilcoxes found her changeable; sometimes she craved society and then with exasperating suddenness she would "slip back into herself". It was not yet fashionable to be a self-obsessed blue-stocking.

Amateur theatricals and charades were a frequent form of entertainment but Clara, who obviously suffered from a sense of artistic creation for which the time and place gave no possible outlet, horrified her aunts by evincing a desire to become 'an actress' or, to put it more accurately, to learn dramatic parts and recite in public. It was a relief to them when, at the age of twenty-four, she married the man of her choice. None of her early letters survives and, apart from the oil portraits and memories of her children, very little has been recorded. But through the veils of sham virtue and hypocrisy with which most anecdotes of the time were swathed, it is possible to perceive the outline of a person who caused consternation by not accepting the usual. Clara loved what she could not understand. Perhaps that is why she loved Leonard Jerome. She certainly loved him all her life.

[1] "More panther than woman," wrote Lord d'Abernon of her grand-daughter fifty years later. The description would, it seems, have fitted Clarissa well.

Clara Hall Jerome
Painted in Trieste, 1853
by Schiavoni

The Jerome house in Rochester
Drawn by Carl Raschen

Corner of Leonard Jerome's house in Madison Square (today)
Drawn by John I. Leslie

After bringing his bride back to Rochester, Leonard acquired the red brick house next to Lawrence's, and built a connecting passage so that the three brothers and two sisters and their offspring need not cross the lawn to 'visit'. Clara delighted at having an independent home of her own, a framework of red plush, tasselled curtains and dark mahogany furniture in which to entertain her husband's varied and "oh, so interesting friends". Chief of these was the brilliant young attorney-ethnologist, Lewis H. Morgan, who had been at Union College with Leonard. Morgan had just started writing up the customs of the Iroquois, and defending the Red Man with an outraged sense of justice. He was also an expert on the beaver, and would sit in the Jerome parlour discussing the unbelievable engineering feats of this little animal.

Leonard was inundated with work. Apart from the Whig cause, the chief issues of importance in the forties were Anti-Slavery, Temperance and Women's Rights. The Female Charitable Society, the Ladies' Temperance Society and the American Female Moral Reform Society deluged Rochester with conventions during these years. Although they used men speakers and were without a vote, zealous public-spirited women were fiercely beginning to prove their power.

For over ten years the Rochester Anti-Slavery Society had been hammering its views into the Press, and in 1849 the city's newly elected Whig representative declared his sympathy for the negro cause at an Anti-Slavery bazaar. Funds were collected to build a City Library, to aid the Irish Famine, and to form a Rochester company which sent young men out to California, as 'diggers', in the rush of 1849. There was agitation for a ten-hour day for working men, for new bridges and sewers, for gas to replace the sixty oil lamps which illuminated the City, for a larger jail, for the abolition of bawdy houses, and curbing of wayward women. The battle for free education aroused stormy controversy, the principle of taxing one citizen to pay for the education of another citizen's children being considered 'undemocratic'.

In all these matters Leonard Jerome was vitally interested for he directed the leaders of his paper. Appeals to improve the city sanitation, and clean up those hovels inhabited by Irish and German immigrants were ignored until, in the summer of 1849, a couple of months after Leonard's wedding, cholera broke out in that county almshouse which provided "correctional treatment for the indolent poor". One hundred and sixty died, and people who could afford it retired from the overcrowded city. As the sensation occasioned by the plague diminished the two Fox sisters stepped into a world which had not heard of mediums or poltergeists, and startled large audiences with loud unaccountable rappings which followed them. In November they gave the world's first public performance of spirit communication and when one committee after another announced they could not detect fraud the unbelieving audience attempted to storm the platform. Quakers accepted the phenomena as proof of the possibility of communicating with the departed, thousands of words were written for and against the rappings and the conflict continued in the Press long after the harassed sisters had departed for New York.

Rochester's flair for preening itself in print caused a neighbouring city's paper to declare with more jealousy than grammar:

> "No peacock ever swelled into larger proportions or strutted about in a more complacent and happy air, than our Rochester neighbours assume when they talk of 'our position', 'our location', 'our advantages. . . .' What adds to the exceeding richness of all this is the fact that the [Rochester] editors actually believe what they say."

Most enjoyable of outings for Leonard were the Saturday afternoon trotting races where he could train his keen eye for a horse while Clara attired in the latest fashion chatted with her friends. Satin gowns, high-buttoned boots and ostrich-feathered bonnets were regarded as indispensable outward signs of inner virtue for respectable matrons on public outings. Unconventional as her character may have been, Clara assumed the exterior trappings of respectability, and both the Hall sisters were considered perfect matches, fit to curb and mould their exuberant spouses. Only Uncle Hiram (now a Judge of the Seventh Judicial District of New York State) remained unimpressed.

During the week-days when Leonard and his brother disappeared to their offices Clara redecorated the rooms and changed the settees from corner to corner. Soon she was begging to replace the mahogany furniture by more fashionable rosewood and walnut and the Turkish carpets by those of Brussels; new figured papers started to cover the walls and around the windows heavy damask curtains were held back by gold lilies to reveal the muslin curtains which were presently superseded by sets of *real lace*. The parlour blushed crimson and purple around its white marble fireplace and those shell bouquets in glass domes which had seemed so ornamental to the old aunts in Palmyra were cast aside for expensive ormolu mirrors.

With scorn she recalled the plain Georgian style in which her father had built his houses. Not for her were bare rooms and pale colours. The fungus of Fancy-Gothic was spreading through the land, darkening windows, laying stripes on wallpaper and insisting that Mrs. Leonard Jerome as a lady of high fashion should dress in the same shade of deep red with which she draped her dining-room. But the Jeromes blossomed happily amidst magenta hues and a year later into their nest of plush, gilt and ebony a daughter was born. She amazed them with beauty all the more enthralling because it was so unlike their own. Little Clara threw back to some fair ancestor and her parents could rave over her blue eyes and golden hair. Leonard walked about as if bewitched, the arrival of his first child seeming to be an event unique in human history.

In 1849 the Jerome brothers had participated in Silver Grey rallies of the Whig party. When the two wings of the party agreed to resolve their differences Leonard and Lawrence, already dreaming of wider horizons than Rochester could unfold, decided to sell the *American*. They made known in Washington their availability for political appointments. Then, as now, America employed two types of diplomat: professionals whose lifelong careers corresponded to those of their European counterparts, and political appointees who were given posts in acknowledgment for their work on behalf of the party.

Leonard was rewarded for his services to the Whig cause when, in March 1850, the United States Senate confirmed his appointment as Consul to Ravenna in Italy (then in the Papal States). Clara was delighted for she realized what a promising diplomatic career might open up for her husband. But Leonard kept several other irons in the fire. He never actually left for Ravenna and two months after the appointment had been confirmed newspapers announced his election as Secretary-Treasurer of the Merchants State Telegraphic Co. Rochester had already been the scene of conflicting telegraph ventures. Several important business men had invested in the Morse line across New York State and when local control had been lost several of them undertook the construction of a House line across the State. A firebrand Irishman, Henry O'Reilly, formerly of Rochester, who had been frozen out of the previous telegraph ventures, had decided to launch a line in competition. There was general surprise when Jerome, a Presbyterian and a Whig, became linked with an Irish Democrat. Leonard, however, had no intention of relinquishing his rugged individuality.

In the early summer of 1850, when Leonard was thirty-two years of age, he left Rochester for New York City where he opened his own office from which he helped O'Reilly press forward the construction of the Merchants State Telegraph. Such energy was poured into this effort that the Morse faction eventually found itself forced to buy up the new telegraph line for $65,379.

Ravenna went without a Consul while Leonard fought O'Reilly's battle. In December 1850, somewhat belatedly, he resigned the appointment. During the following winter the Leonard Jeromes lived at 292 Henry Street, Brooklyn, a red brick house just large enough for Clara and the baby and brother Addison and his wife. Addison was well ensconced as a broker in Wall Street, and Leonard found him congenial company. The two men were out every evening together while Clara kept house as best she could amidst the half-unpacked crates, trunks and boxes which she had packed so diligently in Rochester with "belongings suitable for Italy".

5

WHILE Clara followed her own sedate existence in Brooklyn village the Jerome men ventured into that high-paced extravagant world which surrounded Wall Street. There were as yet only nineteen official New York millionaires. The Jeromes intended to add their names to the list as quickly as possible. Every morning the brothers left the house together "in great hurry and spirits", and took the South Ferry to Manhattan, where they debarked in the heart of the turbulent city. Clara spent the days alone, supervising the negro servants who flounced around in bright bandannas, scribbling notes to friends, and walking along the quiet leafy streets where it amused her to look into little gardens. The cult of the glue-pot and fret-work saw whiled away many hours for her contemporaries, but never amused her. Her excitements were few. Occasionally a fire might occur in the neighbourhood and then she went out to see the Volunteer Fire Brigades racing their equipment to the scene. Competing fire companies frequently arrived in such a state of exhaustion they were unable to man the pumps. It was customary for spectators to shout encouragement to the red-faced gentlemen volunteers, who were usually clad in ruffled shirts, long-tailed coats and high beaver hats.

On fine afternoons she took baby Clara to Brooklyn heights where she could feed pigeons and watch the paddle boats and tugs and sailing skiffs on East River. A kind gentleman sometimes let them peer through his telescope and they could see right over the low roofs of Manhattan Island which lay fringed by a narrow forest of masts.

Occasionally Mrs. Jerome crossed by ferry steamer and once Leonard walked her up Wall Street to show her his office in a pleasant three-storied house with tall windows and green shutters, and to point out the office buildings of their acquaintances. One or two banks had recently put up new buildings for themselves, replacing 18th-century houses by heavy stone façades with thick columns designed some two thousand years previously for Roman temples, but the majority of brokers' offices were still in simple spacious Georgian houses. Leonard always insisted his office should face south and have a large window easily opened "to let the sun in". All day long carts and barrows rattled over the cobbles and gentlemen in top hats strolled along the pavement shouting financial news into each other's ears. When the offices closed there would be a flood of famous personages walking towards the omnibuses of Broadway and many diversions were laid open to them on the way.

The Jerome brothers soon became an integral part of the lively New York scene. They were popular and the moment office hours ended professional friends begged for their company for the evening to talk over new projects and enjoy themselves at the same time. Leaving 'the Street' they stepped into an atmosphere of seething excitement. Sometimes they dined in one of the splendid new hotels which were being built to catch the stream of business men who poured forth from Wall Street each evening. Famous restaurateurs provided cushioned seclusion for those who wished to continue their business discussions; and no little thought was given to the many 'overworked' gentlemen who would be eager for relaxation and pleasure. The pious owner of a famous *bordel* declared at the time: "American men are driven to bouts of dissipation by the relentless pressure of money making." Never had the potentialities of a new continent been reflected as in the brain-storm pace of mid-century New York. Leonard loved it all, the clatter of huge horse-drawn omnibuses, the thronged sidewalks, and the hundred gas-lit bars and restaurants of Broadway, where pretty teen-agers from every state were recruited as waiter-girls. As the numerous new millionaires grew boisterous and self-assured, the straight-laced old families deplored their ostentation, but they were powerless to stop the tide. Caught by his business associates for dinner and supper parties Leonard came home to Brooklyn later and later. Clara began to wonder if she liked being the wife of a financier. Leonard's wife had been brought up to admire subdued manners and quiet tastes. Yet she could not but notice with interest those large brownstone houses, elaborately carved and colonnaded, which the new rich were building above Madison Square and along Fifth Avenue. There was a steady movement towards the open country where Central Park was being planned. Old Astor had died worth twenty million dollars, an unprecedented sum for one man to have collected, and his ruthlessness had set the pace for the next generation.

Leonard wholeheartedly enjoyed the vulgarity and flourish of New York. In Wall Street and at gay men's dinners "the new Mr. Jerome" became famous for wit and quick repartee. However, a contemporary recorded that in the tough unmannered metropolis Leonard kept to his own set of rules. "I never knew him to take a drink in a bar or public place," wrote this person. "Yet Jerome belonged to the city with all its garish brilliance. No man ever became more completely a New Yorker."

While Clara developed a small circle of friends whom she liked to entertain 'at home', Leonard ventured into the musical world. With relish he attended concerts and operas, often alone, for Clara's lack of ear caused her to be hesitant about accompanying him. "Oh dear," she once wrote, "it's such a pity I can't *appreciate* more." When Leonard did persuade her to leave the housekeeping and attend a concert with him she would find herself lost in a mist of sense impressions. Next day she had to fall out of the voluble family criticisms. Leonard's facility to concentrate enabled him to talk glibly with professionals and Clara's heart sank when the subject of counterpoint and *leit-motif* arose. No Jerome could understand that to her, music meant only a flood of sound that swept through her mind arousing strange emotions. Not one bar could she remember. In shyness she let Leonard go out increasingly often without her.

New York had a capacity for enthusiasm which exceeded that of any city in the world. When Jenny Lind, the greatest concert singer of the century, arrived in New York, cheering crowds lined the streets to watch Showman Barnum drive the 'Swedish Nightingale' to her hotel. Twenty thousand fans spent the evening shouting for her, and the New York Musical Fund Society, accompanied by red-shirted firemen carrying flaming torches, serenaded her Broadway hotel until after midnight. Tickets for her first concert were sold at auction for unprecedented prices. "Twenty or thirty dollars to hear Jenny are paid by those who live hand to mouth." Leonard went of course, battling his way through an hysterical mob to reach Castle Garden. The thirty-year-old singer with her plain features and serene shining eyes appeared in a white ball gown. She responded to the wild reception which the audience accorded her with deep curtseys and donated the $12,000 received for her first appearance to charities. Leonard missed few of her performances, and when she was criticized for 'lack of passion' he retorted "her voice is indescribable in quality like the dawn—who wants more?" When he met her he apparently wanted considerably more, but Jenny Lind was famous for virtue as well as for generosity. Leonard had always liked pretty women. Miss Lind changed his taste. He was fascinated by the simplicity of a great artist uncaring of her appearance. And amidst her triumphs, and despite her 'purity' (which unkind critics called a 'publicity stunt'), Jenny Lind could not help remarking that of all her admirers, Mr. Jerome was "the best looking".

Meanwhile Clara produced a second daughter, and showed some disappointment the child did not prove to be a boy for she had set her heart on a son to be called Leonard.

"Why not name her Jenny?" suggested her husband.

Elegant preparations for the new baby had kept Clara too busy to read the papers which resounded with the wonder of Miss Lind.

"Why?" she remonstrated. "Just plain Jenny? No Jerome has been called that before."

Leonard did not press the issue but he firmly ruled out Aurora. "Let her have one short pretty name," he said. " 'Jenny Jerome'," exclaimed Clara. "It sounds outlandish."

But Leonard smiled winningly and, as always, he obtained his own way in the end. "Very well then," agreed Clara. "It shall be as you wish, but I think it is hard on a girl to have to go through life as just plain Jenny."

"She'll manage," said Leonard softly. He walked to the frilly cot, stared down at the small object which lay there in a ribboned bonnet and marvelled at the miniature grey eyes which looked up, they were so bright and so like his own.

6

ALTHOUGH he had resigned his appointment to Ravenna, Leonard, hoping for more political favour later, assured Clara that he would enable her to travel to Europe at the first opportunity. For nearly two years she had to wait in Brooklyn while Leonard and Addison, always on the brink of making fortunes, hustled their way around Wall Street and spent their evenings in the garish brilliance of the new gas-lit restaurants and theatres. When they returned a few hours before dawn, Brooklyn village lay dark and quiet with shutters drawn and curtains pulled. Clara and the baby daughters were fast asleep when the brothers tiptoed in. And in the morning there was hardly time for greeting before the men had flashed away, leaving the chubby hands waving in one window and Clara's wistful smile in another.

Always observant of her surroundings and eager to improve her home, Clara accepted implicitly the standards of her age. In the West she had seen classical houses of the Colonial period superseded by fancy brick and darkened rooms. Now she regarded with interest a city blossoming into sham-Gothic. Not unnaturally she shared the general enthusiasm for reproductions of Italian masters hung in ornate frames. New York copied everything it heard of, Greek, Turkish, Egyptian or Chinese. Harriet Beecher Stowe scolded the rich citizens for their pretentious taste: "Of what use are brick houses whose fronts are plated with brown sandstone with expensive entrance doors trimmed with carving, lacking bathrooms and a good kitchen?... Household ornaments, rich showy food, and elegant garments are more important than sanitation."

Clara, with hours to spare, immersed in books and magazines, studied every new trend. Occasionally she and her sister-in-law Julia crossed on the ferry to take a horse omnibus and observe the mammoth shops of Broadway and those surprising castles, Scotch-Baronial, Venetian, Indian and early French, which were springing up to accommodate the new millionaires in Fifth Avenue. Although an unluxurious person by nature, Clara knew what the fashionable world expected and her fastidious eye enabled her to walk the tight-rope between over-dressing in those bright colours deemed

Wall Street in 1856

Leonard Jerome on his coach

incorrect and any hint of dinginess. Dresses must be sober, but *obviously* costly, and etiquette decried "any material however expensive which might give the look of calico to even the most decided lady". Worse than the stigma of cotton was that of wearing "reddish lilac", a colour considered sufficiently ungenteel to endanger social status. As a gentleman grew wealthier, the hoopskirts of the female members of his family grew wider, and trimmings and ornamentation more elaborate. The invention of the sewing-machine, far from helping the housewife to run up quick garments, led to a surfeit of braiding and embroidery. Clara used materials as heavily embossed as the rest but she looked lovely in some of the new gowns, particularly those with fragile transparent undersleeves and wide collars. As Leonard obtained successes in the city he urged her to spend more lavishly, and she tried in all ways to please him. But the pace of New York did not suit her. With a trace of wistfulness she saved from her personal income to buy him a bejewelled card case, and with her own inexpert hands she embroidered a velvet smoking-cap, hung with a tassel. But her husband had become too busy to notice trifles.

In January 1852 this life, so arduous and gay for Leonard, and so conventional for Clara, abruptly terminated. The Senate confirmed Mr. Jerome's second political appointment, and with joy Clara started to prepare for a term in Trieste. What little time could be spared from shopping and packing she devoted to solemn efforts to absorb the history of the Austro-Hungarian Empire "so that I should know *something* about the place to which we were going, but what a complicated and involved story it did seem". Leonard, kept occupied day and night by business arrangements and conferences concerning his future duties as Consul, had to leave preparations for departure entirely to Clara. She stored furniture, obtained new places for the negro domestics, supervised crates of 'necessaries for the Italian clime!' and ordered a suitable trousseau for the journey. It was the age of special costumes. No lady travelled without procuring a travelling dress, or stepped on a boat except in a sailing bonnet, or dreamt of appearing in a new city without trunks of ensembles devised for that place alone.

Although steam passenger ships were running a regular service between New York and Liverpool, Leonard, who always loved to see the great clipper tacking in from Sandy Hook, insisted that they cross the ocean by sail. They must have traversed the north Atlantic in the westerlies, and then turned south, entering the Mediterranean through the Straits of Gibraltar. The harmony of this Atlantic crossing was not enhanced by the addition of a young songstress to the family party. Miss Lillie Greenough, deeply in love with Leonard ever since her mother's fancy dress party in Rochester, had spent a year persuading Mama to allow her to accompany the Jeromes to

Italy. She was pretty, romantically minded and the possessor of a charming singing voice. Thoughtlessly Leonard had offered to pay for her training—now the poor girl must not be disappointed. The propriety of the arrangement did not in any measure alleviate Clara's irritation. She was busy with her own family, and not interested in Italian singing technique, or the possible renown of Lillie in Grand Opera. Yet she found herself forced to chaperone and supervise 'a feather-wit' who hero-worshipped Leonard in an embarrassing fashion.

In April the party disembarked at Marseilles and travelled along the flowering Riviera to Northern Italy, the whole of which lay within the confines of the rambling Austro-Hungarian Empire. Passports were unknown in those days except for a barbaric land such as Russia and the troubled Italian states. Lillie promptly lost her special papers, and Clara exploded with wrath, "She cannot even look after her own pass. *I* have to look after everything."

Venice, Padua, Milan and Turin were governed from Vienna, and Trieste itself had been under Hapsburg rule since 1382. During several centuries this city had remained the Empire's sole outlet to the sea; in 1852 it counted as the most important Mediterranean port, and three years before the Jeromes' arrival Emperor Francis Joseph had granted it the status of *Reichsunmittelbarkeit*, making it subject to the Imperial Government only. Trieste, in fact, was a tiny city-state within the vast empire.

Perched on the blue Adriatic with all the exports and imports of Austro-Hungary flowing through its great harbour, the city was packed with rich merchants who, like the Venetians of earlier times, traded with the entire world. America was just beginning to open up interests in the Adriatic and Jerome found it easy to stimulate trade between his country and the eastern Mediterranean.

Having settled into a pleasant villa, and familiarized himself with the un-onerous duties of the Consulate, Leonard organized a pleasant life for his household. Singing teachers were found for Miss Greenough, who trilled away at her exercises, and Clara, venturing forth in an open carriage, enjoyed the views of bay and mountain, and the lively people. It was a different world for her, a throbbing little world full of ancient history, and her letters home were studded with romantic stories of Venice. Since every port in the Adriatic had been founded by emissaries of the Doge, all villages near the sea were Italian-speaking, and despite Austria's sovereignty, this remained the chief tongue of Trieste. Clara tried valiantly to master her Italian and German grammars, but she had as little ear for languages as for music. During drives in the country she was forced to notice that not only the townsfolk but many unlettered peasants seemed able to pick up a foreign language more easily than she. Within the Austrian ruling class, it was granted that three or four languages should be perfected in the schoolroom, and Clara now determined that her daughters must learn languages while young.

The Governor of Trieste, to whom Leonard presented his credentials, was a Viennese aristocrat who enchanted both Jeromes "by his manners, the art of his conversation and his supremely unpractical outlook on the world". Later, when they were invited to the castles and manor houses of those Italian counts and dukes who held whatever posts they could procure befitting their rank (this last was of immense importance to all of them), Leonard often experienced tedium in their company. "They spoke more languages than I, but none paid for their own education, and surely it is more important to think clearly in one idiom than to chatter in five."

It was not so to his wife, for whom the charm of all foreigners proved irresistible. A few evenings at the Governor's Palace, where she met the nobility whose villas lay scattered around the bay, completely bewitched her. Her eyes were opened to a way of living she had never glimpsed among the successful men of America, and from now on everything Austrian must be deemed perfect.

Concerning the merits of the Italian aristocracy she remained more guarded. They amazed as much as they beguiled, for the men, apart from those who procured posts in the Austrian Government Services, obviously had no intention of ever doing a stroke of work if they could help it. As for the *contessas*, they appeared to be more interested in lovers' compliments than husbands' careers. Moulded by her strict Puritan upbringing, Clara grew slightly shocked.

Entertaining in Trieste with well-mannered servants and perfectly trained cooks, proved easy. The blue bay surrounded by pastel-coloured mountains made a background of theatrical splendour for the Jerome villa which possessed a large garden set with "exotic blooms and English lawns" where the babies could romp all day and their parents could give open-air parties at night. During the summer no Triestians ever seemed to go to bed and the formality usually attendant on diplomatic entertaining faded away in the warm enchantment of the Adriatic. Clara wrote, "the gorgeous picnic seems as correct as a formal reception for ambassadors and princes as well as our merchant friends".

When Leonard became the proud owner of a small white yacht the Consulate saw little of "that energetic American gentleman". He had never owned a boat before, and was forever "missing lunch while taking sailing lessons from a dreadful old fisherman in a red cap". There were also hunting parties with Austrian friends to blue Lake Zirkintza, and Monte Nevoso, the Snow Mountain of legend.

In winter most of the Viennese departed to their capital, and as the bitter *bora* blew down the stark treeless mountains the Jeromes, creeping cautiously out to dinner in their closed coach, saw ropes fastened along the streets for people to cling to, lest they were blown into the sea. Entertaining on the grand scale started again in early spring, and Clara, growing more vivacious and talkative every day, forced Leonard to take her to all the balls given in the castles and mansions built along the coast. The flickering candelabra and masses of Southern flowers, the old tapestries, and mixture of Latin-Slav-Germanic tastes, enchanted her. And so did the dancing partners. These were largely provided by the battleships of the Austrian Navy, which could disgorge large numbers of well-polished officers for all parties.

Clara, "an elegant brunette with American vitality and Paris gowns", found herself inundated with compliments "so daring one blushes, and yet too graceful to offend".

She met the Arch-duke Maximilian, a naval officer of twenty-one, and danced frequently with his friend Baron William Tegethoff who, she admitted years later, "seemed to be, though one should not say it, rather taken".

Trieste was a tiny world, glittering and light-hearted. Night after night, Clara found herself dancing into daylight, and as Leonard drove home beside her he would be whistling a haunting new Strauss waltz. Never before had life permitted them to be so carefree. She would lean back, close her eyes and, as the stars died out of the pale pink sky, completely forget about Miss Greenough practising scales in the attic.

7

TRIESTE was so different from Rochester and New York, that Leonard could not at first notice the brutality with which the pieces of the old Empire were kept glued together. Behind the pageantry ticked a slow time-bomb which would explode amidst the pressures of the next century.

When the Emperor Francis Joseph had succeeded four years previously, he quickly subdued the Italian provinces and placed wicked ninety-year-old Marshal Radetzsky in charge. The Marshal quickly imposed martial law, hung and imprisoned thousands of remonstrating Italians and ordered the flogging of fifteen respectable Milanese including two young girls, for hissing an Austrian. In 1851, the year before the Jeromes' arrival, a professor of the University of Milan had died under the lash. The murmur of anger which arose through Lombardy became the signal for the Emperor's secret police to be sent swarming through his provinces. Meanwhile, the Austrian Army of Occupation conscripted Italian subjects, and Radetzsky lined his pockets by selling exemptions from military service. Later the same men were conscripted anyway. These appear unlikely methods of winning popularity for any regime, yet Francis Joseph, proclaiming himself a Liberal, found it "unbelievable" that north Italy should recoil from his visits, while its aristocracy avoided all court functions.

Hungary proved far harder to crush than Piedmont. In fact the Austrian Army could not do it without the aid of Russian troops which were presently supplied by Tsar Nicolas I. When in 1849 the Hungarian rebel army had capitulated to its double foe, Francis Joseph acted with a mixture of vacillation and treachery. He spoke magnanimously, and then approved the hanging of the defeated Prime Minister, of thirteen Hungarian generals, and a hundred leading citizens. The governor he installed grew notorious for publicly flogging women on political grounds. Only the Arch-duke Maximilian, whom Clara called "a sweet-faced boy", had the courage to record his disgust:

"Posterity will regard with amazement and horror the chambers in which without any question of law, mere force has, under the influence of hateful revenge, condemned people to death at a few hours notice, perhaps because they wanted something different from that desired by the power that stands above law."

Francis Joseph now found it more extraordinary than ever that his subjects did not like him! In order to cope with the torrent of daily reports from his *agent-provocateurs* and personal spies, the Emperor started his famous life-long habit of rising at 4 a.m. to work at his desk until late afternoon. Would to God he had stayed in bed!

In Austria there was every appearance of gaiety. Dissentients might be flogged, but pretty young countesses danced *le beau danube bleu*.

Fine-drawn, educated minds arose among the aristocracy, but they were not questioning minds. Nothing in Vienna *could* be taken more seriously than the importance of thirty-two quarterings. A foreign Consul, however, was prone to see the more light-hearted side, and Trieste was a city of many enterprises packed with people from different nations. Ambitious professional men flocked there for a few years to make quick fortunes before retiring to Paris, where the art of living had reached a supreme height. Vienna emulated Paris but despite her older royal family never quite attained her grace.

Leonard liked the Austrian Governor of Trieste, at whose palace receptions the rich cosmopolitan merchants of the port mingled with local counts and dukes, presenting the most entertaining assortment of men, all weaving their small destinies in the structure of the swaying Empire. Amongst them, Leonard Jerome, the north American, stamped a vivid impression. He was a character, this "ricco Americano". The 'gay dogs' of Trieste tried to draw him to the gambling clubs but hours at the tables bored him. Seeing him grow restless at Faro, friends urged him to the theatre, but he never mastered Italian sufficiently to enjoy the witty if licentious topical plays 'for men only'. Only the Stadt Theatre with its opera company, to which the stars of Milan and Vienna were frequent guest artists, held him riveted night after night. Verdi, Donizetti and Bellini were his favourite composers and he often travelled to Venice for star performances. Those of his companions who had grown up knowing the score of operas by heart, laughed at the zeal with which "*ce cher Jerome, ce business man Américain*" became a connoisseur.

He showed almost as much interest in the Imperial Stud at Lipizza, a few miles from Trieste, where the famous Lipizzaner stallions were bred and kept on show for foreign visitors. Polite comment (from Englishmen in particular) was expected, but Monsieur Jerome showed himself '*passionné*'. After he bought a pair of Lipizzaners, Clara decided that, as a topic of conversation, she would rather bear with musical scores than equine pedigrees.

Her poetical feminine mind veered away from technicality. And even Lillie began to look pained when the subject of Lipizzaner sires arose. So Leonard, finding a poor audience in his home, would cry out: "Send for the children." And the Misses Jerome toddled in, accompanied by their Italian nurse. Neither child understood a word of Italian but they loved Papa, whose long moustaches could be pulled with impunity. Mama proved quite a different matter, for fragments of valuable lace inclined to tear off her gowns, and when beads, braid and ribbon littered the floor, maids had to be rung for and gaiety ended. Eager to please Leonard, Clara ordered all her dresses from Paris. "Do look well, Clit," he would urge, and he faced with equanimity those bills which arrived in the wake of enormous boxes containing hoop skirts of satin, brocade or muslin. A lady had plenty of time to devote to her toilettes, time to change into two or three dresses each day, and to "attire herself for the evening", a complicated process necessitating several hours and the help of several maids. Here in the romance of this Southern setting, such efforts were well repaid. When Mrs. Jerome swept forth in a cloud of fichus and muslin she had a sparkle in her eye that had never been seen by the aunts of Palmyra. It was about this time that Clara ceased to strive to attain "intellectual heights which just wear one out". She laid by her French and Italian grammars, because they "spoiled too many precious hours", and took to sight-seeing instead. With some trepidation, wearing an enormous sun hat and swathed in veils to protect her complexion, she even accompanied her husband on yachting trips down the delectable coast of the Adriatic.

They tried the Brioni Islands, anchoring amidst wide beaches and rustling woods of oleander and myrtle. "Paradise," sighed Clara. But Leonard fidgeted and longed for a brisk wind. One autumn they reached Venice, glided across the glass-green lagoons in a gondola, and then travelled overland to Florence buying pictures and gazing at cathedrals along the way. After passing through Rome they ventured with some trepidation into the little State of Naples and Sicily, where Mr. Gladstone, splendidly British and nosey, had just paid a visit of enquiry and found 40,000 military and political prisoners working in chains.

In January 1853 Leonard took Clara to Vienna where the winter season was proving particularly gay with "a great passion for Court Balls". These were "informal but exclusive, only the diplomatic corps, and families with the required number of quarterings, were invited". The melodies of Johann Strauss were inundating the city, and the Emperor and the Arch-duke Maximilian, two handsome royal bachelors, created a flutter by attending even informal dances. On Shrove Tuesday their mother, sour old Arch-duchess Sophia, ended the Winter Season with a ball which crowned all the others, and lasted from 8 p.m. until midnight. Then the Court retired into seclusion for Lent.

As visitors to the glittering capital, the Jeromes fancied they could feel the pulse of the Empire. But they each counted a different beat. Leonard observed Vienna with coolness. Clara, completely captivated by Viennese society, could only find everything "quite quite delightful".

8

THE Presidential election of 1853 replaced President Fillmore, a Republican, by President Pierce, a Democrat. Jerome and other American diplomats who held political as opposed to professional appointments tendered their resignations. Clara sighed. She could not help feeling that she would have made a perfect Ambassadress for Vienna or Paris, posts which might have been offered had her husband's diplomatic career continued longer. Knowing the end in sight, she spent the spring in an orgy of sight-seeing, exploring the caverns of Postitana by candlelight and peering from the shelter of a beribboned parasol at the old churches of Trieste. Brow-puckered beneath poke-bonnet she laboured through guide-books verbose on the amalgamation of Byzantine and Gothic. But "one has to be a very diligent student to understand the muddles of Mediterranean architecture and the afternoons are so hot".

Leonard regarded the date of departure gladly enough. He had enjoyed Italy for a time but the tempo was not his. In the mornings he had driven from villa to office admiring his prancing horses all the way. After attending to business, he strolled to a club for an *apéritif* before a late lunch. The usual Italian siesta terminated with a sail or a swim. Then drying whiskers and moustache Leonard drifted to various entertainments along the coast. He and Clara had both been amused by the long-drawn-out Italian dinner-parties. Back in New York they would miss the torrents of conversation which were elegant and subtle if not quite proper, and they would miss the light wines and heady laughter, the old silver gleaming by candlelight and those eyes, languid and blazing in turn, invariably full of admiration for the tall American Consul and the *bella bella signora* his wife.

Before leaving Trieste, Leonard and Clara commissioned an Italian named Schiavoni to paint their portraits. In July these were shipped off with a collection of what they hoped were old masters and a huge crate of antique furniture which fell to pieces in transit. Leonard had not much to pack. His Consular uniform was laid in moth balls and his Court sword, with its fine steel blade and engraved motto *Vive le roi* (hardly appropriate for an Ameri-

53

can Whig), sent home for a future son.[1] He was eager to introduce the Lipizzaner strain to America and visualized the day when his own carriage would be drawn down Fifth Avenue by high-stepping beauties of the blood royal. There was much to attend to. Babies and maids must travel one way, two horses and a groom another.

In late summer Leonard and Clara with the children and their Italian nurse started a leisurely journey across Europe, by horse-drawn coach. They crossed the Alps and tarried on the lower slopes of Mont Cenis. Jennie wrote, "I remember how, as we crossed the Mont Cenis in a *vettura*, the deep snow filled my childish mind with awe and astonishment." In the autumn, attended by maids and nurses, they reached Paris where Clara wished to bide while purchasing gowns at the *grandes maisons*.

After the tension of north Italy, where feelings ran so high against Imperial Austria, Louis Napoleon's city of gas-light and crinolines appeared remarkably content. The new Emperor distracted attention from governmental difficulties by rebuilding the capital Roman fashion for his amazed citizens. Gigantic buildings, new boulevards, monuments and columns sprang up daily, and a glittering court was being created "in great haste", its tone becoming not *nouveau riche* but *nouveau royale*. Clara decided that here, not in Vienna, lay the centre of the world she loved, and Leonard promised to bring her back. If she could not return as ambassadress then she must come for love of the fair city. The fact that France, England and Turkey were at war with Russia seems to have affected the lives of ordinary people scarcely at all. The incidents of the Crimea were hardly mentioned in the Jerome ladies' letters. Far more pertinent to the general interest was the rumour sent across the Atlantic by Clara herself, that bonnets would shortly be replaced by straw hats.

Then news arrived from Addison that his firm of brokers had failed. It was imperative for Leonard to return hastily to America. Clara sighed. When the family embarked, one glance at her husband's keen face showed that he felt no grief at leaving. He had been yearning for that palpitating financial vortex of New York. Amidst the potentialities of the high-strung city he had always been sure he could battle in his own fashion and win.

In Trieste he was long remembered. People walking along the Corso missed his phaeton with its high-mettled horses. "Where has he gone, the American gentleman who was mad about horses?" And they sighed, for Mediterranean folk are romantic-minded and they had liked to see the smart vehicles which drew Mr. Jerome in his impeccable top-hat while by his side (let it be whispered now that his diplomatic career had ended), more

[1] The son never materialized but the sword hangs today in Castle Leslie, the home of an Irish grandson.

54

often than not, there sat the loveliest *prima donna* of Venice. *"Quand même il avait du style,"* they said. *"Ce Jerome il était un chic type."*

On a sailing ship plunging across the south Atlantic, two different faces looked westward. The Jeromes came home with different eyes and aspirations. Leonard remained an American to the core. Clara left her heart in Europe.

9

THE city to which Leonard Jerome returned in November 1853 was the centre of a blunt brilliant world. He was glad to get back to those limitless horizons and to the companionship of men who rose from nothing to fantastic financial power, men who thought in terms without boundary. They were a different breed from the Europeans who climbed from, but never forgot, their ruts. Clara veered naturally towards the snobbish seclusion of old New York society while Vanderbilt, Jay Gould, Jim Fiske, Daniel Drew, were Leonard's contestants in the toughest financial arena in the world. Courage belonged to them all; kindness to very few. "These boys did not like to be clamped down on." They were fussy to see that "sufficient freedom was granted to the individual" and inclined to take the law into their own hands if they could not buy out a Legislature! Walt Whitman, living near the Jerome house in Brooklyn, wrote: "New York is more than a city; it is a way of life." And it was to this life that the Jerome brothers belonged by inclination and understanding.

After a brief visit to Lawrence in Rochester, Leonard brought his family back to Brooklyn, where he and Addison purchased a house lying two blocks nearer the South Ferry than their previous joint home. This residence, 8 Amity Street, became the base from which the Jeromes conducted their Wall Street forays during the next few years. Addison's firm had recently failed, but what of it? "Leonard did not wait to unpack before he plunged. Every dollar he had not settled on me was in constant use on the market," said Clara. Having provided for their wives, the brothers considered themselves free to gamble away the rest, or to make fortunes if luck held. Clara sighed at her enforced return to America, but Leonard swore he would be a rich man within a year, and once again every morning early he and Addison vanished towards the South Ferry which carried them to work. It would be late at night when they re-crossed the river and walked home through the dark streets and quiet gardens of Brooklyn.

Leonard devoted all free time to his one pair of horses which he drove jubilantly among the swarms of fast-pacers exercising on Third Avenue.

Elegant carriages and sleighs abounded, but Leonard's turn-out proved the cynosure of all eyes. He had always been a natural horseman, and years of practice now made him an artist with the reins. Many a girl whisked by amid the jingling bells of her fur-covered family sledge, sighed on hearing that Mr. Jerome was already married.

Despite the failure of his firm, Addison recovered his prestige and amidst the grand-scale ventures which began to sweep America the brothers grew steadily richer. Many of the new projects were being launched as financial tidal waves which grew completely out of control. While vast rivers were being harnessed and new cities sprang up on the edges of the ever-receding wilderness, many an incandescent fortune shot up and died as speedily as rockets soaring against the night sky. Leonard called Wall Street "a jungle where men tear and claw". But jungle air suited him. The all-powerful operators were 'fair game'.

At this epoch the development of railway lines throughout the continent was just beginning to cause financial pandemonium. Most lines were sketched out on paper and built too quickly for their ultimate effects or worth to be assessed by the company founders. Every State in the Union became linked by gleaming metal tracks flung across the prairies, or through virgin forest. Untold reserves of wealth suddenly opened up as Atlantic and Pacific were joined by an iron ribbon.

Leonard recognized the potential dangers of many of these projects, which were out-of-hand financially before the first engine ran. At that time, over-issue of stock could be considered normal procedure, but when the New York and New Haven Railway Companies sold forged stock, and were involved in enormous scandals, the public grew resentful. Mr. Jerome stepped forward as a kind of Railway Reformer. While buying heavily in companies whose stocks he had ascertained were in existence, he simultaneously exhorted political friends to "clear up the chaos". He saw that if railway investments grew safer they would immensely increase in value and he persuaded the Congressman for Rochester, Freeman Clark, to secure the passage of a Railway Reform Bill restricting several forms of over-issue. Leonard Jerome's name began to resound through the Street as "a man who could get things done". Amidst the incredible corruption and gigantic swindles one man of integrity and nerve could stand up boldly and gain the confidence of an outraged public. A sour rival said: "That damn fellow has cashed in on honesty."

While the big-shots battled a way to fortune their womenfolk conspired to enter the tiny nucleus of the 'old aristocracy'. It seems that when sudden wealth lays the world at women's feet they only wish to scale some pinnacle where they aren't wanted! The portals of the New York *noblesse* proved exceptionally strong. Unable to storm certain citadels the 'rich nobodies' built a new social ring which gave original entertainments and the grandees became stiffer than ever. Apparently Clara knew the way in through the barricades. She would soon be able to add to the phalanxes of brownstone mansions which were creeping up Fifth Avenue. Her breeding through Ambrose Hall would allow her to drop cards on the *élite* (no mention was made of her beautiful mother's antecedents one may be sure!).

While Leonard, refusing to belong to any one circle, was always inviting a mixture of people to the house, his wife drove diligently around in her new carriage dropping cards on the 'right people'. She gave formal dinner-parties for guests carefully selected to match each other's tastes and Leonard noted with pleasure her Paris gowns modelled on those designed for the Empress Eugénie. The Italian pictures were hung in a rented house while Leonard decided where to build a permanent home and Clara's discourses on Italian art caused much admiration. The taste for antiques had just begun to spread through America; starting in Boston this cult was to obsess the upper classes for generations. The new rich speedily learned they simply had to have old furniture. Not being able to drag it from attics they were only too grateful to learn from Mrs. Jerome that it was genteel to "snoop in junk shops".

On the fringes of society it was becoming the habit for the wives (as well as mistresses) of successful men to load themselves with jewelry for dinner parties. Clara issuing from the fastnesses of well-bred drawing-rooms dropped quiet snubs to those of Leonard's friends who were newly emerged from the welter. With disappointment they learned that only pearls could be worn by a lady on informal occasions.

When Leonard spent his first sensational gains on a diamond necklace for his wife she counted the entertainments and operas at which she would be able to wear it and then looked at him with shining eyes: "And if we ever went to a Court how splendidly I could show it off!"

"Don't worry, Clit," he laughed. "You shall have your Court too." In the fifties ladies dressed in velvet to show their affluence, they also hung rooms with velvet and sat on velvet but they cultivated steel-sharp thoughts and were forever watching for an opportunity to 'cut' some unfortunate of whom they disapproved. The manœuvre for 'cutting' had been developed into a minor art. The deliverer of the thrust would step forward as if to speak to the intended victim, then as that person moved or smiled in antici-pation, would deliberately stare through her. Clara with a gentle nature had no wish to assert such powers and she quite liked some of the upthrusting families, but the strident note of New York jarred her. She did not sense the drive which made it the most exciting machine on earth. The flamboyant new set whom Leonard met through his business connections often sighed at the number of restrictions which followed the lofty pursuit of social climbing but nevertheless they learned what they could from Mrs. Jerome's hints.

Meanwhile her husband continued on his hurried way, making a friend of Commodore Vanderbilt, fourteen years his senior, and planning to enter into certain railway lines with him. He did not perceive, or did not care to perceive, how much of Clara's activity took place in the hopes of catching *his* attention. The pace of his own life was such that he saw little of his wife save at the far end of a dinner table, and as they grew richer the table grew longer. Clara fretted for she sensed her hold on Leonard lessening and her heart grew restless while she sat amidst the dark glory of her drawing-room, arrayed in her silken hoop skirts, handing out tea and admonition to people who did not really interest her.

During the summer of 1854 Leonard, whose taste for sailing had been whetted in the Adriatic, bought a yacht the *Undine* in which he made several trips to Newport, an old-world fishing village, which he thought would be a satisfactory summer base for Clara and the babies. He could visit his family by sea whenever the fray in Wall Street eased.

By 1855 Addison had made a complete financial recovery. Having re-established himself as broker-banker, he proceeded to build a mansion at 33 West 20th Street, then a fashionable part of the city, and to settle two million dollars on his wife to prevent the poor thing worrying. Leonard, himself grown into a magnate of no mean repute, spent most of the summer shark fishing. He left Clara and the children in the country and wrote complaining of the exorbitant cost of a professional crew (not an unusual shock for gentlemen of fortune who take to the sea).

> "I wish we could always keep a yacht. I had rather have one than all the other luxuries that are indulged in by people of wealth. My dear little pickininies and you, my ever faithful and true wife . . . how happy I shall be to see you again. The boys are pulling me by the coat tail, so goodnight. *Dite Talla che Papa vena a casa subito . . . tre o quatro jorni . . . addio.*
>
> Leonard."

Talla, who was little Clara, received the news joyously but her mother sighed. She did not approve of "the boys".

In November a third daughter arrived and was christened Camille.

LAWRENCE joined Leonard and Addison in New York. The brothers shared a quick wit which kept them in constant demand for dinner parties. By day, the Jeromes strolled Wall Street playing the roles of broker-merchant-bankers; by night they became Manhattan's gayest gentlemen. They earned and spent in unison. Addison's mansion in West 20th Street became the scene of many entertainments and here in 1856 the famous firm of Travers, Jerome, which lasted so long in Wall Street, came into being. Addison, without social aspirations but liking to astound intimate men friends, had given a dinner with particularly good wines. The guests sat talking and drinking, until, in the early hours, Leonard rose to his feet and amidst roars of laughter announced the founding of a new firm by himself, Addison and William Travers (the celebrated lawyer-wit, owner of a stable of fast trotters). The Three Musketeers as the directors called themselves toasted this partnership in rare port, and towards dawn those who could stand gave a smart salute to each inauguration speech.

This was the evening when William Travers, creeping home on tiptoe, originated the reply which has become a famous music-hall joke.

"Is that you, Bill?" his wife called to the creaking floor boards.

Travers always stuttered. "Y-yess," he said, "wh-who did you expect?"

Within a month, the Musketeers proceeded to work. Their attacks in Wall Street produced spectacular results until Leonard, over-confident from success, took a tip from a friend. This man, who was Treasurer of the Cleveland and Toledo Company, knew his stock to be false, but just before it crashed he off-loaded on to the firm of Travers, Jerome.

Leonard's entire personal fortune disappeared. He had settled a considerable amount on Clara, and she accepted with complacency the news that the move to Fifth Avenue mansion must be postponed. "Leonard Jerome never flickered an eyelid in public, but he was sore displeased that one he trusted had let him down."

To everyone's surprise he announced a year's retreat for himself; this period was to be devoted to the study of Wall Street psychology. While he took no part in active speculation Clara ran her reduced household with tact. She did not care if he made money or not; in fact she seems to have been slightly ashamed of her husband's financial flair. And for the first time, Leonard was grateful. "How dear seem Clara's airy notions in comparison to the shoddy values I meet elsewhere."

She believed in her husband. He had made money before and would probably do it again. Did it matter so long as their life together remained smooth and the correct moral tone was upheld? "I will not find it in me to worry," she told her sister. They were not tempted to sell their pictures for none of the new millionaires, intent on furnishing private art galleries, would have thought of purchasing unobtrusive early Italians.

Leonard suffered secretly for his lost fortune represented years of effort, and the sneers of enemies in Wall Street galled. Jerome was mocked as "one of the brightest meteors that has flashed by". But the children saw more of their adored papa, and Clara seemed content. "Only dear Leonard's *real* friends now enter our parlour. I know them and like them." Among those who stood by him in the parlour and elsewhere were Henry Clews the banker, and August Belmont, famous financial adviser to the Rothschilds and the Democratic party. Neither of these men had started life in America. Henry Clews, educated in England to take Holy Orders and accept a country curacy under his brother, had made a trip to New York before going to the University, and this brief kaleidoscopic vision "turned the dear boy's head" to such an extent that he resolved to combat his parents' wishes, break away from quiet country security and plunge into the maelstrom of Wall Street. He became one of the city's greatest financiers, teased by few save William Travers whose inimitable voice was heard in the Jeromes' drawing-room: "I s-s-say, Clews, s-s-since you are a self-made man why the devil didn't put m-m-more hair on y-y-your head?"

The other friend, stocky staunch August Belmont, said that no man in America delighted him as much as Leonard. Belmont and Jerome shared a very special passion for horses (and, rather more complicated, for ladies of high mettle). Some of their upbringing corresponded; they had been born in the same year and started work young, but August Belmont was the son of a well-to-do yeoman farmer in the Rhenish Palatinate. Apprenticed at the age of thirteen to the Rothschilds in Frankfort, he had been sent in 1837 to America as their first agent. During the next forty years Belmont's advice regarding United States securities enabled the Rothschilds to build a new financial organization of immense power and he became New York's outstanding magnate.

Clews from the English gentry, Belmont from the Rhine, and Jerome bred of the frontier: the friendship of these three became consolidated by

61

inordinate school-boyish enthusiasm for sport and horses. The German and the American in particular shared exuberant tastes; their country breeding on soil which had not been corrupted by artificial processes may, to some extent, have given them the strength to enjoy all they won. They lived like tornadoes, apparently nothing ever went wrong with their liver or nerves, and Leonard accepted occasional 'ruin' as a good steeple-chaser does a fall— just a passing event to learn from.

The lean year passed. Clara bore patiently the impossibility of going to Mrs. Schermerhorn's famous costume ball, to which only the "six hundred indisputable members of New York's *élite*" were invited. Leonard had no great urge to shave his whiskers and gambol in Louis XV period attire, but his wife did sigh a little when she heard that for the first time in America the two-hour "German *cotillon*" would be danced as in the Tuileries Palace where the Empress Eugenie considered the one, two, three, hop of the polka too vulgar for her balls. Clara having learnt the endless cotillion steps in Vienna would have been *dans son assiette*. "Never mind, Clit, dear," said Leonard, when he realized what she had missed, "you will have more balls than you want some day. Wait and see."

New York society, which Astor's grandson was now jeering at for "tyrannical exclusiveness", did not open its portals to Commodore Vanderbilt. His language kept him beyond the pale and though the handsome old man made occasional efforts to get invited he just could not 'quit cursing', and his inability to restrain his admiration for the weaker sex caused even his house-maids to fly from his proximity. During the fifties when Cornelius had only reached the ten-million mark the uppercrust of New York society ostracized him heartlessly. Finally, the Commodore built the *North Star*, an enormous luxury steam yacht, and turning his back on home snobbery sailed away to astound and conquer Europe. Across the Atlantic, no one cared if either his grammar or his ladies were 'correct'.

When his year of contemplation terminated, Leonard hazarded a new gamble and the flag of the Three Musketeers flew once more over Wall Street. Scraping together every available dollar he threw for high stakes. Within a month he had multiplied his firm's capital ten times. Once again Manhattan swallowed him soon after dawn, and returned him past midnight. Clara sighed: "All this for a brownstone house in Fifth Avenue?" But Leonard dreamed more of stables than houses. With his first winnings he started a racing stud to equal August Belmont's. "After all I'm fond of the fellow, but one can't let him have the pick of everything—he's got the best pictures, the best porcelain, and the best chef in New York as it is."

The Three Musketeers exasperated Wall Street. They were ruthless, frivolous, and a law unto themselves. In a luxurious room, high above the junction of Pine and Nassau Streets, the firm of Travers, Jerome inaugurated what it airily called its 'Observatory'. Here, in a setting of red plush and polished woods, Leonard entertaining his business acquaintances thoughtfully 'observed'. The luncheons and dinners served in this room were kept unhurried and the conversation stimulating. Wines showed the choice of a connoisseur and tycoons and newspaper men seldom realized their views were being dissected as under a microscope.

Among the most frequent visitors to the 'Observatory' were the financial editors of two New York papers, the *Herald* and the *Tribune*. Since his own venture in Rochester, Leonard had comprehended the developing powers of the Press. If these men wished they could break a company, and in the instance of the *Cleveland and Toledo*, Leonard decided that such action would be beneficial. After careful research he knew the whole company to be rotten but only an unprecedented Press campaign could reveal its true state. Both the *Herald* and the *Tribune* started to publish the facts dug up by Leonard, and not only was this company exposed and smashed, but also the corrupt *Michigan Southern* (which Leonard had sworn to break even if it carried down the whole market). His threats had been laughed at but, during the panic that followed the Press exposure of these companies, Leonard made a far greater fortune than the one he had lost.

A story is told that one day Leonard was standing on the pavement near the old Stock Exchange predicting the failure of certain securities of which he disapproved, when a broker stepped up pointing to the edifice of the *Ohio Life and Trust Company*.

"Say what you please that company is good stock at all events." Leonard scowled and said he would not give 50 for its stocks, then standing at 103. The word went around. None believed him, but two months later the *Ohio Life and Trust Company* failed for several millions and dragged not only Wall Street but the entire commerce of the country with it.

His frankness became famous. "Those Jeromes are doing well," wrote a contemporary, adding not without a touch of irritation: "Sometimes it pays to act like a gentleman."

II

WHEN Leonard thought it safe to leave his various businesses he acquiesced in Clara's pleadings to return to Europe for two years. He strolled down to South Street. It felt good to wander past the trading schooners and ocean clippers whose raised bowsprits stretched almost across the street with the busy dockyard traffic passing underneath. Had it not been for his family Leonard would have dearly loved to choose a ship and sail off round the world. Clara did not enjoy ocean crossing so he chose the most seaworthy barque he could find and booked passage for her and himself, the three children, a maid and a nurse. In the early spring they reached France.

Paris was in a ferment of excitement wondering if the Emperor Francis Joseph would blunder into war with Piedmont Sardinia. Leonard rented an apartment at 63 Avenue de Champs-Elysées and strolled off to investigate the studs of France. On September 13, 1858, he wrote lengthily to Lawrence:

"Paris is not yet as agreeable to me as New York except on Sunday. The pleasure carriages that passed my window yesterday, 12 a.m. to 8 p.m., averaged about 50 *a minute*. I amuse myself with music in the morning, walking or riding in the afternoon and theatre visiting and billiards in the evening. . . . I think I shall spend next summer at the Isle of Wight, a great place for yachting and horses. . . . I advise you to teach languages to your sons young. Boys run to things they shine in. Whatever they *succeed* in, they are inclined to do well.

I wrote Travers by the last mail to send me a wagon and harness. If not already dispatched, cancel. I find horses here abominably dear. 2,000 francs is nothing for a pair that you would not drive a second time. They do not admire speed. Showy, high-stepping, short switch-tail and arching neck is the description that generally answers. I have been looking about only to find French horses so little to my fancy that I have ended by buying nothing. So if you happen to see a pair of horses you think would suit my driving, good size, good travellers, you may send them over."

Clara bloomed at Leonard's side in this new element. They drove, they visited, they saw theatres and operas, and went to private concerts and *salons* and gave "delightful intimate little dinners". Dukes of this and that paid calls, and Leonard sent flowers to more than one *prima donna*. Voices remained long in his memory, longer than the faces of lovely women. According to family research, Clara was the only woman he ever looked at twice who could not *sing*!

While Leonard visited racecourses with the dandies of Paris, Clara ventured gently into the Imperial Court. Apparently the Empress simply heard of an interesting American lady and invited her to the Tuileries Palace. Clara, fluttering with pleasure, assured the Empress she liked dancing and when she came home tried on her diamond necklace before the mirror saying: "I have found the Court I want!"

In January 1859 Leonard wrote again to his brother:

> "We have been to the grand ball at the Tuileries and were presented to the Emperor and Empress. It was universally conceded that Clit was the handsomest woman there. I never saw her look so well."

And then with a sudden blast of bugles came war, and Louis Napoleon heading a new Grande Armée hurried to the rescue of the Italian states. His enemy Francis Joseph, obsessed with the importance of "nipping in the bud" revolutionary movements within the Austrian Empire, could not conduct any army with efficiency. For the second time within sixty years Europe saw the noble House of Hapsburg trounced by an upstart Bonaparte.

The French victory of Magenta was followed by Solferino and by June Napoleon had entered Milan at the head of his troops and the French fleet was blockading Venice (where Clara's dear Archduke Maximilian held an inefficient nominal command allowing him to take no proper action).

Napoleon won the war within a few weeks but he was too ill to think clearly or take advantage of victory. When the obvious moment came to reduce Venice, push into Austria and form a cohesive Italy the oppressive summer heat seemed to sap all his powers of decision. After one hideous day looking over a battlefield strewn with wounded, Napoleon III, who loved humanity, felt his nerve falter. Weakly, at just the wrong moment, he let armistice proposals begin. Francis Joseph's elaborate 'system' of centralization, Germanization and police repression had completely broken down, and the dawn of Italian unity lay in sight; but Napoleon's fatal conclusion of a half-won war merely humiliated Austria and left the Italian peninsula as unsettled as before. The two Emperors, the loser and the victor, returned to their respective capitals in equal unpopularity. What have you done with *our* triumphs? raged the Parisians; did you go to war just to stop *en pleine gloire*?

To allay the discontent of his capital Napoleon ordered a grand parade of returned troops to take place on August 14th—tiers of seats were built around the Place Vendôme, and for hours on end the Emperor and his little son took the salute, while Eugenie sat enthroned beneath a canopy of green velvet and golden bees. The stage management was very impressive. As the Second Army of Italy marched past with tattered banners and trophies of war, regiment after regiment showed gaps in their ranks. These were the places of the dead.

It was impossible not to be moved! The Parisian mob cheered and wept —but it was the showmanship they applauded, not this new Napoleon who led soldiers to war and threw away the prizes.

Mr. Jerome witnessed the March Past but with all her zeal for "history in the making" Clara dared not move from St. Germain-en-Laye. Next day on August 15th, Napoleon's birthday, she gave birth. Again the hoped-for 'Leonard' turned out to be a girl, a funny little brown-eyed creature. Rather sadly they christened her Leonie (French feminine of Leonard). She was their last child.

WHEN Leonard no longer dared to remain away from New York he returned by steam packet with his wife and four small daughters. He found his friends Vanderbilt, Belmont and Clews obsessed by the possibility of Civil War. President Lincoln had stated:

"I shall swear that I will, to the best of my ability, preserve, protect and defend the Constitution of the United States. It is not the Constitution as I would like to have it, but as it *is*, that is to be defended . . ."

The clash of interest between industrial north and agricultural south might have been resolved, but the Southerners took high-handed action, and Lincoln was unflinching in regard to secession. "Can a squabble over high tariffs and free trade lead to civil war? Surely not?" wrote Addison. But slowly the momentum of events was moving towards that moment when, against the will of all thinking men, blood instead of words decides an issue.

Meanwhile Clara was to be given her mansion . . . "I'll build you a castle yet!" Leonard had often called, as he hurried to the South Ferry. "Wait and see!"

She had waited and now she saw.

The fashionable were creeping northward. By 1859 Madison Square had been incorporated in the domain of elegance and the new houses there contained the city's first indoor water closets (which the Press attacked for being not only "insanitary but immoral"). Leonard bought a large site on the corner of Twenty-sixth Street overlooking the Square, and adjacent to the mansion of Mrs. Schermerhorn, redoubtable leader of New York society, who had decreed like the Empress Eugenie that the polka was too vulgar to be danced at *her* balls. Unfortunately even Mrs. Schermerhorn could not effect the removal of an immense marble palace called the Louvre, which also overlooked Madison Square two streets down. Despite the installation of several formidable social matrons in the vicinity, this establishment defiantly continued to flourish as a rendezvous for the city's most expensive *demi-mondaines* and boasting sparkling chandeliers, marble columns, gold-panelled walls and plashing fountains it naïvely advertised itself as the "most refined of its sort in the World".

Not sufficiently refined however for Mrs. Schermerhorn and Mrs. Jerome who launched a 'jehad' to have the Louvre banished from their neighbourhood. Their efforts always remained handicapped by the fact that they were not supposed to know about 'such things'.

Professional architects had only just begun to exist and Leonard with a free hand redesigned the plan offered. Unlike the usual ornate brownstone, his mansion was to be of red brick and white marble, a strawberry pie amidst rows of chocolate blancmanges.

Long before the central portion could be ready for occupation, Leonard enticed the builder to deviate from the original design by adding a rambling fancy stable and a private theatre as wings to the main structure.

According to the New York *Tribune*:

"Jerome was the friend as well as the patron of artists and actors. His passion for the theatre and opera was only surpassed by his love of horses. He built his stable before he built his house. It was of brick, faced with marble, three stories high, with a mansard roof. He filled it with horses and carriages of the finest makes. Except for the Emperor's Mews in Paris, it is doubtful if any stable in the world at that time surpassed Jerome's. Black walnut, plate glass, carpeted floors and other costly decorations ornamented the place. Above the stable he built a private theatre, handsomely adorned. . . . In front of his stable Mr. Jerome built his house and for years it was the centre of fashion. From its doors one Sunday afternoon he drove the first four-in-hand ever seen in this city. . . ."

Clara looked askance at these additions to her home. Did she really wish to live in a house "built in front of a stable", a house that might be described as an annexe to an opera? It was all "very very trying", and despite her bathroom "with French fittings" which really did shock the older generation Mrs. Jerome hankered increasingly for Europe. The Court of the Second Empire, where distinguished Americans were fêted, offered a setting more to her taste than the restricted *haut monde* of New York. The lure of foreign climes seemed yet more attractive when neighs and *arpeggios* began to resound through the windows. Parisian friends wrote her that interesting events were taking place in Europe. The Archduke Maximilian had once complained of the Napoleonic court:

Mrs. Ronalds

Jennie Jerome

Minnie Hawk

"the Emperor is lacking in nobility . . . Eugenie quite a thoroughbred but lacking in the august quality of an Empress . . . parvenu etiquette keeps coming through . . . whole impression is of a make-believe court occupied by amateurs who are not very sure of their parts."

But the American Mrs. Jerome, quite sure of *her* part, disagreed with all the Archduke's criticisms save one concerning St. Cloud where "a very improper piece was performed which, according to our ideas, ought not to have been played before ladies".

Now, after the military humiliations of Imperial Austria the Archduke had again visited Paris to ask for French backing in Mexico where his brother wished to install him as an Emperor. On these occasions *parvenu* rifles are as good as any others.

La belle Madame Jerome had naturally attracted admirers in French society and this partly compensated for Leonard's inability to keep at bay that circle of vulnerable feminine hearts which sprang up around him in every land. In contrast he (almost unique among husbands in Paris) had no cause for jealousy. Clara brought up in the Puritan code was "too good to occasion aught but fair comment". This, however, did not help her countenance Leonard's lapses. Her pleasure when dear Miss Lillie Greenough was finally married off had been made known to all the family. No more musical evenings to arrange for the doting songstress, no more chaperoning, no more eulogies necessary for Lillie's mama! Leonard also seems to have shown a slight relief. His protégée had a few charming notes but her emotions exceeded her art.

Lillie's first letter to Leonard after her marriage survives undated:

"Trouville.

My dear friend,

   I have not heard from you for such a long time. I believe I entirely lost your good opinion because I am no longer a young lady? Oh don't forget to love me just the same. I am the same to you. I love you more than ever because I feel you are never getting as strong love from anyone else. Have you really not written a word of kindness or congratulation? Is it possible you can give me less in this way? What am I to do with my temper is a question I ask of myself every day. It is an unpleasant thing to live with is my temper. It worries me and I cannot help getting angry. You know it is my nature and it kills me. Ah well enough. You will say a pleasant beginning. My husband (the first time I have written that hateful word) is kind and I am living just as I have always wished to, at Trouville (you know that is the fashionable watering place in France) in a house to ourselves. We have hired the house for the season, have plenty of room and are going to have the two boys and Mama (who will come to spend a little time with us), a yacht of our own, carriage and horses, two men servants, plenty of nice neighbours and so you would think I would be happy. Well I am in one way, very, but you know. Then we have a nice piano and I sing and Charlie composes for me and accompanies me. We first thought of travelling in England and when we got to Dieppe in true bridegroom fashion (we were four days getting there) we went to the same hotel where we went, Mama you and I in our first travels and I was so continually reminded of you and kept so constantly talking about you that my worthy husband was frightened at the contrast I would probably draw and after staying in Dieppe for five days we decided, I say we because I was afraid myself, if we went there, I should probably bring on a fit of the blues for my own benefit and one of jealousy for his, so we decided to come to Trouville. I have not heard once from Paris owing to our moving about so and having no settled plans about anything, but I expect letters today. Just think how lonely poor Mama must feel all alone. I have written to her to beg her to come here and spend a little time with us. . . . Do write to me and congratulate me won't you? Say something kind at least. If my life is going to be as long as these first two weeks I shall not want many birthdays. Poor America I have almost forgotten about her as you forget me. What are your plans? Don't for heaven's sake forsake me. If you can't love me as you used to, don't let me know it.

Yours as ever Lillie."

13

THE Jeromes moved into their new home along with the carriage horses, the champion hacks and two angular trotters. No sooner had the clang of workmen's hammers died away than the voices of practising singers arose from the midget opera. Leonard was never at a loss to know what to do with money. He became a music patron in the grand manner.

Meanwhile Clara laboured to decorate her own rooms appropriately. The ball-room shimmered white and gold beneath its immense chandeliers and the drawing-room flamed in dark red. She tried to enjoy it all while secretly dreaming of a small *salon* in Paris where ambassadors whispered state secrets and a poet or two strolled in to read their work. The poets of New York were unsuitable Bohemians who caroused in smoky cellars and were really impossible to invite to a lady's drawing-room.

As Lillie Greenough's sighs faded into the distance, Mrs. Jerome had dared to hope that certain aspects of life would become easier. But the private theatre had risen on her doorstep, and worse trials lay ahead.

Adelina Patti was now famous in New York and before long Leonard met the seventeen-year-old phenomenon. She told him of her surprise when, on being pushed suddenly into the role of *Lucia* by her brother-in-law, on an unfashionable evening, she found the half-empty house rising in uproar at the end of each act. In one night she blazed a trail to the stars.

"They say my voice equals that of Jennie Lind? Does it remind *you*?" she asked Leonard. He answered truthfully: "The only one that ever has."

Now she was the darling of New Yorkers, their first artist to reach supreme heights. Four times a week she sang through an opera to exulting crowds. She was so young and her gift so perfect. What could any man have to offer? Flowers, jewels? No! No! That, to use the favourite adjective of the age, would be 'vulgar'. Only kind Mr. Jerome could produce a toy out of the ordinary for a little *prima donna*. His private theatre was placed entirely at her disposal for the trying of new roles. And who gave her the most stimulating criticism? Who spoke of a woman's soul as well as of her tech-

71

nique? And who was always ready to drive her home in his superb sledge? New Yorkers saw them often together.

Leonard Jerome

"dazzled society with the glitter and novelty of his carriages, the costliness of his blooded horses. He excited its dubious admiration by his extravagance and assurance. Both were obvious in all his activities: his fantastic speculations, his scandalous love affairs, his incredible parties. . . . He made, lost, and again made fortunes; he was reputed to be worth more than ten million dollars."[1]

But this was only half the story. He had a strength that never flagged, a capacity for attending to detail, and a violent interest in everything he touched.

When the Jeromes gave their first tremendous ball the new house had to be transformed into a fairy palace with walls of sweet-smelling roses and gardenias and plashing brooks. Piping difficulties arose concerning the access of the water-main to the dining-room where two fountains were supposed to cascade amidst hillocks of flowers. Leonard swept aside the decorators. "I'll fix it up," he said, "send the plumbers to me." Fountains that spouted champagne and eau de cologne were then devised. Guests inebriated in the vicinity of one could recover beside the other.

A person present at the Jeromes' ball recorded:

"Invitations were eagerly sought by the 400 of that day, and all the wealth and fashion and beauty of the metropolis took part in the dance. Two fountains were placed in the centre of the auditorium playing cologne and champagne and the floral decorations were marvellous. The front of the theatre was illuminated and the sidewalls covered with crimson tapestry. The Supper must have cost thousands."

Clara's diamonds and satin ball gowns now required an inventory to keep in order but she knew the rules. She never appeared in the latest fashion; that would have been considered 'showy' and ill-bred. She simply kept the Paris importations in her wardrobe and wore them a year later when the Empress's approval had stamped them as 'good taste'! Gowns and gossip and calling on the right set took a certain amount of time but as Leonard slipped from her clutches Clara turned more and more to the consolations of the nursery where her eldest daughter was now a dreamy ash blonde ten years old.

[1] *Incredible New York*, by Lloyd Morris.

Meanwhile the 'Observatory' continued to function and the financial editors of newspapers were constantly invited. Leonard used the power of the Press to reveal corruption and in 1860 he purchased one-quarter of the shares of the New York *Times*.

"The Observatory set the moral atmosphere for Wall Street. Mr. Jerome did well through his climb to virtue . . . his name became known throughout the country as one of the boldest, coolest and most successful manipulators in the Street."

The 'sixties certainly presented an amusing epoch in which to be suddenly rich. So much *could* be done to a house. Furniture arrived in crates from the leading cabinet-makers of New York. Pieces of walnut, ebony, tulip wood and rose wood ornately carved or inlaid with pearl crowded the large darkened rooms. Chandeliers threw rainbows of crystal in the centre of her ceilings, glass decanters and goblets were bought from the new Brooklyn industries and electro-plating and pearl-handled knives made yet more opulent the large dinner table. Bronze statues supported gas jets, while cast-iron mirrors, fountains and balconies were inserted surreptitiously into unused corners; light had to be kept out by foliage as well as by sets of curtains. Sèvres, Dresden and Worcester porcelain stood in niches until the only rooms in which it was possible to move freely were the nurseries hidden behind a final filigree of carved woodwork where the four lively daughters lived in the charge of a beloved coloured mammy and a governess.

Delmonico, the famous restaurateur, found his talents stretched to the utmost when Leonard, August Belmont and William Travers arranged a competition between themselves in sumptuous dinner parties. "Here three gentlemen come to me and order three dinners and each one charges me to make his dinner the best. I am given an unlimited order."

The chef, a true genius, threw hysterics but managed to improvise novelties at them all—truffled ice-cream, etc. Leonard added to the originality by placing a gold bracelet with a jewelled pendant in every lady's napkin and Belmont capped this by platinum trinkets. Travers could only add the diamonds of his wit.

Fifth Avenue watched Mr. Jerome's social audacities with amazement. "That any man could have so much *energy*." Was it really very well bred? Clara wilted and turned pleadingly for companionship to the prim old families who maintained their pride behind social fortifications of increasing complication.

Yet in the stiff dark drawing-rooms where an iron decorum existed Mrs. Jerome maintained a brave front. No complaint concerning her husband's activities ever slipped out. The sufferings of a lady in such circumstances must be accepted without a sigh. The code was rigid, but she received indirect sympathy.

The most unsuccessful of Leonard's extravagances was the *Clara Clarita*, the family steam yacht (named for wife and daughter) on which he spent $125,000. The interior was left to an unsupervised contractor and the daughter wrote years later: "Mamma's face fell a fathom when she first stepped aboard and saw the luxurious impractical furnishings in pale-blue silk and hammered silver. 'What *has* all this cost?' she asked."

Leonard, who had given no thought to this project soon became irritated at the constant mechanical troubles.[1] He replaced the engines but when he realized his family did not want to live aboard relegated her to the "limbo of expensive failures." His heart belonged to sailing ships henceforth.

---

[1] According to Press cuttings, *Clara Clarita* knew one brief moment of fame in 1865 when the Atlantic cable was reported broken. "Mr. Jerome having been informed of the difficulties under which the Company laboured, and that Mr. Everett the able and skilful engineer, was willing to undertake the repairing of the cable if a proper steam yacht could be had, gracefully offered the use of his beautiful steam yacht the *Clara Clarita* and we are informed that she will proceed at once with Mr. Everett to the Gulf of St. Lawrence. This liberality on the part of Mr. Jerome will not only prevent any delay in the transmission of cable messages but will enable the Telegraph Company to meet the expedition with a vessel of which not only American yachtsmen but every man in the country may be proud." Every man except her owner.

14

THE Civil War was about to break, and a restlessness disturbed the whole country. Ignoring rumours Leonard opened a new office and began to operate along the whole line of stocks. Then Addison suddenly died (leaving two million dollars to his widow) and the Jerome brothers congregated for the funeral. They got together and all decided to work for President Lincoln's Northern party. Leonard wished to join the Army but he was persuaded into becoming Treasurer of the Union Defence Committee.

Through the New York *Times* he exerted considerable influence. The war enormously increased the circulation of newspapers, and fresh power fell into the hands of the owners. The New York *Herald*, which had been launched twenty-five years before from a rented cellar by old James Gordon Bennett, obtained the largest sale. Its impropriety could be guaranteed to fascinate the masses. Every edition contained amorous scandals, few of which were mentioned a second time, and even the personal column made salacious reading. Bennett desired not to mould public opinion, but to become a millionaire. Having achieved this ambition, and been snubbed by society, he retreated into sulky isolation in his country place and only saw a few business acquaintances amongst whom was Leonard. The New York *Times* in which Jerome held a quarter of the shares aspired towards "correct grammar and unbiassed reporting". In fact, it attempted to emulate that unique organ the London *Times* regarding politics and foreign affairs. Henry Raymond, its founder and editor-in-chief, shared Leonard's enthusiasm for the theatre and drove a smart span of bays. The two were often seen whispering together.

"Reckon I'd like to know what Raymond and Jerome are talking about," said a man in Central Park.

"I'll tell you," responded his friend. "Just 'osses."

What *could* a millionaire do in New York if he didn't like fast horses? Stay outside the pale presumably, a sinister spider like Jay Gould, or living in seclusion in a marble mausoleum, like A. E. Stewart, the "richest merchant in the world", while the other boys showed off their teams.

Leonard made society giddy. "He outdid all who were bent on cutting a figure." The shocked, the cross and the weary scolded in vain. He drove turn-outs with horses which were "trained to rear and prance as they turned the street corners". Old ladies as well as young lost their emotional balance as he careered by. His team of trotters, competing in Harlem Lane, evoked a popularity with the masses of the type which in England goes to those who enter a horse for the Derby. It is difficult to conceive the calm prevalent in civilian life during conflicts prior to the 20th century. Those who were not in the actual firing line considered it natural to carry on with normal pursuits and amusements. For example, on the outbreak of the Civil War, horse-racing was suspended in the Southern States, and many owners brought their stables North for safety, and letters of the period redound with chit-chat concerning fashion, sport and 'delightful soirées'. In this hour of national crisis Clara busied herself defending, not the Constitution, but a fashion launched by the Empress Eugenie of "coyly looping up the skirt at one side to show one foot and ankle". In this atmosphere no one thought it curious that owners of Southern studs should hurry them into enemy territory to ensure the animals' safety and comfort.

Leonard took a keen interest in these horses (the only refugees of the period), and devised plans for building racecourses and instituting an American Jockey Club similar to the English one. "Impossible," snorted contemporaries. "The gambling laws will never allow it."

"I'll raise it above all that," retorted Leonard. "Wait until war ends, you'll see."

Throughout the bitter years of fighting, the New York *Times* ardently supported President Lincoln and the Republican administration. Wall Street speculation continued as before, and the intelligent analysis of economic and political issues which only the *Times* offered, kept it indispensable to the serious reader. While political activities held him in New York City, Leonard continued to run his brokerage business. He gambled heavily but always seemed able to make another fortune to glue to the disappearing tails of those which had gone before. Over ten million dollars ran through his fingers and disappeared.

Leonard's one unlucrative venture concerned a Government Emigration scheme. When in the second year of the War President Lincoln signed the Emancipation Proclamation, various amateur attempts were made by Union supporters to solve the race problem by deporting freed Negroes to Brazil or Africa. These projects were not successful, but Lincoln was so anxious to get any colonization schemes started that, without being able to go into the matter thoroughly, he permitted a contract with a Mr. Kock who offered to lease a suitable island in the Caribbean, and Leonard became involved in what

The Empress Eugenie
A signed portrait given to Miss Clara Jerome

Opening of Jerome Park

The Inauguration Race at Jerome Park in 1866 is won by the five-year-old bay Kentucky

appeared to be a benevolent Government scheme. The Jerome firm raised the money to pay for the voyage and five thousand Negroes were shipped off to a dot, known as the Île des Vaches. But cows had only been seen there in mirage. Having landed the bewildered Negroes on what seems to have been a desert island composed of sand and cactus, the authorities in charge realized that all food and water would have to be shipped from Haiti. Mr. Kock disappeared with the lease money and was never seen again. When official investigators reported an unlikelihood that the island could ever support human beings, tempers flared both up in the Department of the Interior and in the Jerome office. Mutual accusations of irresponsibility flew faster than the enemy's bullets. Barrels of food and water had to be sent at large expense until the island could be evacuated. This hardly seemed what Yankees meant by 'colonization', and the ex-slaves must have puzzled at such uncomfortable freedom. Despite losses in this fiasco, Leonard was still able to contribute large sums to the War Wounded and he wrote a cheque for $35,000 to help in the construction of the *Meteor*, a ship designed to catch the blockade-running *Alabama*. His gifts, however, could not approach those of Commodore Vanderbilt, who presented a steamer costing $800,000.

Meanwhile Clara worked away at "sanitary commissions" for the soldiers. Bandages were rolled, and lint scraped by the "highest-bred hands of the city", which may have given some solace to the wounded in an age before anaesthetics were invented.

During all these war years Clara kept in touch with her friends in Europe, and when the arias, floating up from the red and gold theatre which was just too near her bedroom window, grew over-trying, she found distraction in reading her Paris mail.

The "dear Archduke Maximilian" now laboured deep in that labyrinthine dream of a vast South American Empire. Idealistic, unpractical (except as a sailor), and the most likable of the Hapsburgs, he allowed himself to be influenced by his lovely ambitious wife and nagging brother. France vaguely backed the project but the situation was confused. As Maximilian's wife Carlotta put it with youthful candour, "Francis Joseph grasps things with difficulty. . . . Louis Napoleon seems not quite straight". More ominous still, Queen Victoria was "very cool". The Jeromes' acquaintance, Mr. Motley, American Minister in Vienna, writing from the city which had been parched by a summer drought, stated:

"We have nothing green here but the Archduke Maximilian who firmly believes he is going forth to Mexico to establish an American Empire, and that it is his divine mission to destroy the dragon of democracy and re-establish the true Church, the Right Divine and all sorts of

games. Poor young man . . . that a Prince of the House of Hapsburg
should become a satrap of the Bonaparte Dynasty and should sit on an
American throne which could not exist a moment but for French
bayonets and French ships is most galling to all classes of Austrians. . . ."[1]

But after Napoleon had deceitfully laid out a glowing account of pacified
Mexico Maximilian succumbed. In April 1864 he departed from Trieste on
the verge of a nervous breakdown from indecision. As the Mexican flag
was run up at Miramar the Archduke sadly wandered through the rooms
taking a last look at his beloved castle and gardens. Then he walked down
to the marble jetty and sailed away for ever.

[1] John Motley—*Correspondence*, Vol. II, 1889, ed. G. W. Curtis.

15

THROUGHOUT the Civil War Leonard Jerome had two enemies whom he held in open loathing. These were the Democrat Governor Stephen of New York, and Fernando Wood, a Tammany Hall power and terrorizer of polling booths whom the Irish vote had held in place as Mayor of New York until just before war broke out. These two men were greatly responsible for the riots of 1863. Mayor Wood had, in 1857, deliberately allowed two rival Tammany gangs to riot and murder each other. Consequently the Republican legislature was forced to amend the city's charter and set up a new police force over which Mayor Wood could have no control. Criticizing this procedure as 'unconstitutional', Wood refused to disband his private police, and much blood flowed. He was still holding extraordinary power when in 1861 against violent Democratic opposition Lincoln declared war. Wood had publicly proposed that New York follow the example of the Southern States by seceding from the Union and, amidst acclaim, an association was formed to carry out this project. However the actual outbreak of hostilities nearly always arouses public enthusiasm and while it was still a novelty for the crowds to cheer regiments marching down Broadway Democratic grumbles went unheard.

After a year of dreary conflict had passed, emotions cooled. Democrats called a public meeting to protest against any continuance of military operations. Anti-war feeling created "as dangerous an enemy to contend with at home as that which our armies were confronting in the field".

Governor Seymour, of New York, and 'Boss' Tweed of Tammany Hall opposed President Lincoln with considerable power behind them, and in 1863, when Congress passed a Conscription Act, they seized the opportunity to make inflammatory speeches. "One out of about two and half of our citizens are destined to be brought over into Messrs. Lincoln and Company's charnel house," protested the Governor, and he openly threatened to incite disorder. One Monday morning in mid-July, 1863, the draft was scheduled to begin throughout the city. At ten o'clock mobs of armed men and women, proceeding according to well-laid plans, started to attack the city's main strong points. Enrolment offices were smashed, police and crippled veterans were killed, and by noon whole blocks of houses crackled in flames while pitched battles raged all over the city. Reports drifted in that the leaders of the riot were obviously being directed from some hidden high command. Such large-scale attacks all carefully co-ordinated could not be regarded as a spontaneous outburst. After pillaging shops and residences, the rioters started to kill Negroes indiscriminately. Even the Negro Orphan Asylum was burned to the ground and the terrified children scared out of their wits. When five thousand armed rioters marched down Broadway to capture police headquarters, only two hundred policemen could be marshalled to meet them. After an hour's pitched battle, the rioters fled, leaving their dying and wounded behind them.

Towards evening, a mob burst across City Hall Park towards the big newspaper offices. The New York *Times*, prime backer of President Lincoln, expected trouble, and built barricades around its offices, in the midst of which Leonard, unaware of the atrocities committed since dawn, proceeded to enjoy himself. A journalist records the scene in the inimitably sticky style of the day:

"At the broad entrance, and pointing outward were planted two of those revolving battery guns, of the newly invented Gatling type, and Mr. Jerome was in command of them. . . . The formidable things had been loaned to the *Times* by order of President Lincoln. I recall Mr. Jerome, tall, mettlesome, proud-looking and with power in his face, standing by the battery, ready for action and awaiting the approach of the rioters. Ruffians were lurking about: a gang of them could be seen near the upper end of the City Hall Park. . . . Reports got out which I may say were largely true, that there were soldiers in the second storey of the building and that rifles were held ready for use by editors and reporters on the third storey, and that there was on the roof another Gatling gun about which there was some merriment, for according to a yarn, it had been so placed as to bear directly upon the editorial quarters of the *Tribune*. Calmly and alone stood Leonard Jerome by his death-dealing machines. He was a gallant friend of the Editor of the *Times*, in defence of whom he risked his life, in defence also of the Government of the United States against whom the rioters had risen. There was something like majesty in his mien. Were I an artist I would paint the scene as I then beheld it and as it yet exists in my memory."

In fact, rioters smashed the windows of the *Tribune* building and sacked the lower floors. Police drove them out by nightfall, but violence did not abate. Leonard and his staff remained by their guns all night while indiscriminate murders continued throughout the city, and terrified families poured out into the suburbs over the few bridges left undamaged.

During the following day fighting continued, and the rioters organized barricades in studied Parisian fashion along Ninth Avenue. An acquaintance of the Jeromes, Colonel O'Brian, who commanded troops in one engagement, was caught by a gang of ruffians, tortured and killed.

Leonard hung on in the *Times* office, aching to let off his Gatling guns, until Thursday, when five fighting regiments were returned by the Army of the Potomac. By Friday, thirteen regiments held the city in control, and the printing presses again started to roar.

The New York *Times* puffed smoke and thunder. It issued a bold first edition making no secret of its views concerning the guilt of Governor Seymour, but the Federal Government never disclosed the identity of the true instigators of the draft riots. Twelve hundred people had been killed, and two million pounds worth of property destroyed.

Leonard Jerome, whose commitments with Commodore Vanderbilt were making him exceedingly rich, handed a quarter of a million dollars to the fund for families of those who had suffered.

16

DURING the late summer of 1863, seven-year-old Camille, the loveliest of the four Jerome girls, died in Newport of a sudden fever. Her desolate parents brought the child back for burial in Greenwood Cemetery.

During the remaining months of the war, Clara hid away in her villa, and Leonard attended only to urgent political business. When General Lee's army was finally brought to a halt at Appomattox and the South surrendered to General Grant, New York City speedily forgot it had once given acclaim to Mayor Wood's proposal for cessation and rejoiced wildly in Yankee victory. The Jeromes had returned to New York at the time of President Lincoln's assassination, and Jennie has described what she saw of the funeral: "our house in Madison Square draped from top to bottom in white and black, and the whole of New York looking like one gigantic mausoleum".

Lincoln alone had been great enough to understand the urgency of healing his country. After his death few individual Americans strove to eradicate the fratricidal wounds. Leonard who, throughout the war, had earned thousands for charity by the performances in his theatre, now opened a campaign for a Southern Relief Fund. "We must ease the bitterness," he wrote. When Henry Clews (who with Leonard had subscribed for every Government Loan and organized all the Union meetings during the war), built up plans to help the South recover its lost wealth and prestige by diverting foreign capital to regenerate Southern agricultural and commercial interests, Leonard placed a large amount of his own money in Georgia Bonds.

The Civil War had quadrupled many fortunes. Cornelius Vanderbilt who had been the government's war-time shipping agent was now a unique citizen. He possessed over twenty million dollars. Leonard found his own modest three million slipping up in the general expansion of railways, but he could not say like Daniel Drew, the Commodore's rival, that "I got to be a millionaire afore I knew it, hardly."

Old Daniel Drew, tattered, semi-literate ex-cattle dealer and his young henchman, Jim Fisk, were the outstanding 'smart guys' who made overwhelming fortunes out of dealings with the army during the Civil War. Through working with Vanderbilt in the Harlem-Hudson railway battle Leonard had cleared several million for himself, but no matter how much he made Mr. Jerome expended most of his energy on enjoying life.

Although her husband had won a foremost place, the dynamic rhythm of growing New York never struck a responding chord in Clara. She seemed impervious to its verve, its raw splendour. Even Leonard's most cultivated friends, witty William Travers and clever English Henry Clews and weird brilliant August Belmont, slightly jarred her. She preferred Europeans in their own settings.

Travers' humour which exactly fitted the America of the time left her unmoved. He and Larry Jerome took a schoolboy delight in boarding a horse-drawn Broadway bus treading on each other's toes and pretending to fight violently, shouting "How dare you, sir!" and demanding to be set down so they could take their coats off. When the frightened passengers stopped the bus and looked for a policeman they would walk off arm-in-arm roaring with laughter.

At dinners Travers could silence bores with jokes which only they did not grasp. A deadly talker running out of subject matter once asked if oysters had brains.

"Well, y-y-yess," purred Travers, "just enough to keep their mouths shut."

A famous shaft was launched when a crowd of Wall Street business men were watching the end of a yacht race at Newport—as the boats passed the winning post the name of one rich broker after another was called out. Then came the inimitable voice of Mr. William Travers echoing from the club steps: "And w-w-where are the c-c-customers' yachts?"

There was no answer.

August Belmont, educated on the Rhine, contrived to dominate New York City 'at almost every level'. Enigmatic, dapper, short, strong, limping from an old pistol duel, hard as nails and uncannily astute in finance, he became Leonard's rival in more matters than one. Belmont boasted the best chef, the best paintings, the best porcelain and the best trotters. Added to which, according to Frank Griswold "his connoisseurship of horse-flesh and women were considered authoritative". Whatever that may mean. He certainly possessed a very dashing wife. People like Belmont and Jerome did not enter society, they created it as they went along.

Despite her shyness, Clara was sure of her own judgment concerning things artistic. However, few New Yorkers saw any virtue in the panels of angels she had brought from Florence asserting they "had been done before artists learned how to paint properly". And in time she grew slightly ashamed of liking them. Indeed perhaps they did look rather odd amidst the dark mahogany and striped wallpapers. Happily Leonard purchased a Raphael as well, and her friends had at least heard of *him*. The horsey world was one in which Clara could never shine. She admired, but could not seek to emulate Mrs. August Belmont, who with elegant French manners and amazing jewels won renown as 'Queen of High Life'. The niece of famous Commodore Perry, hero of Lake Erie, she had been born into the highest stratum and after marrying August she soared naturally to elegant leadership. Not only could Mrs. Belmont converse, enchant, put people at their ease, and yank them out of it, but she electrified the common herd by allowing a nude by Bouguereau to decorate her home, and by driving herself at speed around Central Park. Clara did not envy painted nudes in the drawing-room, but light fingers and quick nerve, and an all-round ability to show off with horses would have served her purpose, her pathetic everlasting purpose of catching Leonard's eye. "So silly to admire courage and have none," she said. Unable to handle any reins adroitly, she determined her daughters should be of harder fibre, and supervised their upbringing in detail.

Already they rode and danced and skated with expert precision and in an age when the vapours were still fashionable Clara Jerome insisted on cold baths, fresh air and strenuous exercise. "Strong women make beautiful women," she coaxed. They showed every sign of having inherited Leonard's immense physical vitality and people turned to smile at the rosy-cheeked girls driving their donkey-cart along the new wide avenues of Newport.

Despite her antipathy to certain professional singers Clara entered whole-heartedly into her husband's charitable schemes. It must have been extremely convenient for Leonard to be able to entertain himself while raking in large sums for charity at the same time. "I believe you *can* serve God and Mammon if you try hard enough," said a prominent New Yorker. "Look at Jerome."

The most memorable artists to grace the Jerome stage after Patti left for Europe were Minnie Hauk, for whom Clara evinced a particular tenderness, and the fabulous Mrs. Ronalds whose singing voice and beauty added to her social talents elevated her to a unique niche in New York's history.

To the chagrin of many less talented ladies, the exquisite Fanny Ronalds could not only hit high C but drive her own drag in masterly fashion to Newport picnics. It was impossible to compete with such feats. Clara wisely did not try, for Leonard's horses trained to rear and caper caused her to close her eyes.

For years, Leonard had worked to perfect himself in the art of showy driving. From boyhood he felt an instinctive understanding of the high-mettled horse: riding around Rochester, trying Lipizzaners in Trieste, gallivanting down Harlem Lane with his first trotters, he had never ceased to study and improve his hands. Now he heard that the Duke of Beaufort had taken to driving a four-in-hand around England seeking to revive the romance of old coaching days. Leonard's eye lit up. Such a pastime appealed to him.

Soon, from the stables in Madison Square emerged a spectacular vehicle, "built to Mr. Jerome's special requirement", and New York saw amateur coaching for the first time.

Social-snob chronicler of the time Ward McAllister recorded Jerome's inauguration of what was later to become the smartest sport of the city:

> "He turned out daily with his dray or coach loaded with beautiful women, and drove to every desirable little country inn and about the city, where one could dine at all well, crossing ferries, and driving up Broadway with the ease and skill of a veteran whip which he was."

August Belmont followed suit. Being a multi-millionaire, he devised a still more costly coach, and with German thoroughness mastered the high art of four-in-hand driving. The two friends astounded New York with the spectacle of their rival coaches, but Belmont had not the natural showmanship of Jerome. Having avoided church since his father broke his violin, Leonard devoted every Sunday morning to this new amusement. A shocked newspaper criticized him for driving up Fifth Avenue waving to friends who had turned out for the smart church parades:

> "Gay and laughing ladies in gorgeous costume filled the carriage. Lackeys, carefully gotten up, occupied the coupé behind; Jerome sat on the box and handled the reins. With a huge bouquet of flowers attached to his button hole, with white gloves, cracking his whip, and with the shouts of the party, the four horses would rush up Fifth Avenue, on toward the Park, while the populace said, one to the other, 'That is Jerome'."

17

In 1865 Leonard bought a race-horse for $40,000. This was great-hearted Kentucky who was to prove 10 lb. better than any horse of his day. In August, soon after entering the Jerome stable, he won the Inauguration Stakes, the first race ever run at Saratoga Springs, and Leonard in impeccable spencer and morning coat knew the pride of leading in a winner to the cheers of the crowd. He and William Travers had vowed they could raise horse-racing from disrepute to the high standard it obtained in England. They would maintain a royal sport, not rowdies' outings.

Saratoga Springs enchanted Leonard. He had studied the course with William Travers (who presented the Travers Stakes, the first stakes ever given for a flat race in North America), and they decided that a race-course for New York City ought to be laid out on the same lines. They named it Jerome Park and founded a Jockey Club which they hoped to keep as strict and incorruptible as the one in England.

New York in the sixties sizzled beneath its elaborate social ramifications and diverse methods of showing off. Behind the accumulating fortunes, behind the façade of brownstone mansions which crept ever further from the vulgarities of Broadway, lay interlapping a strange tangle of crude, tough, corrupt circles of power. Where respectability began and ended did not always distinctly show.

'Boss' Tweed who was Street Commissioner, head of Tammany and ruler of the city's polling boxes, used as his right-hand man one John Morrisey, a gangster-pugilist who ran luxurious gaming-houses both in New York and at Saratoga Springs. The whole of New York feared Tweed. It knew the machinery of the city lay in his hands, and that millions were extracted by him in bribes. But he was efficient and by making the law conform to his wishes he remained legal. New Yorkers were hardly surprised when the 'Boss' took up with Morrisey the notorious leader of the dreaded Dead Rabbits gang which commanded the immigrant Irish vote in the Bowery; but they suffered a real shock when Commodore Vanderbilt made friends with the ex-prizefighter in his gambling house at Saratoga. When they saw Morrisey matching his fast horses against the Commodore's in jovial competition in Central Park they wondered where the underworld ended and respectable society began.

If a man trod on the fringes of high finance where gangsters met bankers he needed to 'know his way around'. Leonard Jerome did. Clara would have fainted had she understood the calibre of the men with whom her husband dealt. Leonard, however, stuck to a straightness that the gangs understood and seem to have respected. They knew where they were with him, and some curious trait in his character—his deliberate frankness perhaps or his flamboyance—appealed to the riff-raff. At any rate, John Morrisey, having instituted a system of repetitive voting in city elections,[1] and bribed the City Council in order to secure the appointment of Tweed's nominee as City Chamberlain and made a fortune from his sumptuous casino on Twenty-fourth Street, had the grace to announce that he "sure liked Mr. Jerome's driving".

Now that Leonard was devising a new sport calculated to enthrall the multitudes he had to beware of tough twisters only too eager to enjoy a rake-off. The moral responsibility lay on his shoulders from start to finish. He had battled in New York City for sufficient years to understand how a 'racket' started. But the gangs appeared to be hypnotized by the novelty of this new venture and the verve of its inaugurator. Gangsters were not very lurid in those days, they hardly ever pulled a gun and could be charmed by a man they thought 'a sport'. If Mr. Jerome would provide a race track where they could honourably gamble and flaunt their bejewelled lady-loves, they wished him luck.

Leonard started by purchasing the old Bathgate estate of two hundred and thirty acres at Fordham where, for half a century, the Bathgate family had privately bred and tried out their horses. The property possessed a unique formation, with a large hill, called the Bluff, standing in the centre of a natural race track. On this eminence the stands and club house were to be erected, while the course curled in full view around it. With William Travers and Lawrence enthusiastically sketching, and making notes and suggestions, Leonard walked every hillock. Already they could visualize the horses, hear the thunder of hoofs. To August Belmont, who joined in the project with zest, Leonard wrote: "It will pass Saratoga in charm. We have the most picturesque scenery, hills, a hollow and a really good view and I am insisting on a competent engineer." This turned out to be Charles Wheatley, designer of the Saratoga course.

In the following April, the American Jockey Club held its first conference in Leonard's office, at 46 Exchange Place. The committee laid down its aims thus:

[1] According to Tweed's evidence in court later.

"To promote the improvement of horses, to elevate the public taste in sports of the turf, and to become an authority on racing matters in the country."

The moment it was finished, Leonard leased Jerome Park to the Jockey Club, and volunteered to stand an annual loss of $25,000 if the expenses could not be paid. He possessed a childish enthusiasm and drive which brought flat racing into repute throughout the country in one day. Thousands of people who had never previously heard of 'the turf' now found it their favourite subject.

In September 1866, with unsurpassed fanfares the Jockey Club of America held its first race meeting. According to the Press this opening of Jerome Park "proved the social event of all time and started a new era in the horse-racing world". General Grant, victor of Appomattox, presided as guest of honour in the 'royal box' of a grandstand holding 8,000. New York's smart set turned out in magnificent clothes, and the pleasure-hungry masses followed joyously. Every woman present from richest to poorest had a new bonnet for the occasion, and the shimmer of silk and satin covered all Leonard's green hill. Newspapers could hardly find space to print the race results such were their exclamations over the well-known faces, beauteous ladies and gorgeous gowns. And in the centre of it all, serene in their Club House, the Jerome brothers and August Belmont and William Travers surveyed the perfectly laid course and scintillating crowds. Mrs. Belmont all beaded and befringed, and Clara rustling in deep-puce silk, could fan themselves and sigh with satisfaction. Nearby in white, beneath a ribboned parasol, the exquisite Mrs. Ronalds, songstress and socialite, distributed her soulful enigmatic smile to a band of top-hatted admirers.

Needless to add, the leaders of the great New York 'rings' were there, John Morrisey "in sober black", and 'Boss' Tweed (with nine years to run the city as his own, before imprisonment), and diamond-covered Jim Fisk the partner of Jay Gould, whose plan to effect a corner in gold would be broken by Ulysses S. Grant who now sat with Clara Jerome in the grandstand. But Tweed, Fisk and Morrisey were the refined froth, the *crème de la crème* of the underworld. Mannerless gamblers and rowdies had somehow been kept away, overwhelmed, perhaps, by the fragrance of expensive scent, or suffocated in the crowd of feathered hats.

Every lady present did not necessarily possess a diploma of respectability, but those without one atoned for lack of virtue by stylish turn-outs. Josie Woods, the young and lovely owner of New York's most expensive *bordello*, arrived in her luxurious victoria, escorted by liveried footmen. "I wonder what is engraved on their buttons?" whispered William Travers.

The virtuous declaimed it "impossible to follow such a profession and look so good, and dress with such taste". For doe-eyed Josie wore only costly silks in subdued colours as a real lady should, and her manners were affectingly genteel. To the relief of many, the millionairess-abortionist Madame Restall did not appear. She had built herself a colossal brownstone palace at the corner of Fifth Avenue and 52nd Street and outraged society by whirling around Central Park at fashion parade hour in a magnificent barouche with her nose in the air like a duchess, but she did not care for a day in the open and the respectable were spared the sight of *her*.

Strange characters, rich and poor, had trekked from every part of the city, and a babel of different tongues arose, Italian, German and the Irish brogue that was the seal of New York's core. The green grass blazed with human beings, and a roar of voices echoed long after the last race, when the white dust driven from a hundred departing carriages rose high in the evening sunlight. "Never was there such a day for pomp and glitter and excitement."

Clara drove home "faint from so many people but all a success," she wrote, "only very bad for Clara and Jennie. He would take them to the Club House."

New York retained an inordinate enthusiasm for its racecourse, and the 'social glories' continued to occupy Press headlines. The Jockey Club obtained power with a membership of thousands held in firm control by the Committee, so Leonard was never called upon to donate his $25,000 but he stipulated that the Club should not be allowed to degenerate into a mere money-making concern. Jerome Park was to be run as a cherished creation, a kind of untarnished sportsman's dream. Money must be earned elsewhere.

An old newspaper article reads:

"L. W. J., who was the master spirit of the club, began collecting a stable of racers with characteristic dash. He purchased *Kentucky* shortly before that famous horse won the Inauguration Stakes, and bought an elegantly appointed stable west of Jerome Park, where *Kentucky* was installed and a select stud of brood mares was acquired. But Jerome will be remembered more as a promoter than as an owner. *Fleetwing* came to his stable late in life, and with brittle hooves: *Clara Clarita* was only fair; *Redwing* quite moderate; and *De Courcy* was about the best of the racers under the 'blue and white stripes'."

It is evident from contemporary letters and articles that Leonard's personality made a vivid impression on all he met. He was an "odd cove" but "none could squander money with his espechal artistry, or was kinder to those in trouble". An old lady wrote years later: "he had such beautiful

89

manners and despite his dashing ways many young people nowadays could learn from Leonard Jerome how to behave in public". And another said: "Jerome will not write his name in dollars alone. His name brings a smile to the faces of all . . ." a smile or a frown of annoyance, but never dislike. The crowds loved him, they called him "a sport", and in him many poor men perceived some aspect of themselves, a facet of how they would like to be if rich. It was his attitude to life, not his fortunes (which were always disappearing), that singled him out among Americans.

Unfortunately most of the anecdotes concerning Leonard's speculations have long ceased to bear any point. One newspaper reporter writes: "There are a host of stories afloat about Jerome illustrating his ready wit. One of them concerns a person who had been carrying a heavy load of Michigan Southern in anticipation of a rise. . . ." And then follows a long-drawn-out, almost incomprehensible story studded with Wall Street jargon the gist of which is this: A Rochester acquaintance who had newly opened a banker's office in Manhattan met Leonard in Broad Street and asked if he would give his firm orders on a commission basis. Leonard refused saying: "You'll never make money in the Street. You can't keep a secret. If I gave you an order you would run off and tell everybody. All the brokers hereabouts would know what I'm doing. . . ."

The representative of the new firm pledged his word to keep Jerome's orders secret, so Leonard gave him a trial order to buy 5,000 of Michigan Southern.

As result the whisper went round that "Michigan Southern was a mighty good thing to hold, for Jerome was buying the block". The stock soared and Leonard, guessing what had occurred, sold all that his own office held. The market immediately began to falter, and a few days later his acquaintance arrived with a long face to admit his house was indeed "busted for he could not resist telling a few friends and had bought Michigan on his own account until swamped".

Leonard teased him heartlessly and suggested he learn to be more meticulous about divulging secrets. But in the end he relented and helped the man out. It was his nature.

A fellow operator wrote:

"He was a daring man in speculation, being guided implicitly by an almost blind confidence in his own destiny. And yet he was not reckless. He would risk $100,000 on a turn of the market with a cold calculating coolness which was not altered by either loss or gain. During the period when he was floating on the top of the tide with his *Pacific Mail* deal he used to paralyse his friends by the magnitude of his transactions.

'How is business, Leonard?' I asked him one afternoon as I met him sauntering leisurely up Broadway. 'Oh dull,' he said, 'confoundedly dull. I've only made $25,000 today.' And with that he passed on."

Another contemporary wrote:

"He spent money as freely as he made it and never was happier than when contributing to the welfare and amusement of others. No matter how busy he might be he had always time to talk of racing, yachting and sport of any kind. . . . Any half decent fellow who failed in Wall Street could borrow enough from Mr. Jerome to start anew.

Always surrounded by a crowd of business or social acquaintances and seemingly engrossed in affairs or amusement he succeeded in observing all his acquaintances closely, learning when any of them was in trouble, and hurrying to them with open hand and sympathetic heart.

A fine young fellow who had more energy than money was working himself to death. Mr. Jerome urged him to give up business for a few weeks and run over to Europe with his wife for a rest.

'I can't do it, I haven't enough money.'

'How much have you?'

'About $2,500 and I daren't clear myself out.'

'Let me have it,' said Jerome. 'I'll send for it and as soon as I'm ready I'll make a turn for you. At the worst you shan't lose anything.'

Within the week the young man received a statement showing nearly 3,000 earned to his credit on stock operations but his own cheque had never been sent for."

Another man who knew him wrote:

"He had not the character to hold on to money and in the years after the opening of Jerome Park there were constant rumours of financial loss. The 10 million he had made certainly grew less but he continued as a public spirited benefactor."

The rumours about Jerome never ceased. Slightly less polite is Henry Collins Brown's[1] account of the Grand Union Hotel at Saratoga where

"You couldn't walk along one of these verandas without stumbling over the boots of a Vanderbilt, a Jerome, a Gould or someone else

[1] Founder of the Museum of the City of New York and author of *The Story of Old New York*, etc.

positively filthy with money, seated in a rocking chair, discussing the water-holding capacity of a new railroad."

But whereas "Bill Tweed, Peter Sweeny, Pete Connolly and the rest of the 'boys' wearing velvet waistcoats, big diamond rings and shirt studs" would be chewing tobacco and drinking at bars Jerome and Vanderbilt behaved 'aloof'. They simply talked horses and sailing, which must have been exceedingly boring for the diamond-studded tobacco-chewers.

Rumours about Jerome never ceased. Clara said she did not think he himself knew how many millions he had made or lost. Too many other interests held his attention. Now with Jerome Park added to his passion for trotters, coaching, sailing, music and ladies, it seems extraordinary that he could keep a finger on the pulse of Wall Street at all, but he owned huge blocks of railway shares and almost all the Pacific Mail Steamship Line to California.

Leonard evidently spoiled his daughters, who pressed him into combating their mother's strictness. Jennie has described these years with

"lessons, and matinées at the opera 'to improve our minds', sleighing and skating for pleasure, and on red-letter days a drive to Jerome Park on my father's coach, where I always occupied the seat of honour next him. Sometimes, from afar, I could see the blue and white of his racing colours come in first, which was a great excitement. On one occasion I was hoisted upon the back of his most famous race-horse, the celebrated Kentucky, whose sire Lexington, and dam Magnolia, by Glencoe, were of the best blood in England."

There were

"several delightful summers at Newport, where my father had built a charming villa more in accordance with one's idea of a seaside residence, than the gorgeous white marble palaces which are the fashion nowadays. There we were allowed to run wild and be as grubby and happy as children ought to be."

Jennie made her worldly debut at the age of ten, when August Belmont gave a fancy dress party. Leonard had ordered a pretty little costume to be made for her, copied from a print of a French *vivandière*. She did not sleep for a week with excitement, but on the evening her father found her in floods of tears, "because I don't look as I thought I was going to". Years later she added, "a situation which alas! was often to repeat itself".

18

MINNIE HAUK was rumoured to be Leonard's daughter through an early romance. She had been born in New York at about the time of Jennie Lind's visit and curiously, the gift Leonard admired most seemed to have been wished into this small dark-eyed creature. Song came as naturally to her as to the nightingale. After a childhood spent in the wilds of Kansas where she had rambled with Indians and gathered prairie flowers while "singing at the top of a baby voice" Minnie travelled back to New York during the Civil War. A man-of-war brought the Hauks up from New Orleans and Minnie's mother, whose whole life centred on this precious and precocious only child, launched her as best she could into the musical set. Leonard first heard Minnie sing after a dinner party when she was still a schoolgirl, with hair in long plaits. He could hardly believe his ears. With August Belmont he promised to finance her musical education and as foremost patrons of the Old Academy of Music they arranged for her to be given an audition there. Minnie hoped to please with the 'Casta Diva' from *Norma*. The manager listened with surprise to this small person's rendering of the opening recitative ending with pianissimo *La* in *Alt* developing into a forte and then dying into a pianissimo. "Enough," he cried, "study and you will be great."

Leonard and August Belmont now vied with each other in encouraging their 'discovery'. They took her out to be petted and spoiled, treating her to cakes and ices along with their criticism. After a year she had mastered ten or twelve Italian operas, and her poetic renderings of the more emotional airs gave promise of real art. An untrammelled out-of-door childhood had given her strength and perhaps the very lack of any early forced education had kept her mind receptive. She certainly showed an unusual capacity for learning long passages of music by heart. At fifteen she was ready to make a small debut, "with the aid of Mr. Jerome and other kind friends who had taken great interest in my progress, I succeeded in doing so".

From the first Clara found something touching in the fiery little brunette and Minnie's memoirs record many happy days spent with the Jerome family:

93

"During this period I was quite at home at Mr. Leonard Jerome's house in Twenty-sixth Street, near Madison Square Gardens. His wife and three daughters, Clara, Jenny and Leonie, welcomed me very warmly. Almost every Saturday Mr. Jerome would take us girls in a dog-cart to his country seat near New York—later known as Jerome Park and Race-course—and there we used to stay over Sunday, returning to New York the following morning.

Mr. Jerome possessed some beautiful saddle-horses, and his daughters were in the habit of riding many miles before breakfast. They rode like Amazons and wished me also to mount a horse, which I had never attempted before. Desiring to avoid the appearance of fear, I allowed myself one morning to be mounted on a horse which Mr. Jerome himself had selected. It was a very gentle, beautiful black pony, with the prettiest head and shapely legs, and I felt as proud as a peacock when at last I sat in the saddle. Although I observed all the instructions that were proffered to me as to the handling of my pony, I must inadvertently have touched him with my whip a little too smartly, for without warning he galloped off right across the paddock and back into his stable.

This might have put an end to all my operatic aspirations and career, but, clearly, my star was not destined to such extinction. Fortu-nately the stable door was not hooked back, and I had sufficient presence of mind to push the upper part of the door so that I could retain my seat, while the horse walked quietly up to his manger. I was safely taken from the saddle. Thus ended my first essay as a horsewoman.

My second attempt was not more successful than the first. We had all cantered into a newly-ploughed field, and while the others urged their horses into a gallop, my pony evidently thought it would be heavenly to take a roll! Before I realized it he was down on his knees, but, as I had no inclination to share in his fun, I slipped from his back, while he continued to roll about to his heart's content. This trial was my last. My sporting ambition was nipped in the bud, for I found that I had absolutely no talent for horsemanship; nor have I ever since been able to find pleasure in outdoor sports.

The day of my debut was fast approaching. I had chosen for it *Linda di Chamounix*, and in addition to my studies I had to prepare my costumes. I was particularly anxious that they should be as rich and as correct historically, as possible, and I longed to get one of *rose moiré antique* for the second act. Mr. Jerome kindly presented me with it, while Mrs. Jerome lent me all the jewellery required to perfect my appearance as a grande dame. My happiness was complete, for it must be realized that I was then a very unsophisticated child of fifteen!

The theatre chosen for my 'private debut' as an opera singer was Mr. Leonard Jerome's own theatre, a few doors from his house in Madison Square, at the corner of Madison Avenue and Twenty-sixth Street. In later years it was converted into a fashionable club-house. It was a perfect bijou building, decorated in the most extravagant style, with a seating capacity of about four hundred, and at my debut all of the so-called 'Four Hundred' of New York were actually present. I remember that on either side of the stage there was a fountain of scented water.

The rehearsals passed off very well, and when the great evening came I was perfectly self-composed, without the least stage-fright.

My appearance was a pronounced success, and all New York rang with my name as 'The Wonder Child'. Demands for invitations had been so numerous that Mr. Jerome very kindly arranged a second performance, and this was equally successful."

A few notes from Minnie to Leonard survive:

"New York. Aug 17 1866. Won't you come and take us out from the farm? You know I love to go with you better than anyone else. Please try to come and see your child Minnie."

"Oct 11, 1866. Come and see me tomorrow if you have time. I feel very unhappy about some things before I make my Debut and I should be so very happy to have my best friend try to help me out of it."

"Philadelphia. Oc. 24, 1866. Could you not send me those stockings? I should love to have those stockings worked with blue for *Sonnambula*. I am wearing those stockings worked with pink that I sing in every evening. Goodbye my Dear Friend. Kiss Jennie and Clara for me and my regards to Mrs. Jerome."

She was only fifteen.

Never had Clara taken such an interest in any singer, and her nervousness exceeded Minnie's before a performance. On the night of her public debut at the Academy of Music[1] Minnie's mother trembled with anxiety. Backstage an old singer saw the young star jumping for joy in her blue silk costume. He warned her: "In later years you will not dance before your looking-glass before appearing on the stage." And she was to learn from Patti herself the increasing nervousness which besets mature artists, but now at fifteen, fresh from the prairies, with the high true notes ready to burst 'from her childish heart', Minnie made so guileless a picture that Mrs. Jerome could hardly refrain from kissing her. That exuberance, that disregard of all save the moment's excitement . . . where had she seen it before?

[1] Forerunner to the Metropolitan Opera.

On the back of a photograph of Minnie, now faded to pale sepia, Clara pencilled one indiscreet clue, "so like Jennie, but less good-looking".

Her own girls, galloping wildly on their ponies, had indeed become her very life, but here she found another version, a high-strung incarnation of Leonard in song. She could not but be fascinated.

Minnie's career launched in the Jerome Theatre to that picked 'Four Hundred' swept forward without a hitch.[1] Destined to become the first great American *prima donna*, she toured the States and then, well-chaperoned by a forbidding and stately mama, left for Europe. She conquered Paris and Moscow before accepting contracts with the Imperial Opera House in Vienna and the Berlin Court Theatre, neither of which had heard an American singer before.

Adelina Patti became, through Leonard Jerome, her inspiration and her friend. It was Minnie Hauk who first sang *Carmen* in London, and although this opera aroused consternation on account of its novelty she "made people like it".

Towards the end of her life Minnie found herself sitting amid the faded costumes in which she had won fame in so many cities and she wrote nostalgically in her Memoirs:

> "At my feet I noticed a piece of stuff which had fallen out of my very oldest trunk of all. I picked it up. It was a remnant of the *rose moiré antique* dress which I had worn when I made my first appearance in opera at Mr. Jerome's theatre in *Linda di Chamounix*. A world of memories of the past came rushing and flooding through my mind. I sat with this lovely piece of rose moiré clasped in my hand. . . ."

Seymour Leslie, a grandson of Leonard, has written:

> "The end of Minnie Hauk was romantic as her beginning, for she bought and restored Wagner's famous villa of Triebschen, on the Lake of Lucerne . . . the house where most of the *Ring* was written. I went through it in 1928, just before she died. Royal photographs, silver framed, cluttered the piano, every table, every vitrine. She willed Triebschen to the City of Lucerne as a Wagner Museum; and here in

[1] A letter written decades later by Frank Griswold to my grandmother Leonie reads: "I remember my first opera. I went in 1866 to the debut of Minnie Hauk—your father had educated her voice and morals I believe? Clara and Jennie were both in the box. The Opera was *Lucia*. . . ."

A postscript adds: "I see on looking it up that Minnie Hauk made her debut in New York Nov. 30 '66 in *L'Étoile du Nord*, so that it must have been later in the winter that your father took us to the opera. I am sure it was *Lucia* for I remember the Scots in the first act with drawers on which were meant to represent bare legs and also remember the prima donna with a Scotch cap and plaid."

1937, took place one of the most moving and historical of musical events. Toscanini conducted a picked orchestra of the finest musicians in Switzerland in a programme that included the exquisite Siegfried Idyll ... played for the first time since that far-off morning when Frau Cosima Wagner awoke to receive the most immortal of childbirth gifts. There, we sat, with Wagner's grand-children and Minnie's old admirers. It was a glorious day and even the lake steamboats had been muted for the occasion. Few of us knew that we owed it indirectly to the inspired Testament of Minnie Hauk ... or perhaps to her far-away and forgotten patron."

19

THE year 1866 was an eventful one. Financial panics rocked Wall Street; Commodore Vanderbilt and Leonard Jerome fought together in the Hudson-Harlem railroad battle; the Atlantic cable was laid; Clara's youthful beau Tegethoff created naval history at Lissa; the Empress Eugenie started to wear humming birds in her hat; Mrs. Ronalds gave her famous fancy dress ball and the Jerome brothers participated in the first Ocean Race ever sailed.

Meanwhile, a skating craze developed which kept the smart set with their rude health and strong ankles whirling and gliding on every pond in Central Park. The Jerome girls of course became star performers. Leonard flooded a large area near his racecourse, and a special train ran guests out to waltz and pirouette while a band played encouragingly in the crisp air. Two cottages by the skating rink were furnished, and Clara supervised hot luncheons. "It would take Leonard to devise the details," wrote a bruised visitor; "we were comforted by waltz tunes and sausage rolls. I can't tell you how lovely a scene it made, with the band playing, and everything glinting in the sun." And, the centre of attention, her whole little body given to the rhythm of the waltz, legs twinkling, and cheeks scarlet with excitement, skimmed Miss Jennie Jerome. Clarita, less daring, and baby Leonie, unable to equal their sister's fancy steps, circled precariously around the edge.

Mrs. Jerome sat by the sparkling lake wrapped in furs and worry. She worried about Jennie who obviously ought to have been a boy, such zest and energy might then have been in keeping. And she worried about the gay ladies and queer men whom Leonard and Commodore Vanderbilt liked. The old man's bluff ways and untempered tongue amused Leonard, and the Vanderbilt trotters, yachts, shipping lines and railroads all backed by a maelstrom of millions gave them plenty to joke about. Leonard could not stand glum tycoons. Vanderbilt had charm—for men, if not for refined ladies—and if high-society recoiled, there were wider worlds which appreciated his dauntless character. Clara had to admit she liked the Commodore, "not despite, but because of his lack of airs and graces". But now that Vanderbilt had taken such a fancy to John Morrisey, she quivered with anxiety. Such a person could not be asked to *her* home.[1] Dressed soberly in black, Morrisey allowed only a few large diamonds to sparkle in his cravat, and on his fingers. He did not drink and after watching the brother of New York's Mayor Wood lose $10,000 in a night, at faro, he would remark piously: "I never gamble myself." "A character," Vanderbilt called him, when he established Morrisey as his 'political agent'. After Jerome became Vanderbilt's partner in the Harlem Railroad he was often seen appraising horses with the Commodore and Morrisey.

Respectable citizens frowned. Unable to stomach such intruders socially, they yet feared the power of Tweed's Ring. No one wanted to fall foul of John Morrisey, or to delve too deeply into his affairs: they merely wished he would 'stay put' in his sumptuous underworld casino, and not be seen about. Well-bred folk disapproved but could not resist watching as the suave intruder with the broken nose matched his horses in Harlem Lane against those of Vanderbilt, Jerome and Belmont. Not daring to speak out the snobs shook their heads and muttered to the grass and cast angled glances to see how Mrs. Jerome was taking it.

Clara did not think Morrisey at all a nice person, but she feared to say a word of reproach lest it result in Leonard leaving home even more than he already did. Her husband never mentioned the cards he had to play, or who the real powers might be in that strange background from which he emerged with an occasional fortune. How could she understand those hard-hitters and corrupt politicians against whom he had to pit himself? Less and less did he discuss mutual plans. Perhaps it was her fault. She could not understand music, horses or finance, and yachting made her sick. How could a quiet, motherly person amuse such a husband when all glamorous ladies of New York went out of their way to catch his eye?

For Mrs. Ronalds the road opened very differently. It was only too easy for her to obtain attention. A graceful skater, she practised figures of eight, in a shortened hoop-skirt while little Jennie swooped after her. Only Fanny could show so much leg and not be criticized.

Fanny could sing and manage horses. Fanny could skate in circles. When Fanny went out in boats, her cheeks turned pink instead of green. Everyone wondered at Fanny. Had she so wished, in her enchanting authoritative manner, Fanny could have got away with murder very prettily.

Clara's thoughts took refuge in Europe when Leonard's eyes had lit each evening as she appeared in a lovely new gown. She would never forget the night when they went together to their first Tuileries ball, and he had said as they came home in their carriage, "Clit, you were the handsomest woman

---

[1] Morrisey eventually entered Congress and when he died 19,000 citizens flocked to his funeral.

there." She cherished that evening's approval—could she ever win it back? How could she shine before him? Certainly not on ice skates.

When summer came they all went as usual to Newport where the little 18th-century town, with cobbled streets and vistas which came to an end "like the quick steps of old ladies", was fast disappearing. Here Mrs. Ronalds took daily driving lessons with Leonard. She showed exceptional talent with the reins. Everyone gaped, and everyone talked. Comments were not always kind.

Meanwhile Clara busied herself with the children who had a tendency to 'show-off'. She found this extraordinary, and very hard to curb.

Then in July 1866 the Battle of Lissa occurred between the Austrian and Italian navies, which stunned technical spectators, and awoke romantic memories in Clara's breast. All the world spoke of Admiral Tegethoff, and as she read of the first conflict of iron-clads, it seemed that a faint echo of Viennese waltzes stole through the Newport villa. American newspapers printed the odds against which the Austrian ships had won their sea-fight.

Even ladies ignorant of warfare could understand the following:

"12 iron-clads against 7.
208 rifled guns against 74.
20,392 pounds of metal in the broadsides against only 1,776."

The manœuvres of Tegethoff were slightly confusing to the feminine sex but other paragraphs could not but stir the emotions. Here was classic proof "that courage and enterprise can reverse, in the actual fight, the conditions that beforehand, would seem to make defeat inevitable". The American Admiral Farragut had said, "Give me plenty of iron in the men, and I don't mind so much about iron in the ships". Now a commentator wrote: "There was iron enough in the Austrian sailors Tegethoff and Petz, to outweigh all the iron in the guns and armour of the Italian fleet." And of the young count who had danced with her till dawn lit the Illyrian hills, they said: "His successful ramming of a fleet that should have been able to destroy every one of his ships in an hour, will remain for all time a proof that skill and courage can hope to reverse the most desperate disadvantages."

Tegethoff had not yet reached forty and the crews under his command, drawn hastily from creeks and islands of the wild Dalmatian coast, were chiefly fishermen to whom he had given one month's intensive training. Most of them, unissued with uniforms, had fought in their picturesque native costumes. Clara fluttered. How clearly she could see it all—the burning blue sky, the fair islands in a haze, and the violence of that brief brilliant battle which would live for ever in history.

Taking a quill, she scratched a long letter to the Admiral at Pola. She destroyed it and rewrote it twice.

"I did not know he was *such* a friend of yours," said Leonard, and there was a tinge of respect in his voice. "My dear, you certainly chose well."

20

THE wandering eye never ceases to wander, a fact which presents consolation to certain wives. No one had held Leonard's attention for long, not even Patti with her unbelievable octaves and dramatic fire. But Mrs. Ronalds, siren of New York society, became a lasting friend.

Born in Boston she had overwhelmed family opposition and persuaded reluctant Puritan parents to send her to Florence to train a natural singing voice under the best masters. She might have stormed every musical citadel in Europe, but Pierre Ronalds, a young American of fortune, persuaded her into early matrimony. They returned to New York where the alliance disintegrated. Fanny bore three children, and then according to a first-hand account: "The husband neglected his wife. In fact, he would disappear for months at a time. She had to look to her brave men friends for sympathy and these she found in abundance."

Then Mr. Pierre Ronalds disappeared from the picture; contemporary memoirs do not allow him even a peep around the frame. Most of those who were lucky enough to meet Fanny gushed about her beauty, her voice, her expressions. One habitually reticent Englishman Mr. Greville Moore, in his *Memories of an Old Etonian*, otherwise written in the traditional British style of understatement, bursts forth: "Her face was perfectly divine in its loveliness, her features small and exquisitely regular. Her hair was of a dark shade of brown and very abundant."

Leonard met her when she had just shed her husband and become the sensation of New York, but a very *well-bred* sensation. She dressed perfectly, entertained on the grand scale and showed herself a gracious patron of music; in fact she represented what any respectable mother might have wished for had her daughter proved irrevocably and through no fault of her own to be *une femme fatale*.

The story of the first meeting of Clara and Fanny became famous. Leonard had not known Mrs. Ronalds for long, but gossip flared easily in that small slippery social world and when Mrs. Jerome, on entering a ballroom, was unexpectedly introduced to the lady whose name she must have heard linked to her husband's, an embarrassed hush fell on the immediate spectators. Might she use the deadly weapon of the public 'cut'?

Clara took the proffered white-kid hand. "I don't blame you," she said softly. "I know how irresistible he is."

After opening her house in New York Fanny continued to study singing, but as an amateur *prima donna* she found fulfilment difficult because she could not demean herself by 'going on the stage'. The problem was neatly solved by Leonard Jerome's private band-box opera.

She began to sing in aid of wounded soldiers, and took the leading part in four Italian operas, beginning with *Hernanie*. Audiences were enchanted by such vocal range and magnetic personality "in a lady". Tickets sold at a premium, and enormous sums poured in for the soldiers. Mrs. Ronalds could never know the excitement of a professional working her way to the top, but from Leonard she received the critical adulation which every artist craves. She flowered into fresh beauty with the attainment of self-expression, and when at the end of the Civil War Leonard switched to the aid of Southern charities, she sang herself to exhaustion. Then they decided on a new venture. The Jerome Theatre would be thrown open for "Tableaux Vivants" to be presented by society belles. These persons were more easily managed than singers, and the delectable Fanny could star among them without straining her throat. The theatre dressing-rooms now overflowed into Clara's bedroom. Rehearsals and costume fittings took place every afternoon, and the elect, who had previously been allowed to listen to Fanny, were now to be allowed to look. Tickets cost the same for either favour.

According to a newspaper cutting the first Tableaux presented to an "audience rare and radiant" earned thousands for the Southern Relief. Fanny appeared modestly as an Italian Madonna, while Mrs. Belmont, "a miracle of taste and loveliness", pole-axed spectators by personifying Winter "all hung with icicles made of *real* diamonds". Everyone had their fun and the charities reaped rich profits. Only Clara and the exhausted servants were glad when the Tableaux season ended.

Lovely Mrs. Ronalds—the best of every world was hers for the asking, but she walked carefully among proffered bouquets, and if she seemed to over-sparkle at Leonard's fabulous parties, the malicious were forced to admit she seemed to have become a dear friend of Clara's as well.

All the summer mornings she drove with Leonard at Newport, learning how to conduct her own plunging horses, his hands on hers, gently showing how to send the message along the reins until she could skilfully manage her own four-in-hand on crowded Belleville Avenue. All the evening she would be singing at the piano. But afternoons were spent with the Jerome children, who 'allowed her to become a favourite'. She gave them "a species of small dog cart and two donkeys, which rejoiced in the names of Willie and Wooshey". With these they spent hours tearing up and down Belleville Avenue, "a terror to the smart folk in their silks and feathers who drove majestically by".

Naturally Leonard was not alone among Mrs. Ronalds' admirers. August Belmont, usually able to mask his feelings, was becoming only too visibly affected. The two men had been friendly rivals so often but now neither could fathom what tactics the other would try to employ. Only Fanny knew and she kept silent.

A New Yorker whose mother was an intimate of Mrs. Ronalds wrote in his privately printed memoirs:

> "There were two outstanding men at that time who were most prominent in all social and sporting matters. They both drove coaches and four, and had large racing stables; both were married and in the prime of life. These two men fell desperately in love with Mrs. R——. L—— and A—— were rivals who kept the house of their lady filled with flowers and attempted to satisfy her every desire. She proved to be an accomplished general, for she managed these two great men, as well as other aspirants, with much skill."

One day Fanny seemed wistful and full of sighs. She thought it would be delightful to give a fancy dress ball but complained that she could hardly afford it. "Too bad," Leonard agreed. Then, after some thought, he suggested she deposit a few hundred dollars with his firm to see if he could improve matters. A week later the investment was returned to her, multiplied into thousands.

Mrs. Ronalds set to work with ardour. She would give the best fancy dress ball ever seen in New York. A guest wrote:

> "It was the talk of the town. Invitations were sent out three months ahead, so there should be time to get special costumes from Paris. Such hot-house fruit and flowers, such music, canvas-back ducks, terrapin and old wines had never before been seen on Manhattan Island. The ball was a grand and glorious function which produced some little sympathy for the absent husband, owing to the extravagance of his young wife. Thousands of dollars had been spent on flowers alone and the ball lasted until six in the morning."

The hostess excelled herself. She impersonated *Music*, and wore a wonderful white satin gown embroidered with bars from Verdi's *Ballo in*

Maschera. Her crown, especially designed and constructed in Paris, consisted of sparkling quavers and crotchets lit up by the tiniest gas jets which were supplied from a holder hidden in her hair. A guest wrote: "This made a great impression; the harp glowed and sparkled all the time that Mrs. Ronalds received her guests. . . ." Everyone quivered with excitement. How daring and how explosive!

Exquisite as ever beneath her ingenious head-dress, Fanny caused the sensation she had intended. But many guests were shocked, for peeping from her satin skirts were red boots hung with tinkling bells. Not quite good form for a lady, even when representing Music.

Happily this stupendous outfit did not have to be relegated to oblivion. It reappeared thirty years later when Mrs. Ronalds attended a yet more famous fancy dress ball, that of the Duchess of Devonshire in London. But times had changed; now the crown could be lit by an electric battery!

Frank Griswold, well-known American sportsman, recounts a nice ending to Fanny's party. He happened to be present on a day twenty years later when Leonard Jerome and August Belmont were lunching together at Jerome Park. Mrs. Ronalds' name was mentioned, and Leonard looking across the table asked: "August, do you remember Fanny's celebrated ball?"

"Indeed I ought to," replied Belmont, "I paid for it."

There was a sad faraway look in Jerome's dark eyes as he said:

"Why, how very strange. So did I."

21

DURING the late sixties Leonard worked with Vanderbilt in several financial skirmishes.

Since 1860 the Commodore, entertaining the notion that railroads might supplant his own steam-boats, had begun to buy entire lines. Daniel Drew came up against him on several occasions. When Vanderbilt had induced Albany to allow certain tracks to be built Drew bribed the Legislature to rumour the privilege would be granted, but later, on Drew's signal, to report adversely.

Leonard and the Commodore had organized a five-million-dollar pool. On the Legislature's change of tune stock fell heavily. Vanderbilt rose in wrath and swore that he would teach the honourable members to break their word, that he "would hound them, etc., break every mother's son, etc.". The Commodore then purchased 27,000 more shares of Harlem than existed, while Morrisey got to work on the political side, prying and forcing and frightening. In a month the stock soared from $150 to 280 and then 300.

"Put it up to a thousand, Tobin," chuckled Vanderbilt to his agent. "This panel game is being tried too often."

But Leonard Jerome prevailed upon the Commodore to abandon so splendid a revenge. "If you should carry out your threat," he insisted, "it would break every house in the Street."

Vanderbilt relented; he would be content to break the Legislators and "send them home without paying their board bills".

One line after another came into the Commodore's hands. "By subtle machinations that are not, almost a century later, quite clear to historians of stock and bond operations, he pounded Harlem railway shares down to nine dollars, then took control."[1] He then shook the Hudson Line down to $25 and bought out that company. Leonard worked with him during these transactions which were packed with incident and kept darting down from Newport yacht races for confabulation at the Commodore's house in Washington Place.

A New York newspaper has written of Mr. Jerome:

[1] *Age of the Moguls*, by Stewart Holbrook.

"It was impossible that such a man would not provoke enmity as well as make friends. He was exceedingly disliked by a large proportion of brokers. Sometimes they united and struck at him hard. But Jerome could bear a square blow without flinching better than anyone. His sangfroid was inimitable. After a hard day of ill luck at every point he would sit down with his friends at supper, brimming over with animal spirits, telling a story or singing a song with the gusto of one who had just made half a million. He never acknowledged a moment of despondency except in reference to one occasion. This happened in connection with a corner in *Hudson*. Jerome had made all his combinations and satisfied with the outlook, took his yacht and set out on a pleasure trip, up the river to West Point. Beginning to have misgivings he steamed back to the city and on reaching the pier heard bad news. The scheme did not work. Everything was at a dead stop. Leonard kept his own counsels and turned the problem over until daybreak. By that time he had laid out a fresh line of strategy and canvassed it point by point. Satisfied with his plan he gave orders and went up to West Point again. The result of that night shortly showed itself in the rapid culmination of one of the most brilliant corners ever known in stock speculation."

Having obtained control of both *Hudson* and *Harlem* railway lines Vanderbilt decided to buy out a competitor, the *New York Central*, which met the *Hudson* line at Albany but only actually crossed the bridge to pass on freight and passengers to the *Hudson* when the river was frozen. Under normal conditions *New York Central* trains stopped short and handed over all goods to the steamboats with which they had an understanding. Vanderbilt jumped at this weak link. One winter day he ordered his *Hudson* trains to stop west of the Albany depot so that passengers had to walk two miles through the snow carrying their luggage. He even raked up an old forgotten law which legally prohibited the Hudson Railroad from running across the river. Despite public outcry, outraged committees and angry legal debates no legislation could force Vanderbilt's trains to cross the river. *New York Central* stock began to slide and when it had fallen sufficiently Vanderbilt bought 18 million dollars' worth and made himself President of a line that now extended from New York City to Buffalo.

Leonard made several millions while working with Vanderbilt and he managed it without giving up other distractions. His yacht racing with the fresh wind and sparkling waves made a pleasant contrast to the skullduggery of financial manipulation.

So far Vanderbilt's finance had been very simple and pretty rough. When Daniel Drew brought in his 'smart boys' Jim Fisk and Jay Gould a new crafty cunning would evolve in 'big business'. The ordinary citizens of New York, unable to make head or tail of the Powers that ran them, contented themselves with criticizing rich people generally, especially those with 'immoral bath rooms'.

There grew up 'Rings within Rings' in New York City. Boss Tweed the political controller with Tammany Hall behind him induced the astute and gentlemanly August Belmont and the young Astor heir, a millionaire who had nothing to gain, to condone his machinations. He even lured Belmont to appear on the same political platform as Jim Fisk, a man to whom Belmont would not speak in Wall Street.

Two judges of the Albany Supreme Court (Justice George Barnard and Justice Albert Cardozo) were ready to dispense justice as the Tweed Ring thought fit. The Ring controlled the Democratic political machine and bribed and intimidated many of the smaller Republican politicians as well. It was impossible to avoid its octopus tentacles and when Vanderbilt started to prepare for the biggest fight of his career, that with Drew, Gould and Fisk, for control of the *Erie* Railroad he had to employ John Morrisey, pugilist-gangster of Tammany Hall, as his 'political agent' to get the job done efficiently. Jerome had been called "the cleanest man in the Street not called Straight", but no one kept kid gloves on during transactions with Daniel Drew.

Of the unbelievable three Princes of Erie with whom Vanderbilt was about to take up the cudgels fat flamboyant Jim Fisk was the most human. The *Springfield Republican* wrote:

"nothing more gigantic in the way of swindling has ever been perpetrated in this country, and yet it may be that Mr. Fisk and his associates have done nothing that they cannot legally justify, at least in the New York courts, several of which they seem to wholly own."

But at least Fisk gave the public a show for their money. He drove a splendid phaeton in Central Park and the carriage in which he flaunted his gaudy lady loves was upholstered in cloth of gold. The most royal of vulgarians he acquired millions, squandered millions and "was kind to the poor".[1]

Many New York gentlemen waxed indignant when Jim drove to the

---

[1] Jim Fisk came to a sad end in 1872. His beautiful mistress betrayed him and the handsome master with whom she had fallen in love attempted to blackmail Fisk over certain letters and finally brought a case for libel. After this case Fisk repaired wearily to the Grand Central Hotel and there Stokes, who had stolen his mistress's affections, shot him dead in public. It was a sensational end; thousands attended his funeral and wept when his horse was led by with his spurred boots turned back to front.

Jerome Park races six-in-hand, using three pairs of white and black horses with gold-plated harnesses, and mounting two Negro postilions in white livery on the leaders, and two white footmen in black livery on the back of his dray, while a host of young actresses, picked from the theatres he owned, smiled from the seats.

"August! Is it possible he's trying to copy us?" teased Leonard.

But Belmont's face showed no smile. Fisk was his enemy, and a dangerous one. While Fisk remained vice-president of the *Erie* Railroad, no man of repute would sit on the board. Gould would soon beseech Belmont and Astor to lend their names, to share the profits, to clean up the mess—(though not by exposing *too* much). They refused "because of Fisk". He could hardly be more dishonest than the rest but he flaunted mistresses in public!

During November 1866, nostalgic for the days of his youth and perhaps revolted by the crookedness he had seen on high levels, Leonard sat down at his mahogany writing desk in Madison Square and penned a letter to the President of Princeton which still survives:

"My dear old Friend and Tutor:
    I send you by politeness of my friend Judge Field $5,000 of United States 6% Bonds.

    I shall be obliged if you will arrange that the interest on these bonds may be annually expended in the purchase of a medal to be awarded to the graduating Senior who shall be declared by a vote of his classmates to be the *first* gentleman in his class.

    I know you will be surprised, dear Doctor, at the novelty of this request, but you will be still more so when I tell you that you are the cause of it. I have not forgotten the remark you made upon a certain occasion to my class: '*Young gentlemen with all your getting I advise you to get a little more manners.*' I am right then to offer a premium to carry out your views.

    I think that the most pressing necessity of Young America is the article you recommended. We have plenty of science, and are pretty well up considering our years in Art, but our manners I must say are rather rough. If the trifle I offer shall lead to improvement in this respect, I shall feel that I have done the country a service.

    The character of a gentleman I consider within the capacity of all— at least it requires no extraordinary intellect. *A due regard for the feeling of others is in my judgment its foundation.* . . .

    I think very often of Princeton. The scenes of that lovely spot are fresh upon my memory as though they had occurred but yesterday. My two brothers who graduated before me—you remember what noble good men they were—are both dead. Allen is buried in Princeton. Aaron died in Alabama.

I shall always regard Princeton with the deepest interest and affection: and among the many friends I met there, none can be remembered with higher regard and respect than yourself.

Ever faithfully and gratefully yours,
Leonard W. Jerome."

The prize money was not in fact used, the difficulties of selection being considered too onerous for either masters or classmates, but a lively correspondence on "manners" resulted in the Press.

Incidentally Leonard's definition of a gentleman was almost exactly that made by Confucius in the 5th century B.C., "a gentleman is one who thinks of others before himself".

The manners of great magnates in the sixties were supremely well depicted in the great fight which Vanderbilt had with Daniel Drew over the *Erie* Railroad. The Commodore did not stoop to tricks, he was a bluff bold grabber. In amalgamating his *Hudson-Harlem—New York Central* lines he had voted himself six million dollars in cash and twenty million more as a 'bonus'. It was all quite clear and above board. Now he cast eyes at the *Erie* line whose stocks Drew held and fluctuated at will. Drew had come to New York driving cattle which he salted and then allowed to drink their fill before being sold at false weight. Drifting to Wall Street he continued the same tactics; "watered stocks" became a usual term in his entourage.

Vanderbilt announced openly he was going to take over control of the *Erie* Railroad. His agents bought all the stock on the market. To the Commodore's amazement an unlimited amount still seemed to be offered for sale. Vanderbilt's 'boys' started investigation. When they discovered that Daniel Drew had started a backroom printing press and the machines were stamping out new stock indefinitely, the Commodore flew into a bellowing rage. Before he could obtain an order to seize the press Drew and his friends departed by rowboat to Jersey City out of the court's jurisdiction. Here they barricaded themselves in a hotel which they renamed Fort Taylor and mounted three cannon on the waterfront. Vanderbilt did not hesitate to take the law into his own hands if he got a chance and they were terrified of being kidnapped.

At length the Commodore, evading the spies of Gould and Fisk, sent a note which read: "Drew, I'm sick of the whole damn business. Come and see me. Vanderbilt."

The tale henceforth is told by Daniel Drew himself:

"I decided to meet the Commodore's offer of peace, not that I felt any great love toward him. He had been calling me all sorts of names during my stay in Jersey, said I was no better than a batter puddin' and that I would turn tail on my partners any time he wanted me to; that I had no backbone and such-like. And whilst I was starting rumours about him through Wall Street in return for the mean things he was saying about me, he up and said to friends: 'This Erie war has taught me that it never pays to kick a skunk.' It hurt me considerable when these remarks came to my ears. I had half a mind to resent them. But I concluded to forgive him.

So when Sunday came I set out from the hotel, supposedly for an afternoon's walk. When I was out of sight, I changed my mind and skipped over to New York. I found Vanderbilt at his home in what used to be Potter's Field, but was now called Washington Square. It was a fine big house; red brick with white trimmings. I was very cordial in my greetings to him. I thought it best to show a friendly spirit and act as though nothing had come between us. 'How do, Commodore,' said I, and grasped him by the hand, 'the sight of you is good for sore eyes.'

'Come in,' said he. He was short as pie crust. I saw those convertible bonds were sticking in his gizzard. But I made up my mind to keep sweet anyhow, no matter how miffed he might be.

'You've got a fine house here, Commodore,' I remarked, sitting down in an easy chair and crossing my legs in a friendly sort of a way. 'It beats all creation how this city is a-growin'. Why, back in my Bull's Head days this here place where you've got your fine house used to be called Shinbone Alley, and the graves around here were thick as bugs on a pumpkin vine. Those were great old days anyhow. I often think of the time when you and I were in the steamboat business together.'

But Van puckered up tighter than chokerberries. 'Now, see here,' said he, 'let's don't get mushy. Of course, I'd like to be affectionate and chat with you about old times. No one knows how my bowels yearn after you, Drew; but as I understand it, this is a business interview, so if you'll wipe that tobacco juice off your chin and draw up here to the table we'll talk.' So I wiped off my chin and drew up close to the table. We talked the thing over."

Vanderbilt won but the fight had cost him one million dollars.

22

THE blue water sport had, like horse-racing, revived with a flourish after the Civil War, but trans-ocean racing had not yet been thought of. All through the summers of 1865 and 1866 Leonard spent what time he could spare from coaching, and Jerome Park, and the Observatory, out at sea. Since the evenings in Trieste, when he had learnt to sail his own little boat with an Illyrian fisherman for master, Leonard had developed a passion for taut canvas and high wind. He raced *Undine* and *Restless* along the coast of Maine, and as long-shore racing grew in popularity he became a prominent member of the New York Yacht Club, a discriminating group easy with the black ball. To this club he brought an unhappy, uncontrollable boy of twenty-five who did not know what to do with himself or where to turn for headstrong adventure. This youth was James Gordon Bennett Junior, the only child of that old millionaire who had been the greatest publisher of his day, whose press had dared assail Astor at his death, as a "self-invented, money-making machine", and who himself now merited that epithet.

Mrs. Bennett, finding it hard to make headway in New York society, had whisked her darling son off to Paris for a sophisticated education. Now he was brought back to be loosed on the *élite* with a superior accent in French and a large income. Young James found himself much in demand socially—and was bored stiff. He grumbled that he did not want to be 'classy', he wanted to "feel able to breathe". This was rude when the best people were inviting him to their houses. Soon his parents had to scold him hard and, as often happens when this treatment is meted out, the scoldee took pains to avoid future contact. This proved easy as far as his father was concerned, for the old man indulged in picturesque seclusion in a vast house on Washington Heights; but Mrs. Bennett after spending so much time and money on polishing this one jewel, sighed to see her white-headed boy sneering at society, scorning newspaper management and groaning for "something worth doing in life". Like many frustrated human beings, he turned to the sea for escape, but his sailing-master tried to win a race by cutting through Plum Gut instead of sailing over the prescribed course. The opposition papers seized

Jennie in riding habit

Kentucky—1868

By courtesy of John I. Leslie

William Travers

The Duc de Persigny   The Marquis de Tanysier

on the charge and used it as a handle to belabour the *Herald*. James' father, bitterly resentful of his son's inability to keep out of trouble even in sport, banished the youth from New York much as a mediaeval king might dismiss an erring son from court. Stamped as a ne'er-do-well, haunted by reiterated reminders of "that wonderful education" he had so ill-deserved, James finally found consolation in the company of two older men whose early lives had been entirely different from his own. Leonard and Lawrence did not treat him as a wealthy fop. With them he found "the companionship of real men at last". They forced him to raise the courage to live down the ignominy caused by his cheating skipper. With their moral backing, James ventured once more into the yacht-racing world. Lawrence had become as ardent a sailor as his brother. "It is not fair," wrote a cousin, "those middle-aged Jerome brothers don't even get sea-sick." An American sportsman of the time describes the halcyon days when:

"Racing was a social function. Jerome Park was in its glory, and the race horses all belonged to one's friends. The Four-in-Hand Club was Society's most fashionable resort. The Social circle was small and select, and the 'Charge of the Four Hundred' as yet unheard of. After the turf, the most popular sport was yachting. The yachtsmen of the day owned large sea-going schooners, and raced them in the open sea."

When they came back from their ships boasting and arguing as people always do when a hot bath has washed off the salt, the yacht owners of New York would treat each other to splendid banquets, and sail every inch of the way again. It was in October 1866, after such a dinner at the Union Club, that Pierre Lorillard and the brothers Osgood, all sporting millionaires, with no uncertain notions concerning their own prowess with boats, fell into excited discussion concerning the sea-worthiness of the centre-board yacht. Lorillard owned *Vesta*, a centreboard schooner, 105 feet long; and the Osgoods sailed a keel schooner *Fleetwing*, built the year before, with a length of 106 feet.

Lawrence and Leonard, also sitting at the same table, threw forth their opinions, but no one listened in the fray of flying words.

"Don't shout so—try it!" cried Lawrence.

"Try the Atlantic, and give each ship her chance!"

Within a flash, the owners were hurling bets on the table, thirty thousand dollars a side.

And then poor-little-rich-boy Bennett came up, heard of the match and begged with such vehemence to be allowed to enter his *Henrietta* on the same terms that, despite the fact she had been beaten both by *Vesta* and *Fleetwing*, they allowed him in. Ninety thousand dollars lay on the table; the winner was to take all, Leonard holding the stakes.

By dawn they had fixed the date, and set the course. The race would be sailed from Sandy Hook outside New York to the famous Needles Rocks off the Isle of Wight in the stormy month of December, "when there's wind enough for all". Each owner was to sail his own boat, and the match was to be a test of endurance as well as of speed.

As the starting day drew near, dramatic efforts were made to obtain first-class crews. The original contestants, Lorillard and the Osgoods, thinking better, or persuaded by horrified families to think better, of their hasty challenges, decided not to sail themselves. Their boats would venture out to strut their stuff in charge of the finest professional skippers obtainable. Only young Bennett insisted on the privilege of sailing in his ship through the mid-winter storms, and the Jerome brothers thought it would be "good sport" to join in.

Henrietta, a keel schooner like *Fleetwing*, was 107 feet over-all and carried a crew of twenty-four. In an article published later in *All the Year Round*, a journal conducted by Charles Dickens, the following descriptions occur:

> "Some difficulty was experienced in securing seamen to cross the Atlantic in such vessels, and in such weather. The men were willing enough to engage but their mothers, wives and sweethearts, interfered and persuaded them not to sign articles. Moved by such feminine solicitations, the picked crew of the *Henrietta* deserted her a few days before the start, and their places had to be supplied by a lot of land lubbers. . . . Invitations to prominent yachtsmen were declined for various reasons, and the gentlemen who served finally in this capacity, were almost all volunteers. . . . From seven a.m. on Dec. 11, the day of the start, no communication was permitted between the yachts and the shore, partly to prevent any further difficulties in regard to the crews; and partly because several kind but frightened friends had conceived the idea of subpoenaing some of the yachtsmen as witnesses in trials of which they knew nothing, in order to preserve them from the perils of the sea."

Fleetwing had the same crew difficulties but, at the last moment, nine whaling sea captains volunteered to man her. At the start Bennett was loudly cheered as "the only man who goes in his own boat". Spectators noted that *Vesta* and *Henrietta* had both decked over their spacious cockpits, making for icy hardship but greater safety. "A pity the Fleetwing hadn't taken the same precaution, for the seas would be big out there, and cruel and hungry." The three ships scudded away into a fresh wind and *Vesta*, with her centre-board up, clearly set the pace. Then they disappeared into the green sea and snow-filled breezes.

Meanwhile old Mr. Bennett, fuming in his monumental palace, was anything but pleased, for opposition papers declared that everyone who sailed in the race would be drowned.

The ships' logs survive. During the first week *Henrietta* chalked up two hundred and fifty to two hundred and eighty miles a day. Then she ran into a full gale and when Captain Bully Samuels, famous master of clipper ships, decided that she could be driven no longer, preparations were made to heave-to under close canvas.

> "The storm tri-sails happened to be stored in the cabin, and as the sailors came silently down, coiled the tackle and carried up the sail on deck, the scene reminded one of the bringing forth of a pall for a funeral. A pause in a race like this seemed the burial of all our hopes. Nevertheless, it was some consolation to be informed by Captain Samuels that, in his thirty years experience, he had never seen a vessel that could face a gale for so long. . . ."

During this gale *Vesta*, who might have sunk had she attempted to heave-to, scudded on, running dead before the wind, and gained a far lead.

At 6.55 of Christmas Eve, *Vesta* made the lights of the Scilly Isles. Fifty minutes later *Henrietta* picked them up. But in the two-hundred miles up Channel to the Needles, *Vesta* threw away in poor pilotage the ascendancy she had gained in mid-Atlantic driving.

At 10 p.m. *Henrietta* brought land abeam, and raced up the Channel at thirteen knots, compensating for the hours lost while hove-to. Soon after noon on Christmas Day she picked up the Cowes pilot, who set free loud cheers with the news: "*Henrietta* is first boat in, and a good 'un." At 3.45 p.m. she passed the Needles with everything set, and so won the race in 13 days, 21 hours, 45 minutes. Eight hours and fifteen minutes later, at midnight of that same Christmas Day, *Fleetwing*, who had taken a more southerly course, roared past the Needles reefed down in a fierce gale, and *Vesta*, again losing her way through poor pilotage, took last place 40 minutes later.

But *Fleetwing*, who had not decked over her cockpit, bore sad tidings. Six of her stalwart crew had been swept overboard and drowned. The ship's log reads:

> "Wed. Dec. 19th. This day commences with a light breeze from S.S.W. 2 p.m., in all light sails, gale increasing with heavy sea. 7 p.m.

blowing a gale; running under two-reef fore-sail and forestay sail (storm canvas). 9 p.m. shipped a sea which washed six of the crew out of the cockpit; hove to for five hours under two-reef foresail. 2 a.m. kept off; latter part moderate, wind hauling to west; set square sail. Lat. 47–20. Long. 37–27. Distance run 199 miles."

The five-hour search in the dark, with icy seas breaking against the ship's sides, had been almost hopeless from the start. Men cannot live for long in the North Atlantic in mid winter, oilskins and sea-boots shortening their struggles.

One hopes that the millionaire owners of *Fleetwing* looked after the families of these gallant seamen who died trying to win them laurels. Surely they did. Generosity was ever the hallmark of American sportsmen. International interest had been aroused by the Great Race, and the sportsmen of two continents had kept their attention riveted on the Atlantic all that December. The yacht clubs of Europe were waiting for the three brave schooners slashing their way before the westerlies.

Members of the Royal Yacht Squadron hurried to welcome each ship as she anchored in the sheltered harbour of Cowes. The crews were bathed, feasted and sent to receive acclaim in London and Paris. At some of these entertainments we learn that "Lawrence Jerome was the life and soul of the party and told stories that greatly amused the Britishers. He was a very large man, full of humour and wit and a practical joker. . . ."

The tables were turned when a member of *Henrietta's* crew managed to abstract a sheet of royal note-paper from Osborne House, and on it write commanding Mr. Jerome to dine with Queen Victoria on a certain evening.

Jerome was both pleased and distressed when he discovered that he was the only member of the party so honoured. . . .

His shipmates sat about and jollied him along as he dressed for the banquet but did not reveal the truth until the gig had actually put off from the yacht bound for the Royal Landing.

When Jerome was recalled and climbed back on board *Henrietta* his relief was so great that he danced a hornpipe on deck.

A public banquet was given in Paris and "the eulogistic articles in the English and French papers were cabled to the New York *Herald*". Papa Bennett's annoyance faded when he saw his son blossoming into the hero of the hour. According to a writer of the eighties:

"This ocean race was the turning point in James Gordon Bennett's career. When he returned to New York he began to devote himself to business. . . . The foreign staff was reorganized and ordered to use the cable instead of mails. Editorials were telegraphed from London. Stanley (the renowned explorer) was engaged to report the Abyssinian war and repeatedly beat the British dispatches with his news. The *Herald* supplied the London journals with its telegrams and became a power in the English metropolis. The acquaintances which Bennett made as a yachtsman became of the greatest service to him as an editor."[1]

Such a transformation in the Bennett heir caused general comment; in the storm-swept sea he had grown up and even his socially ambitious mama smiled. Did not J. P. Morgan state: "You can do business with anyone, but you can only go sailing with a gentleman"?

"Right, although it depends what you mean by a gentleman," said Leonard Jerome. He was thinking of hard-driving Captain Samuels, and of the stout crews of flush-decked *Henrietta* and *Vesta*, crouching half-frozen behind the lee of weather cloths during long hours of watch, and putting all their heart into the handling of canvas in shifting freezing winds, and of *Fleetwing's* six sailors lost in the roaring ocean.

The world excitement died away but lasting tribute has been paid to this First Great Race in Alfred Loomis' modern history of Ocean Racing. He writes:

"ever since, in a score of ocean races, have seamanship and dogged determination and inscrutable luck mirrored the greatness of the historic match between *Henrietta*, *Fleetwing* and *Vesta*."

Frank Griswold, in his *Clipper Ships*, finishes off the story:

"Leonard Jerome won considerably over $100,000 backing *Henrietta*. I well remember, when a boy, driving to Jerome Park with him during the Winter of 1867, in a large blue and golden boat sleigh, which had been built for him to celebrate the event. It took six horses to pull the sleigh over the snow and what surprised me most was that he drove the ten miles in the cold without gloves."

[1]*Prominent New Yorkers*, 1884, by Stephen Fiske.

23

WHILE Lawrence remained roistering in the yacht clubs of England, playing his impossible pranks, and amusing dinner parties with verve and wit, his wife Catherine remained in New York. According to her in-laws, Sister Kate was becoming rather grim in middle age. Once a grave, modest girl with downcast eyes, years of mingled adoration and disapproval of a flamboyant husband had turned her silent and solemn. While Lawrence had grown famous as a humorist in two continents she only wished to be taken more seriously. Everything the Jeromes did worried her, and they in turn referred to her as "a plague". While Clara shrank from all forms of publicity Catherine brooded because the family name received the wrong sort of recognition.

Both Jerome brothers had contributed financially to the building of a wide avenue leading to Jerome Park, and Catherine took for some reason a personal interest in this procedure. "I admire that Avenue," she announced. Intense grew her indignation when local authorities named it after an Alderman Murphy. This was "really too much!" After some pondering Mrs. Lawrence Jerome set out in her carriage to visit a large metal foundry where she placed a considerable order, and hired a band of craftsmen. Overnight the Murphy name-plates were removed, and impressive bronze ones bearing the words Jerome Avenue were irrevocably riveted and welded in their stead. Evidently the Local Council felt too tired to carry them away. Bronze lasts and the subway goes to "Jerome Avenue" to this day.

Meanwhile Leonard inadvertently received more limelight than he desired concerning two showy white horses from his stable which appeared drawing the carriage of a certain lady. All New York recognized the gift.

Clara had been brought up in the belief that a wife who speaks a cross word loses power over her husband for ever. She merely announced that she was in poor health and thought it would be better if she sailed for Europe to consult a French physician. The three girls and Dobbie their black mammy were to accompany her. She visualized taking an apartment in Paris while Clarita and Jennie in their teens, and little nine-year-old Leonie, could receive a French education out of the ordinary. Leonard would be freer.

He let her go. Within a month she had mustered her personnel, packed belongings, and said good-bye to the house in Madison Square, turning without regret from the rooms she had so carefully furnished with ebony and scarlet plush. Henceforth the address of the Jerome ladies would be 70 Boulevard Malesherbes, and Leonie with Dobbie in tow would be staring round-eyed up the Champs-Elysées.

Paris was at this time about to hold a Great Exhibition. Thousands of foreigners flocked to France eager to see the latest marvels, which included "locomotives, 50-ton guns from Krupp in Germany, aluminium, fuel oil and American rocking chairs". Among the visitors there were of course many crowned heads, Alexander II of Russia, Queen Victoria, and the King and Queen of Prussia. Clara, for whom royalty held much appeal, immediately recovered her health, and prepared for a diverting time. But first she had to organize the girls' education. Because of their special talent, music took highest place, but they must also become "polished conversationalists in French and German". The "Jerome Programme" drawn up left very little time to spare.

No sooner had they moved into "an apartment containing many gilt mirrors and padded chairs" than a series of news bulletins arrived which must have made padded furniture less a luxury than a necessity. Ladies swooned all over Europe, and quills were scratching little notes, dotted with exclamation marks, at every aristocratic writing desk. First, a Polish patriot attempted to assassinate the Tsar as he drove in the Bois de Boulogne with Louis Napoleon, and then the Emperor Maximilian was shot by a firing squad in Mexico. Contemporary letters stress the "inconvenient moment" at which the telegram announcing this news arrived. Eugenie was dressing in the Tuileries to present prizes at the Exhibition and all festivities had to be cancelled. The court went into mourning and so did Mrs. Jerome. Meanwhile the Paris mob raged because their Mexican Loan seemed beyond redemption. If the Emperor got shot it must have been his own fault; why should their small savings disappear in the dust along with that tiresome Hapsburg? Ominous clouds rested on the city, the atmosphere thickened as before thunder, and when Maximilian's Empress Carlotta capped the drama by going mad in the Vatican, the pens of a thousand social scribblers squeaked with horror. Queen Victoria wrote in her inimitable style:

"too horrid, poor dear unhappy Carlotta bereft of her reason, and her husband killed. . . . What a shocking end to their luckless undertaking which I did all I could to prevent, and which dearest Albert was *so* much against."

Clara sympathized with them all but could not resist a twitter of excitement when her gallant Admiral Tegethoff departed for Mexico to retrieve the Emperor's body. It was so dramatic! Every time she came to Paris either a victory or a calamity blazed up.

Leonard, alone in his large sombre house in Madison Square, received the news with coolness. He was himself approaching a tumble. During the past seven years his profits had been immense; never confining himself to single operations, he had made one fortune in *Hudson* and another in *Pacific Mail*.

"He led the street now to the exclusion of everyone. Tobin even, with all Vanderbilt's influence, had not the power of Jerome over men's opinions. The latter was the pet as well as the king . . . almost worshipped as well as watched and imitated."[1]

How long could it last?

By now a contemporary could write, "Jerome had weathered more cyclones, and triumphed over more conspiracies against his fortune, than would have sufficed to ruin a hundred ordinary men." His biggest defeat lay ahead.

In 1861 Leonard had cornered the *Pacific Mail Steamship Company*. He took the stock when its selling rate was $62 and carried it up in the next few years to 329. His realizations, even at the earlier stages of the rise, were enormous. A stream of dollars ran through his fingers and burnt holes in his pockets. Ever since 1848, when California joined the U.S.A., there had been a great need to bring ships to the Pacific Coast at ever cheapening rates, and Jerome's shipping line headed this vital effort. "At the close of the Civil War the Pacific Mail Steamship Company, almost entirely owned by Leonard Jerome, was considered the soundest investment in the country." He believed in *Pacific Mail*. It was his favourite venture, his financial hobby-horse.

In 1872 an article in *Harper's Weekly*, describes the situation.

"In 1868 the leading part in *Pacific Mail* was played by Leonard Jerome. He had made a fortune of several millions out of the stock. He understood Wall Street and the public temper thoroughly. Born a *preux chevalier*, in another age he would have led charges of dragoons [complicated chronologically even for a Jerome]. It contented him to-day to lead Wall Street. To this man it now occurred that if the public were willing to give $240 a share for 6 million of new stock in the Pacific Mail,

[1] *Eminent New Yorkers*, 1884.

it would be well to feed them with more of it while the appetite lasted. He accordingly proposed and the directors sanctioned a further issue of 10 million of stock. But like many other operators, Mr. Jerome was infatuated with his own property. When the new stock was issued he offered to take the whole issue off the company's hands at $200 a share. The offer was accepted. This was the turning point in his own fortune, and those of the Company."

The stock did not find support elsewhere and remained on his hands ruining him. The Directors decided by one vote to reduce the dividend and within two hours Leonard had lost one million dollars.

The failure of this vast expansion of *Pacific Mail* came at a moment when he was already tiring of the role of millionaire. He was too many-sided, too many-gifted, to hang on to fortune. Left alone with his failure, his mansion, his theatre and a half-dozen demanding songstresses, he began to wonder if the chase was worth while. Money had become boring, a bore to make and a bore to lose. The tranquillity of retirement with Clara might hold charms he had not hitherto appreciated. She had demanded little, and other women so much. Patti had long disappeared to capture London and Paris with her trills, and besides, as a jealous rival put it, "her charm only just exceeded her tantrums". Autumn was in the air.

Despite his enormous *Pacific Mail* losses, there would always be the remnants of several other fortunes to live on, pleasantly and quietly. Leonard visualized himself as a family man at last.

In April 1868 he leased his house to the Union League Club and in October, after attending the debut of Ethel Agnes in what the newspapers still called 'Jerome's Private Theatre', he left for Paris. It was rumoured that at fifty Leonard Jerome was "retiring to Europe". He would be known as a sportsman, as the promoter of Turf Clubs and winner of yacht races, but Wall Street would see him no more.

In the apartment which Clara had taken in the Boulevard Malesherbes he found her calm and gentle as always. She was getting plump but the new flounced gowns suited her and the drawing-room was decorated in her favourite way with hanging baskets of flowers and garden vases of terra cotta from which green plants struggled in search of light and air. A jewelled hat-pin delighted her. The smallest attention brought light to her eye and soon she was pouring forth the gossip of the French court. She had stepped into the last brilliant whirl of the Empire. Leonard wrote to Lawrence of gaiety and gas-light and Offenbach and of "the extraordinary architectural changes made by Napoleon and Haussmann."

"It is curious, Clit, dear," he remarked, "to find 'home' in a Paris apartment." Clara smiled at the unintentional compliment. Home would always be where *she* was.

Only the girls were not quite as he had expected. Leonard puzzled at their lack of docility. Clarita at nearly eighteen was, his wife assured him, interested in quite the wrong type of beaux. It was distressing, one might almost say alarming, to have a daughter so blonde and innocent with sweet upturned blue eyes who did not think the way her mother bade. For Mrs. Jerome had decided exactly the type of match her daughters were to make: they must *all* marry into old Huguenot families. Their husbands were to be aristocratic but definitely Protestant. This limited suitors to a very small circle in which Clarita took no interest at all. For a time she had foolishly smiled on the Emperor's companion in exile the Duc de Persigny, twenty years older than herself and married to a jealous lady who opened and read the notes he sent Miss Jerome (which were then censored by that lady's angry mama). And no sooner had that been stopped (if indeed it *had* been stopped, for the Duke's carriage seemed to be always at the door with a message) than Clarita must go and fall in love with the young Marquis de Tamisier, who was out of the question as a husband.

"Why?" Leonard asked his wife.

"His grandfather Carrier de Nantes was responsible for those terrible drownings during the Revolution. . . . Think of it *les noyades de Nantes*. . . . Happily he came to the end he deserved."

"But the grandson hasn't done anything?"

"He keeps proposing to Clara. Such dreadful blood. I couldn't stand it!" snapped Mrs. Jerome. And that was that.

Leonard found his eldest daughter blossoming into a frivolous blonde with a misleading gentleness of manner which made it difficult to speak to her on serious subjects. She herself ventured few opinions to the family save that M. Worth was "mad on azure and pale green". Her eyes were mild but her chin determined. Poor Jennie suffered from her elder sister's habit of smiling on older men, for at a children's party where she had difficulty in dancing the mazurka the Duchesse de Persigny came up and suddenly boxed her ears.[1]

The younger daughters marshalled by a troop of French and German governesses were studying music with the best teachers in Paris. All three of Leonard's daughters had inherited his musical inclinations and they played the piano unusually well. Jennie, whose flamboyant beauty was already beginning to show, might have become a virtuoso. Her master, impressed

[1] The Duchess was a daughter of the Prince de la Moskowa and a great-grand-daughter of Maréchal Ney. As Ambassadress in London she won a reputation for eccentricity, often appearing at official dinners late and apparently soaking wet from her bath.

at such competence had assured her she could earn her living as a concert pianist if she wished, an idea which fired her imagination. "I'm *never* going to marry. I am going to be a musician," she announced with assurance.

Her mother winced.

Leonie had become a quaint little ten-year-old who had no looks at all but a burning vitality. Her short grubby fingers plucked melody from the piano with a plaintive charm which her father found most fetching. He praised and encouraged her renderings of Chopin and insisted that Jennie, who with flashing eyes and no small talent was pounding out the *Sonata Amorosa*, should not reap *all* the attention. Leonie was obviously going to be a real problem; her hasty temper coupled with a habit of naughty repartee caused complaints from all the servants save Dobbie who had managed her since childhood. Leonard could laugh at quick wit but even he was put out by her violent temper. On the first day the girls had tea in the drawing-room Leonie was teased for walking in the Champs-Elysées with her toes turned in (at that time correctly reared young ladies turned toes *out*). In a flash she had seized the table cloth, dashed china and cakes to the floor and was led to bed in hysterics. The peace of home life was not exactly what Leonard had anticipated. "Can't you control the girls? Why are they so wild?" he exclaimed.

"Well, dear," said Clara and the faintest smile flickered across her lips, "they are *your* daughters."

24

DURING the Jeromes' stay in Paris Jennie began to comment on her parents and their surroundings. She has written:

> "On regaining her health, my mother went out a great deal in French society, where her beauty attracted much attention, *la belle Américaine* at that time having all the charm of novelty. Never had the Empire seemed more assured, the court more brilliant, the fêtes more gorgeous. The light-hearted Parisians revelled in the daily sights of royal processions and cavalcades. . . . I remember often seeing the Empress Eugénie, then the handsomest woman in Europe driving in her daumont, the green and gold liveries of the postillions and outriders making a brave show."

According to Jennie, Princess Metternich (the Austrian Ambassadress), and the Duchesse de Mouchy (Eugénie's most intimate friend) and many famous court beauties habitually drove out with four horses in great state, "helped by the magnificence of their appearance to give to Paris that air of elegance and distinction which could neither be surpassed nor emulated by any other capital in Europe".

Among the strollers who most enjoyed the sight of splendid equipages were the two Jerome girls who, "still plagued by governesses", walked sedately along the wide avenues envying their elder sister who met these celebrated ladies in society.

Napoleon's Court had become a rendezvous for international beauty and fashion. "Wandering stars, English, American or Spanish were always welcome there and the permanent circle counted many foreigners besides the Empress." The young Jerome sisters greatly admired Eugénie whose entourage had thrown the other courts of Europe in the shade. They could hardly wait for their turn to grow up and be presented.

Louis Napoleon was teaching other monarchs that it could prove an advantage to be a *parvenu*. Many hereditary princes were apt to wet-blanket their own entertainments. The present royal couple might often be sneered at as "cosmopolitan adventurers brought up in the world and not to the purple" but they had a wide range of friends of various nationalities and with the prestige of a throne and unlimited resources and a sense of the picturesque they were able to turn imperial functions into unique entertainment. Eugénie's flair for the dramatic helped the gayest capital in Europe to dance a swifter more lighthearted rhythm than had ever been seen before.

Naturally the Tuileries provided the court at which Americans were most likely to excel and enjoy themselves. Here no one seemed shy or stiff. What if the monarchs did enjoy wild games of catch and paper chases through the woods around Biarritz! What if the sombre Palace with its inadequate lighting and lethal drainage had been garnished with what the *ancien régime* sniffingly referred to as *couleur de théâtre*? Mrs. Jerome found more charm in Eugénie's famous blush than in all the long-lineaged royalties with their blue blood and shiny noses. Jennie described her as "the handsomest woman in Europe", but this put it flatly. The Empress possessed an indefinable translucent beauty, a variability of expression which no portrait could reproduce. We know that she soared above other women, not from the painter's brush which records only a pretty oval face and large blue eyes but by her effect on those she met. A sneering enemy in the person of the American Ambassador in Madrid (his country particularly disliked Eugénie owing to the encouragement she had given to the Mexican venture) wrote:

"But when I met her yesterday, simply dressed, wearing her hat, and speaking Spanish, her features lighted up, and fingers, fan and little feet all in animated movement as she talked, I laid down my arms on the spot; I lost the battle at the first onslaught. Yes she is beautiful, more lovely than words can express. . . . And how sparkling she was at the Banquet that evening. . . ."

Could mere coquetting have reversed this sturdy Yankee's opinions? Her famous-good night bow, "like a swan curving its neck", caused him to forgive her all unwise political efforts.

Eugénie considered herself well fitted to be an Empress, and the Jeromes were not alone in considering such charm more interesting than pedigree. As for the Emperor, he was the most genuinely sympathetic man in the world, his thoughtfulness of others' feelings gave him the stature of a gentleman even if he did occasionally shock the Hapsburgs. His son's doctor wrote: "It is really curious to see how strongly he has the instinct of practical benevolence, and the satisfaction he feels in doing good incessantly, wherever he goes."

Mrs. Jerome, of course, knew more intimate details concerning the Imperial couple than her daughters did. She said: "You could not know the Emperor without loving that kind heart. His servants idolized him." What if he *were* unfaithful to his autocratic wife? Many another woman suffered that affront without receiving a throne in compensation.

Leonard, who had been horrified by the sombre political cruelties of Emperor Francis Joseph, found in Napoleon III a human being he could respect, "if only he were not so ill, it rots any man's judgment".

While Clara preened herself in new diamonds and court gowns and the girls received a high degree of "French polish", Leonard followed his own pursuits. He bought a few pictures to add to his New York collection, he went to the opera and he investigated the possibilities of racing stables in France.

Almost every morning he rode in the Bois de Boulogne with the Prince de Sagon (later Duc de Tallyrand), a leading buck who had originated the Auteuil racecourse and Circle de la rue Royale. The most eccentric of Paris beaux he liked to astound society by his fêtes and extravagances. Though born of different worlds he and Leonard had much in common, and the Prince showed his pity for the two poor Jerome girls who were not yet 'out' by organizing juvenile picnics for them. Jennie mounted on a 'seemingly fiery chestnut' often accompanied her father and the Prince on the morning rides. Little Leonie had less luck, the governesses hung around her like crows at a corn-bushel. One day the Prince organized a picnic at St. Germain for the whole family and Leonard brought along some of his American friends. Jennie writes "as Mr. James Gordon Bennett was driving us back on his coach, we came to grief near the Arc de Triomphe and were nearly killed". A likely end to any picnic with Bennett Junior. He may have been sobered by wild Atlantic racing but it is unlikely that he ever became the sort of person to put in charge of children!

Once again Leonard saw Adelina Patti, who was singing Italian opera in Paris until, at the height of her fame she accepted an offer of marriage from one of the Emperor's equerries, and temporarily retired from the stage. For a time her place remained vacant. Patti's manager tried new artists in vain. Then Leonard 'pulled a string' and soon after he had the satisfaction of seeing the eighteen-year-old Minnie Hauk selected to take the leading roles in the Italian opera season of 1869. 'Miauk', as the rude hotel concierges called her, was the youngest *prima donna* to have appeared in the renowned *Salle Ventadour*. She became the first American singer to succeed in the great opera houses of Europe.

Her Paris debut as Amina in *Sonnambula* is described by Maurice Strakosch in his *Mémoires*:

"I had done everything I possibly could, for the theatre was completely filled with the *élite* of Paris. The Imperial couple, whom I had specially invited, were present, and the little American girl really sang herself into the hearts of the French. In the last act an unforeseen incident amused the audience hugely, and contributed more to her popularity than the beauty of her voice and her art in using it. When crossing the bridge, she, in her childish way, hesitated and finally stopped . . . frightened. Suddenly the words 'Go on Minnie' were heard by the whole audience coming from behind the scenes. At the tittering that followed Minnie continued her walk faint-heartedly, and when the curtain went down she had won the game. Auber, the octogenarian, who sat in his accustomed corner stall wrote to her with lead pencil on his card: 'Bravo *ma chère enfant!* May "Go on Minnie", become the device of your life.' "

Leonard who only three years before had teased this unsophisticated child into singing after a dinner party, knew strangely moved feelings when he heard her acclaimed a worthy successor to the great Patti. His advice to her to study Patti's technique reaped results for Minnie wrote:

"It was my good fortune to hear Adelina Patti in all her brilliant roles, giving me a chance to make an intensive study of her art of vocalization and breathing, something which I may have imbibed, for both in Vienna and Berlin the critics declared they noticed a resemblance."

One particular evening which remained in Clara's memory occurred when Minnie was asked to sing at a reception in the house of Théophile Gautier where many Paris intellectuals were gathered including Auber, Flotow, the Duc de Broglie, Ferdinand de Lesseps, the younger Dumas, Alphonse Daudet and Ernest Renan. Minnie had chosen two arias from *Rigoletto*, Leonard's favourite opera. A young musician called Bizet accompanied her on the piano. Flushed by success Minnie did not pay much attention to his shy compliments. Neither artist could have foreseen the interweaving of their names in the future. Bizet died unappreciated and unknown. It was ten years after his casual meeting that his opera *Carmen* was produced for the first time and Minnie Hauk sang the lead to an astounded London.

It is hardly surprising to learn that Mrs. Ronalds arrived in Paris at about this time and when winter froze up ponds and lakes *la belle Américaine* skating in a hoop skirt became the sensation of Paris. Her exploits on the ice attracted the attention of the Empress who liked to surround herself with beauties and she was invited to the French Court. Fanny Ronalds with her elegance, her charm and her musical talent found no difficulty in skating her way into the royal entourage. She soon took a place as one of the many lovely ornaments of the Second Empire. She and Mrs. Jerome drove around together paying calls and young Clara was "brought out" ceremoniously in their wake. She made her debut at one of the Tuileries balls and despite her confusion at having to walk up the grand staircase between the *Cent-Guardes* in her first low dress she was able afterwards to give a coherent description of the scene to those two pairs of greedy ears in the schoolroom. "When the company was assembled, the doors were flung open and *Sa Majesté l'Empereur* was announced." Then after a pause *Sa Majesté l'Impératrice* who that evening appeared

"a resplendent figure in green velvet, with a crown of emeralds and diamonds, spiked with pearls, on her small and beautifully shaped head. The Emperor and Empress walked round the circle of curtseying and bowing guests, addressing a few words here and there and then proceeded to the ball room."

An old photograph shows Miss Jerome ready for this ball: she wore a white crinoline, the tulle skirt billowing around her in the style of a Winterhalter portrait and her golden hair hung in ringlets on her neck.

Leonard did not share the womenfolk's enthusiasm for royalty. When Minnie Hauk had departed for the Imperial Opera of Moscow (well chaperoned by her mama) and Mrs. Ronalds towards Algeria where she thought it would be amusing to subjugate the Bey, and Patti had shown her preference for the role of Marquise in a *salon* rather than *prima donna* before the footlights, Mr. Jerome returned to New York. He wrote: "the two Claras are having a wonderful time. I leave them to it."

In New York he found his unwatched finances deteriorating. On Black Friday in 1868, Jay Gould and Fisk brought ruin to Wall Street, and, despite the fact that President Grant stopped their plan to corner the gold market, they paralysed the business of all America, whilst reaping fresh millions for themselves. Gould had secretly tried to bring the President into their scheme, and over-sure Fisk boasted to a Congressional committee that the President was going to 'play ball'. In his last-minute decision to stamp on their gold plan, President Grant made bitter and powerful enemies within the 'Rings', but he could not prevent a national disaster.

Jerome had, when the power lay in his hands such as after Vanderbilt's Harlem battle, always worked to avert the smashing of smaller folk. "I prefer the role of financier, to that of highway man," he wrote laughingly. Now he suffered, as everyone did outside the Rings, from the shaken con-

Clara and Jennie
dressed by Monsieur Worth

Leonie on her wedding day

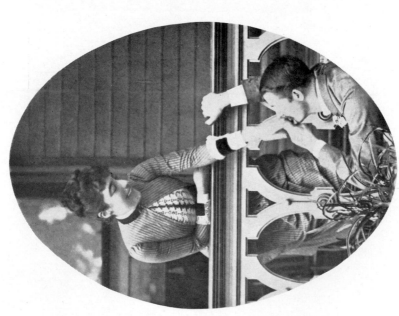

Leonie and her fiancé John
Leslie

fidence and panic of the entire country. He revolted against the jungle which had once excited him. He longed to pull out but he could not. For the first time in her life Clara would be distressed by curtailment of income, for whether at Compiègne or the Tuileries, their eldest daughter needed an immense repertory of expensive gowns. Taking a tip from the Austrian Ambassadress Princess Metternich, who said, "I *made* M. Worth you know —or was it him made *me*?" the Jerome ladies had decided to purchase all their dresses from that expensive gentleman.

Clarita went to a succession of *grands bals* at the Palace, as well as to *les petits lundis*, those informal weekly dances which the young Prince Imperial was allowed to attend. Mademoiselle Jerome—*la voilà!* . . . She could be seen gliding through the drawing-rooms of both old and new nobility (they were just beginning to tolerate each other), and her after-dinner piano-playing caused many hearts to miss a beat. The oldest man she ever danced with was the Comte de Flahaut. "Just think of it," she blurted. "He was Napoleon's a.d.c. at Waterloo, and Queen Hortense's lover!"

"Hush!" snapped Mama. What a word for a *jeune fille* to have learnt! Perhaps there were drawbacks to bringing girls out in France after all.

Numerous Imperial invitations have survived. On heavy cream paper headed *Maison de l'Empereur* they issue from the Chamberlain's office in the *Palais des Tuileries*.

"*Mademoiselle*,
    Par ordre de l'Empereur, j'ai l'honneur de vous prévenir que vous êtes invitée à passer six jours au palais de Compiègne du 10 au 15 Novembre.
    Des voitures de la cour vous attrendront le 10 a l'arrivée à Compiègne du train spécial partant de Paris à 2 h. pour vous conduire au Château."

This, dated November 1869, seems to be the first time she travelled without Mama. One can see the picture . . . a young girl on a Special Train, heavily chaperoned we may be sure, with a frantic lady's maid in charge of her trunk—the fuss of packing and preparation must have brought a flush to her cheeks and made her blue eyes shine.

A letter written to her mother by Clarita at Compiègne gave a brisk picture of palace life:

"This morning I went down to breakfast. The Princess Mathilde shook hands with us, and the Emperor asked me if I would like a ride. . . . We *suivred* very well—and got in at the death of the *cerf*—it was five o'clock before we got home—the rendezvous was beautiful, the whole city of Compiègne and its environments turned out to it.

In the evening I put on my white with marguerites, for the Prince Imperial was to have a Cotillion. We played *chat et souris*, so he ran after me and in and out, and I finally caught my foot in the Duchesse de Mouchy's dress and fell. . . . We have been asked to lengthen our stay until Tuesday—so I shall need another dress—something white, trimmed with anything you think pretty. I think I must have it, in fact two if possible, for these ladies dress so much and never appear in the same. Dear Mamma, I love you and you are so sweet.

Addio,
Clarita.

P.S.—I need a new light opera-cloak badly—merely something to throw around me to go to the dinner table."

It was obviously essential that dear Papa should also remain sweet. If every evening demanded a new white dress, he could not consider it the moment to relax. While his daughter tripped in and out of the imperial palaces, Mr. Jerome struggled alone in the city his family had scorned and deserted. Now was the time he longed for a son, a lad who would be an American, strong and confident as he had been, ready to learn from experience and fight his own battle, ready to take over responsibility.

When it was rumoured that Jerome had passed his heyday, criticisms of him appeared in the Nonconformist press. Had he not driven down Fifth Avenue on Sundays? Was not betting allowed at Jerome Park? Certain persons attributed the failure of *Pacific Mail* and shaking of Wall Street to direct Divine Intervention. The New York *Times* argued in his favour:

"Nothing goes on at Jerome Park which the purest minded person could object to. There is no bribing of jockeys, no 'dosing' of horses with laudanum. Never did the history of racing in any country begin with so fair a page."

The dressmakers of New York rose up to defend the races which gave them much trade: "Has not Monsieur Worth presented handsome stakes to the Ascot meeting? We will do the same!" and a band of well-meaning Puritans asked for croquet to be added to the racecourse as a harmless *divertissement*.

By his own tremendous endeavour, Jerome had created this course. He had raised horse-racing from the disrepute into which it had fallen and placed it upon the level of the English Turf. Now picnics, croquet and dress parades were the defence of his efforts! With a groan of boredom, Leonard wrote to his family: "Everyone getting tiresome here. I'll make you a little something and come across. Paris sounds delightful and a change."

He was in the fifties, physically on the crest of the wave, for his vitality had lasted. The whole wide world lay open to him to explore. He longed to travel, to sail the oceans, to see strange sights while there was yet time; but just as he had begun to tire of finance, it became incumbent on him to fight once more in the tottering frenzy of 'the Street'. His daughters' tastes left no alternative. Sustained by the unflagging health of the frontier-bred he tried to earn afresh.

One evening after working long hours he thought it would be "good fun to take a party to the Circus". At an age when he might have known better (but the very strong never do), he leapt into a contest with a professional weight-lifter. Friends cheered him on while he wielded the hammer which sent a weight soaring in the air, and the pretty ladies who inevitably formed his background applauded, but the effort strained one whole side of his body and he collapsed soon after.

"Will you never learn?" pleaded Clara. Long ago she had been upset when for a bet he beat the strong man at the Foire de Neuilly. He wrote back wistfully. "Can it be, that one gets too old for circuses. I know I *ought* to feel too old but the truth is I enjoy such nonsense as much as before."

25

THE Court circles into which Mrs. Jerome and Mrs. Ronalds drew Clara for a worldly debut were quick-sanded by dissension. Legitimists, Orléanists and Republicans criticized every Bonaparte move while the Mexican campaign had shaken the Empire's popularity to a degree which the daily procession of beauties in splendid carriages could not counter-balance. Eugénie's great charm seemed to be accompanied by an equal lack of widsom. The Emperor struggled against her authoritative attitude and no longer permitted her to attend the Council but it was hardly possible for a man so tolerant of the faults of others to construct a new-model liberal-Europe from scratch. Eugénie surrounded by 'soupirauts', men who sighed for her unassailable virtue from a distance, continued to exasperate all parties. Reared to make a great match for herself she had aimed just too high. Never did she manifest the natural practical statesmanship which in history has so frequently and surprisingly shown itself in common-born women whom destiny has lifted to a throne. The feminine world might strive to copy her hats and her grace, a bewitched American Ambassador might write, "perhaps for an Empress she was too much of a coquette, but as an Andalusian and a woman she was the most perfect creature I have seen anywhere", but none yearned to be governed by the former Melle de Montijo. In the autumn of 1869 the Emperor packed her off to open the Suez Canal, a task for which her dramatic beauty and sense of theatre seemed particularly suitable, but the troubles of France were too deep-rooted to fade in her absence. Already the black shadow of Bismarck flickered on the eastern horizon. The Second Empire sensed uneasily that it might be dancing to its close.

Across these last tinselled scenes of the old Tuileries and of the Château de Compiègne the figure of a dazzling American girl flits like a bird. Miss Clara Jerome in a cloud of tulle, besieged by proposals of marriage and in love with the one man her mother had forbidden, could be seen wringing all possible delight from a first season. The dark old palace with the statuesque Cent-Guardes in their glittering blue and silver uniforms standing rigid at every door provided a background that no young person could forget.

Devoid of shyness she enjoyed an occasional waltz with the schoolboy Prince, who to improve his ease of manner was allowed to attend informal *soirées* at the palace. She has herself described to us one of the *petits lundis* when her mother being unable to attend had arranged for her to be chaperoned to the Tuileries by a married couple.

"As usual you know how impossible I have always found it to be punctual. I was late in meeting these friends and they departed without me leaving a message they would wait at the top of the big palace staircase. I flew back to the carriage with Dobbie our devoted Negro nurse at my heels. She came from the old South and had very definite views on the importance of chaperoning young ladies. For nothing on earth would she allow me out of her sight until I could be handed over to my official duenna. We drove post haste to the Tuileries and there she descended beside me with an indomitable expression on her black face: 'Ah'm not going to leave you until ah sees you safe.' You can imagine the surprise of the palace guards who lined the great staircase as a young girl fluttered up the marble steps closely pursued by a large Negress wearing a green turban on her head and a red shawl around her shoulders.

'*La jeune Américaine* . . .' gasped guests at the top of the staircase and then my friends stepped forward and Dobbie smiled, curtseyed and took her leave satisfied that the conventions had been upheld and that no impropriety could now befall her young mistress."

Among the outstanding hostesses of Paris to whose *salon* the Jeromes were regularly invited was the Princess Mathilde, cousin of Louis Napoleon and formerly his fiancée. Jennie wrote:

"The most intelligent and brilliant woman of the Second Empire she used to give cotillions at her fine house in the rue de Courcelles at which the *collet monté* and aristocratic families made their appearance in greater numbers than in the Tuileries: the noble faubourg (pre-Napoleonic nobility), satisfied that her mother was a Princess of Würtemburg, while her uncle was the Czar Nicholas I, did not look upon her as a parvenue and an interloper.

The Princess loved to surround herself with those possessing wit and talent, and sought to make her salon compare with those of the 18th Century. . . . That these sacred portals were opened for anything so frivolous as a dance, was to please the Prince Imperial and the Empress's nieces, the Mesdemoiselles d'Albe."

Princess Mathilde had not always been a royal highbrow however. At the famous *bal masqué* at the Hotel d'Albe a few years earlier she had pulverized the diplomatic corps by appearing *en Nubienne* in extreme undress with her body dyed dark brown. She survived this scandal, however, and also the misfortune of being sister to the unutterable Plonplon who until the birth of the Prince Imperial had damned Bonapartism by being its heir. It was in the Princess's house that Miss Jerome, a delicious featherwit of eighteen, had the pleasure of meeting Dumas, Sardou, Théophile Gautier and Daudet, the intellectuals of Paris whose names she recorded in a diary but without comment, save for beguiling descriptions of her own dresses from which posterity must suppose the impression *she* must have made.

When he had been a young man with but faint prospect of becoming Emperor, Louis Napoleon had courted Mathilde. Their engagement lasted until his second attempt on the throne failed. Then her father the "old roué of Westphalia"[1] had broken off the betrothal and insisted on a more remunerative match with a Russian Count. This gentleman exceeded the bounds allowed to Muscovy bears by slapping his lady wife's face in public. The Tsar stepped in, ordered his unmannered subject to donate a large share of his fortune to the Princess and she retreated to Paris secure behind the barricade of a legal separation but unable to remarry. The city respected her intellect and liberal views. Mathilde became the leading patron of writers and artists and her lions were of the highest grade. If she entertained more than cousinly feelings for her former fiancé, none could guess it. Her unhappy domestic interlude was never mentioned and carrying her head high the Princess contented herself with the creation of her brilliant *salon*. If she suffered afresh when Louis Napoleon looking for an Empress had to pass her by on account of her unannulled marriage none had been kinder than Mathilde when Eugénie mounted the throne. Now in a time of increasing stress she became a political pivot.

In January 1870 while the Empress, basking in Egypt, was lulled by blue skies and the strains of Verdi's *Aïda*, Louis Napoleon flung the last of his famous country parties and Leonard received the intimation that *une élégante* would need twenty new dresses for a week's stay at the Château. When she had supervised her maid unpacking young Clara spared some observation for the Emperor who "seemed to be in bad health and beset by political worries". As was usual in Eugénie's absence the Princesse Mathilde did the honours. Hunting and shooting and local sightseeing were always provided to amuse the guests and for those who could totter by the time night fell, there would be dancing.

The house parties of Compiègne were intended to resemble English

[1] King Jerome of Westphalia, the last surviving brother of the great Napoleon.

country entertaining, but no one was left alone to dream or to amble or to read by the fire. Visitors groused at being dragged out from the hot-house atmosphere of the great drawing-rooms on perpetual organized excursions. But not so the young. Miss Clara explored all she dared of the Château and missed no possible moment of activity.[1]

"There was a *grande chasse* or stag hunt, on the first day, at which all the guests appeared, riding or driving. Those who hunted wore the royal colours, the men in green coats and the gold hunt buttons, the ladies in flowing green habits and three cornered hats. The stag on this occasion was brought to bay in a lake, the Prince Imperial giving him the *coup de grâce*. At night there was a *curée au flambeaux* in the courtyard of the château, the whole party assembling on the balconies in the glare of the innumerable torches. The carcass of the deer lay in the centre covered with its skin; the *hallali* was sounded; at a signal the hounds were unleashed, and in a moment every vestige of the stag had disappeared."

Clara thought it savage and cruel but she admitted herself impressed by handsome Castelbajac, director of the hunt. "*Il était tellement beau.*" Her mother did not object as long as the girl's attention was diverted from Tamisier.

"The next day an expedition was organized to see the Château de Pierrefonds, a distance of nine or ten miles; the party went in *chars-à-bancs* (the old-fashioned horsed version literally 'benched chariots') under the guidance of the architect who had just completed its restoration . . . the day ended with tea in the beautiful armoury of the castle from which the Emperor presented each lady with a souvenir in the shape of a small weapon.

One day there was a Cabinet Council, and the guests were exhorted to be discreet in their amusements and not to disturb his Majesty. Who knows what fateful questions were discussed. Times were disquieting and *pourparlers* with Prussia had proved anything but pleasant. The Government was in direct conflict with the Opposition."

Napoleon had in fact decided to hurriedly invent a new kind of Constitution and parliamentary Cabinet. Remaining absolute himself he strove to create a Liberal Empire which would win over the Opposition. Small wonder his guests were asked to refrain from noisy games!

[1] After the 1914–18 war, as old Mrs. Moreton Frewen she took her daughter Clare Sheridan to Compiègne to see "the room I slept in as a girl". The guide who accompanied them stared unbelieving as she identified the guest rooms. At last she paused: "And here I stood in front of a mirror in white tulle before going down to dinner."

Among the Ministers summoned to this Council at Compiègne was the Maréchal Bazaine accompanied by his Mexican wife. The Emperor's guests seem to have been less astounded at the Maréchal's idea of disciplining the Chamber by using troops than at the evening *toilette* of Madame la Maréchale. At a time when all evening dresses were white or pastel-coloured this lady appeared in a gown of vivid scarlet with gloves to match. "This was thought *très Anglais*, as no one in France wore such brilliant colours."

"Every night from sixty to a hundred guests sat down to dinner, the Emperor never permitting it to last more than three-quarters of an hour. Sometimes magnificent gold plate adorned the table, sometimes precious *biscuit de Sèvres*. Before dinner the company assembled in two long lines. The Emperor took in Princesse Mathilde, sitting opposite her at the centre of the table, a few seats of honour being reserved on each side, while the rest placed themselves as they wished the ladies choosing the gentlemen to take them in, according to the custom of Compiègne. After dinner there was dancing, in which the Prince Imperial, then only thirteen was allowed to join till ten o'clock, when his tutor would approach him, saying, '*Monseigneur, votre chapeau*,' which meant going to bed. At the close of the visit there was a grand lottery and in which all tickets won prizes. The Emperor stood near two great urns from which the numbers were drawn, and as each guest received one he wished him '*Bonne chance.*' Some little juggling must have gone on, for my mother and the American minister, Mr. Washbourne, won valuable pieces of Sèvres china, whereas the presents for the younger people were less costly."

Young Clara received from the Emperor's hand an inkstand shaped like a knotted handkerchief filled with gold napoleons. As his Majesty gave it to her he remarked, "*Mademoiselle, n'oubliez pas les Napoléons.*"
She never did.

26

IN THE summer-time, when the Imperial couple moved to Biarritz for an informal country holiday, Mrs. Jerome took a villa nearby, where her daughters could continue their studies, and enjoy the countryside. Occasionally they met the young Prince Imperial whom Leonie, three years his junior, thought a very wonderful person.

Meanwhile on the grown-up level the Duc de Lescera, a Spanish relative of the Empress, visited and made advances to the elder Miss Jerome, who was sufficiently amused to encourage him until her mother, "who wanted no Catholic alliance however aristocratic", ordered him from the house, but with the connivance of Clara and Jennie he came back through the drawing-room window. Mrs. Jerome burst in and her trembling daughters expected a scene, but she, somewhat short-sighted, mistook the Duke for their servant and said, "*Pierre, commandez le déjeuner pour sept heures.*" "*Oui Madame,*" replied the Duke, and as he left the house, he passed the message to the cook.

The girls recounted this story with glee for many years.

Mrs. Jerome ran her daughters' love affairs with an iron hand, but sometimes they made use of her strictness to ward off unwanted advances. In March 1870, Leonard took Clarita and Jennie to Nice where they enjoyed the countryside, and drove in carriages along the coast to Genoa. A few letters to their mother who remained in Paris survive: "We shall be addressless for the next few days," they write, and Clarita describes how they twit their adored Papa. After one night's rest "he looked so fresh and handsome, that we told him the ladies would all be after him". This news he accepted calmly and proceeded to organize various exhausting expeditions by horse.

Then follow explicit instructions to Mama:

"Tell the Duke (de Bassano) that you object to my writing him or that I should certainly have answered his letters and that it is not because I am angry. He writes beautifully, and I have kept his letters to show you when I come home."

She was a careful tactician.

The spring of 1870 came with unusual warmth and beauty. Leonard knew he ought to return to Wall Street but he could not bear to depart, and besides he had just taken a fine new house in the Boulevard Haussman, in which his picture collection could be hung to advantage. He was in any case finding New York exceedingly fraying. Old Commodore Vanderbilt had now become besotted by two sisters whom he had set up as lady brokers. They communed with "the other side" and gave spookish advice concerning stocks and shares. They also aroused considerably earthy impulses in the gentlemen who visited their office for astral financial help. "Spirits are the last straw and Tweed runs the city. I dread going back," Leonard told his wife. And off he went for a ride with the Prince de Sagon who, having never heard of bears, save as animals, made a refreshing companion. And in the evenings he had his daughters' piano-playing to listen to, and Minnie Hauk's progress to appraise.

There were a few political excitements this spring. Louis Napoleon, hot from the reconstruction of his new Liberal Empire, launched a plebiscite, asking one question only. Did the people assent to his reforms? Many were too puzzled to answer. Must their approval of reform be tantamount to approval of Bonapartism? Paris and the great cities cried "No" but to the amazement of other countries seven million Frenchmen answered "Yes."

This undeniably proved a triumph for the Emperor but in May his old friend Lord Malmesbury wrote home:

"I thought him much altered in appearance and looking very ill. . . . I naturally began by congratulating him on his *plebiscite* which was just counted up but I found that he was not satisfied as some 50,000 of the army had voted '*Non*'. He, however, explained that 300,000 soldiers had voted for him. This struck me as strange, for I imagined his army was in number 600,000 and I made the remark, to which he gave no reply, but looked suddenly very grave and absent."

Throughout the early spring there were rumours of war but not of a very serious kind, for Prussia was just a cocky little state and King Wilhelm had *so* enjoyed the Exhibition.

Jennie finished her studies and began to talk of the following season when it would be her turn to be presented at court. To Mrs. Jerome's relief the idea of becoming a musician instead of a great lady was fading away. The glitter of the Tuileries had won over artistic aspiration.

"Did your teacher truly say you could attain concert standard?" asked Leonard.

"Yes," Jennie stared up her dark eyes flashing, her cheeks and lips rosy with the natural colour of her tremendous health, "if I continued to work hard but then he looked at me and sighed and said, 'But you won't.' "

Jennie, a more vigorous and dynamic character than her elder sister, could hardly wait to make her mark in the world. Clara brought home what fragments of interesting conversation she could remember and the inmates of the Jerome schoolroom regarded the Palace as a stage on which they would each be allowed to shine in the train of brilliant Pauline Metternich and bewitching Melanie de Pourtales. No one with Leonard's blood in their veins proved remarkable for modesty.

During this year only one slight shadow was recorded. It occurred after a particularly animated *petit lundi* when Count Hazenfeldt, Secretary to the German Embassy in Paris, who was a frequenter of the Jerome *salon*, drew Mademoiselle Clara into a window embrasure and remarked, "I never saw their Majesties in better spirits than they were last night but God knows where they will be next year at this time."

When Clara recounted this to her sisters, both Jennie and Leonie frowned. What *could* he mean?

The Court removed to St. Cloud in early Summer and there the fourteen-year-old Prince Imperial and the Empress's nieces the Mesdemoiselles d'Albe played happily throughout the long golden days.

Old-timers unamused by excess of artless innocence grumbled that the vast Château now resembled a "boarding school" or worse still "a nursery".

June passed. After throwing off the Bourbons the Spanish throne was offered to Bismarck's stool-pigeon Leopold of Hohenzollern. France (and all Europe for that matter), screamed with indignation. Leopold withdrew and war seemed to have been averted. Bismarck (with some reason) sulked and scowled while the entire population of France muttered. The French were determined to have their war, not to pause and prepare, but to have it out now immediately while the blood pounded hot in their veins, and the marching songs had not grown stale. Only the Emperor seemed relieved when he could murmur, "*C'est la paix.*"

Leonard hesitated as to whether he should remain with his family or join James Gordon Bennett in England for what was to prove the first international Atlantic yacht race—a two-boat tussle fated to become as famous as the Great Race of '66.

James had embarked on a fiery and somewhat boastful correspondence with an Englishman, James Ashbury, Commodore of the Royal Harwich Yacht Club and owner of a beautiful schooner *Cambria*, 188 tons, 108 feet over all and with a main mast 61 feet high, above which she could carry a main top-mast of another 35 feet. Ashbury challenged his yacht against any in the world and Bennett (now Vice-Commodore of the New York Yacht Club), had sailed his *Dauntless* over in 1869 to winter at Cowes, refit in the Spring for a trans-ocean race and contest the Atlantic run with her. *Dauntless* was 120 feet over all and spreading seven thousand square feet of canvas. It took a crew of 37 men, expending their utmost, to keep her at best sailing speed.

"*Dauntless* was among the best in 1870 and Bennett had as good reason as Ashbury to believe that in a transatlantic race his schooner would fly the winning colours." The prize was a set of silver ware valued at £250 and the start was dated for July 4th off Daunt Rock, Queenstown, Ireland.

Lawrence had come over for the race, and Leonard could hardly resist joining him. Charles Longfellow, son of the poet, was Bennett's other amateur. Of the professionals, who numbered thirty-four, Captain Bully Samuels, the Browns, Lyons and J. Taylor "constituted a brains trust as formidable as any that modern times have known".

July 4th found a large collection of British and French yachts assembled at Daunt Rock, to cheer in a fresh westerly which soon brought fog and rain, the two yachts began the race. . . . At 2.30 *Dauntless* cast off her tug and stood away on the starboard tack.

The 1870 Race has been so hotly debated in the sailing world ever since that it is irresistible to quote at some length from Alfred Loomis' classic descriptions in *Ocean Racing*.

> "Three o'clock saw *Dauntless* drawing ahead and weathering *Cambria*, which tacked inshore to escape. *Dauntless* followed her in and at 4.30, after another tack, her crew had the satisfaction of seeing the British schooner safely tucked away under the American's lee. An hour and a half later *Cambria* stood in near the Old Head of Kinsale, and *Dauntless* maintained a starboard tack off shore. Here the two yachts parted company. . . ."

They were not to see each other for three thousand miles. In this hard-fought start *Dauntless* had proved the better boat. Among *Cambria's* brains trust "there was evidently one who knew that a boat which cannot go to windward with her competitor, must break with her and seek a different slant of wind".

From this night on *Cambria* battled straight across the Atlantic, while *Dauntless* made the great mistake of taking a southerly route. For July 7th her log reads:

> "At 3 a.m. took in gaff top-sails. At 6½ housed top-mast. At 7½ wind and sea increasing, took in flying jib. In furling it two men—Charles

Scott and Albert Demar—were washed off the boom. Hove to the yacht for two hours, lowered foresail and got out boat, but failed to see anything of the missing men. At 9½ the wind increased to a gale, we reluctantly gave them up, took the boat on board and kept on our course. Double-reefed mainsail, and took bonnet out of foresail. Ends in a fresh gale, thick, rainy weather and short high sea."

They had already lost the race.

"Better favoured by the fates, *Cambria* had worked north to 54-59 her highest latitude, and from the 7th she slanted slowly down taking what current there was on her port beam until she came within the helpful influence of the Labrador current."

By the time three weeks had elapsed the whole interest of New York was centred on Sandy Hook, "hoping against hope that the *Dauntless* would justify the faith of the American patriots".

Gentlemen of the Press were scanning the horizon to eastward, and the New York *Times* relates:

"The operator's room at the station was filled with half a dozen active newspaper reporters, who were constantly consulting Mr. James Farrell, the bronzed and veteran ship-news reporter, who, with telescope in hand, was keeping a vigilant watch seaward. His keen eye swept the water for miles and miles in every direction, but failed to make out anything resembling either of the two anxiously expected vessels. Precisely at 3.05 (on July 27th), he turned from his glass and announced that a schooner yacht was coming up toward the Hook, but that her colours were not discernible. . . . The speck rapidly approached, and assumed plainer proportions until it was discovered to be the sails and spars of a schooner. Nothing was visible of her hull which seemed to be a part of the sea on which it floated. Exactly forty-one minutes elapsed, according to Mr. Farrell's calculations, before she passed the lightship, seven miles outside of Sandy Hook. Her outlines were then fully and clearly distinguished. The wind was blowing off her port quarter due east, and she scudded along under full sail. The flags which she carried at her ensign, together with a private pennon, contained the letter C in the centre. She was at once pronounced to be the *Cambria*.

A sigh of disappointment swept over America. *Cambria* had sailed from Ireland to Sandy Hook in twenty-three days five hours and seventeen minutes. It was only one hour and forty-three minutes later that *Dauntless* passed the winning line—one hour and forty-three minutes in a race of 3,000 miles—it had been a good try but, in the end, it had to be conceded that "*Cambria*, a slower boat, won the first international yacht race because of faster head work."

As soon as he got ashore Leonard wrote an excited letter to his daughters but they scarcely read Papa's account of the fatal decision to sail a southerly route, the loss of the two men, or the shift of wind that favoured *Cambria* at the finish. Very different events filled their heads, for the Franco-Prussian War had broken out, Paris reverberated to the Marseillaise, and cries of '*Vive l'Empereur*' echoed on the boulevards all through the night.

27

THE Emperor Napoleon III stood by with leaden heart while his people shouted for blood. During early July Wilhelm of Prussia was tormented by the French to give impossible guarantees that no repetition of the Hohenzollern episode should ever occur. Bismarck saw that war, for which he had long schemed, materializing.

Never had a country shown more enthusiasm for battle than France in this year, a year in which she had neither a trained army nor a plan of action. The country worked itself into a frenzy. Only the Emperor seemed capable of attempting to assess possible results, and he was dubbed spoilsport. It might have been wise of the Chamber to investigate the Army's efficiency before hysterically voting unlimited war credits, but the nation's enthusiasm exceeded the bounds of sanity. Cafés and cabarets were packed with elated crowds. Over three thousand people danced around the Place de la Concorde. Someone counted them. It was all *très émotionné*. And, of course, the weather was just right.

The Emperor, sick and pessimistic, aroused the indignation of patriotic journalists by his cautious rejoinders. But although sensing catastrophe, he knew himself unable to stem the tide. The horror of battlefield visits never left his mind. He loved his fellow men and could visualize war realistically. The Press scorned him for this. Bonapartes were not expected to be conscientious objectors.

Minnie Hauk, who was at the Opera with her mother on the night war was declared, wrote this vivid description:

"I spent the summer of 1870 in Paris, to get new dresses and to see my numerous friends again. While I was there, Auber came one day and invited me to a performance of his opera *La Muette de Portici*, to be given the same evening at the Imperial Opera. He said the Imperial couple had announced their intention to be present. It was to be a gala night. I readily accepted, Auber himself came to fetch me, and when we arrived at the theatre, all the *crème de la crème* of Paris society was already present. He pointed out to me all the notabilities, the Ministers of State, the Duc de Grammont, Rouher, Maurice Richart, also many of the duchesses and princesses, all in most beautiful toilets and bedecked with sparkling jewels; but Napoleon III and the Empress did not put in an appearance.

The curtain went up, but to my great surprise, instead of the first scene of *La Muette*, I saw on the stage the *prima donna* of the opera, Marie Sasse, dressed in white, with a long mantle embroidered with gold bees thrown over her shoulder, carrying in her outstretched right hand the French national flag. The conductor raised his *bâton*, but for several minutes he was prevented from beginning by the most deafening applause.

In a box opposite ours sat the beautiful young Duchesse de Mouchy, dressed in the French colours, frantically waving her handkerchief. Suddenly she and the other occupants of her box rose from their seats, and at the same time we heard a ringing voice shouting '*Tout le monde debout.*' It was Émile de Girardin, the well-known journalist, who from his box on the *grand tier* had invited the whole audience to stand up. Everybody stood, while the orchestra crashed into the inspiring strains of *La Marseillaise*!

I could not believe my ears! The battle-song of the Great Revolution at the Imperial Opera! What had happened? Had war against Prussia been declared? Why, then, the Republican *Marseillaise* and not the Imperial hymn?

When, after the prelude, Marie Sasse, in her beautiful voice, began to sing the first verse of the *Marseillaise*, the whole audience joined her, finishing up with such hurrahs, shouting, clapping of hands, stamping of feet and waving of hats, sticks and handkerchiefs as I have never witnessed again in any theatre. Through the deafening tumult I heard people shout: '*Vive l'Empereur!*' '*Vive la France!*' followed with ever increasing enthusiasm by shouts '*A Berlin! A Berlin!*'

Auber had excitedly left the box and run on the stage. I followed him, and in the narrow passage we met Ludovic Halévy, the composer of *La Juive*.

Halévy appeared most agitated and shouted to Auber, 'Who has done this? Surely not with the Emperor's consent?'

Auber replied, 'No, it was Maurice Richart (the Minister of Fine Arts), but the Emperor must have been informed beforehand!'

Halévy shook his head and exclaimed quite in despair: 'Where are we drifting to? The song of the Revolution at the Imperial Opera!'

In reply Auber pointed towards the raging audience and said: 'He just hit the right thing, only listen how they acclaim the Emperor!' It was the last time the French did so, for a few months later the Empire had fallen and the Republic was proclaimed!"

From New York Leonard cabled frantically to his wife begging her to move to London, but Clara possessed no sense of danger. She allowed her girls to walk the boulevards with their governess while the crowds roared for victories and ceaselessly repeated "*à Berlin!*"

Leonard calmed down on receiving his wife's description of passing events; she seemed to be enthralled by the general delirium and was advantageously placed to receive gossip for Persigny brought her the latest news from Court daily. Eugénie had been named Regent during the Emperor's absence at the front, and with suitable dramatics the fourteen-year-old Prince was dressed up as a lieutenant and sent out to cheer the fighting men. "Do not worry, Leonard. It will soon be over," Clara insisted, "the French must reach Berlin within a few days; *everyone* says so!"

Leonard, having hardly washed the salt spray from his face, did not wish to return to Europe, except in case of urgent necessity. His New York *Times* had launched a powerful attack on William Tweed, State Senator, 'Boss' of New York City and king-pin of Tammany, and was employing Thomas Nast, greatest cartoonist of the day, to expose the Tweed Ring in brilliant drawing. It would be very inconvenient to leave New York. Moreover Paris seemed safe and far from the guns.

Jennie recorded:

"Exciting incidents crowded on us. One day we saw Capoul, the celebrated tenor, and Marie Sasse of the Opera made to stand on top of an omnibus and sing the *Marseillaise*, an ever-growing crowd joining in the chorus. One night we went to the opera in walking dresses, with our hats in our hands in case there was any trouble and we might have to walk home, which proved to be the case. It was a strange performance, as the singers were constantly being interrupted and made to sing patriotic songs. We found the greatest difficulty in getting home, owing to the streets being filled with huge crowds marching to the cry of '*des chassepots, des chassepots*'. Poor fellows they soon had them, and all the fighting they wanted."

It was very moving, especially for American girls singing the *Marseillaise* in the dusk and moving their paper flags over schoolroom maps. They saw decorations run up on each rumour of victory and blinds pulled down as stark truth filtered through. The Parisians were highstrung, nervy, hot-tempered. They had shouted for 'War' but not for this kind.

The Duc de Persigny came to call almost every day after his visit to St. Cloud where he gathered shattering information from the Empress. Louis Napoleon's first letter to Eugénie read: "Nothing is ready. We have not troops enough. *Je nous considére d'avance comme perdus."* This was followed by an astounding series of defeats. As is usual in such circumstances the Army Commander had to be flung out. His replacement happened to be Marshal Bazaine, that soldier of small talent and large words. The country clutched pathetically at this new name as if by the touch of a wand Bazaine could unmuddle the depots, provide guns for the artillery batteries, turn the bewildered raw recruits into trained troops, and make the whole military machine work.

On August 6th Eugénie returned to the Tuileries where, camping amidst the dust sheets, she worked wildly to dispel the country's chaos. She formed a new cabinet headed by General de Paliakao, an old Imperialist much disgruntled at having been made a Count instead of a Marshal. As Minister for War he saw his chance. His plan for the disorganized armies reached the bewildered commanders just as Bazaine's army suffered its appalling triple defeats around Metz.

The tension in Paris increased. Foreigners drifted away, not because they feared the Prussian cannon might come within striking distance, but because there were better playgrounds elsewhere.

Only the Jeromes lingered on, riveted to their battle maps. Why, because of a rude but obviously temporary invasion, should they desert their chosen city, their chosen Court? "Our house was the rendezvous of the few of our French friends who had not gone to the front," wrote Jennie.

The Duc de Persigny's daily visits became more distressing, his news more unbelievable. Just five days before the regime foundered he found time to write the following note accompanying a little gift:

"Paris,

30 Aout, 1870.

Ma Chère petite Jenny,

Je vous envoie le papier marqué à votre nom, comme je vous l'ai promis. Votre nom est gravé sans ornement parce qu'il m'a paru convenir davantage par sa noble simplicité au caractère de votre jeunesse et de votre beauté. La première lettre de votre nom ne se prête pas d'ailleurs au caprice des combinaisons que comporte celui de votre sœur dont le C ambitieux pourrait embrasser l'univers.

J'espère que tel qu'il est ce chiffre vous plaira et qu'en écrivant vos lettres de jeune fille vous penserez a votre vieil ami. Mille compliments affectueux et devoués a votre excellente mère et à Clara, sans oublier bien entendu votre chère petite sœur.

Persigny."

On the following day compliments ceased. The Duc arrived grave-faced to explain that the armies did not seem to be linking up as intended (they were in fact retreating on Paris). Mrs. Jerome had just fallen and sprained her ankle, her foot could not be put to the ground. She still refused to believe that the Prussian advance could continue.

"Maybe you are right," agreed Persigny unhappily. Next morning he rushed in before they had finished breakfast crying: "*Tout est perdu; l'Armée n'est pas concentrée. Les Prussiens sont à nos Portes.*"

His alarm was so genuine that Mrs. Jerome dragged herself to her feet and told the girls to pack as quickly as possible. They could hardly believe their ears—what, leave their home and belongings with only an hour in which to prepare? Clara retired in consternation to her bedroom, wrote a brief message for the Marquis de Tamisier and started to sort her ball dresses, but Persigny was insistent. Within an hour they must leave; few trains were running and it might even now be too late to reach the coast. No cabs were functioning and Mrs. Jerome would have to be carried all the way to the station by whomever they could hire in the streets. While the Duc gesticulated and entreated, the girls ran around tying up jewellery and treasures in table cloths and sheets. They created bundles far too heavy for their strength and by the time they reached the station they were completely exhausted. So was Mrs. Jerome and her maid. But the Duc found them places on a train . . . any train would do as long as it got them out of the capital and this one was due to head north shortly. Amidst the general commotion Clara could not decide if her maid should return for "the heavy luggage" or not. In the end it was decided that dear Marie should walk home, pack up all their clothes properly in large trunks and hire a cart to bring them to the station next day. The Prussians might be at the city gates but to be stranded in Deauville without one's hats . . . really that would be too much!

Unknowingly they had boarded the last train to leave Paris for many a month. Poor Marie endured the siege half-starved in the Jerome house, looking after her mistress's gowns which were, unfortunately, only edible to the moth.

At Deauville, overcrowded by stupefied refugees, the three girls procured rooms for themselves and their lame mother in the Palace Hotel. Tearful and exhausted, they had flung themselves down to sleep till morning when a tap sounded at the door. There stood Monsieur de Garonne, a Chamberlain of the Empress, begging for concealment "owing to state reasons which they would know later". Clara unenthusiastically assented. This meant she could not leave her daughters unchaperoned for one minute. All day Monsieur waited nervously, leaping to hide behind the curtains if anyone came and greatly intriguing the girls who remained too well brought up to venture questions.

"After dinner when it was quite dark, he departed as mysteriously as he had come. Two days later we were thrilled to hear of the Empress's escape from Paris, accompanied by Dr. Crane, Dr. Evans (the American dentist) and Mme Lebreton, our friend M. de Garonne having helped to make the arrangements."

The Empress, whose orders from the Tuileries had been flatly contradicting those issued by the Emperor, sailed to England in Sir John Burgoyne's yacht which encountered a terrible storm. The wild seas appealed to Eugénie's uncrushable sense of theatre. After all the stresses of the last two months she could still summon enough imaginative energy to apprise the dramatic effect if she were drowned *now* in full flight! Perhaps the dangers of Paris had been exaggerated in order to drag her from the capital. The mob there was fickle but not fierce. Although ready to tear down gilded eagles it wanted no heads.

The yacht landed safely at Ryde in the Isle of Wight and she moved to Hastings to await her son, a chivalrous, high-strung boy of fourteen, who had been subjected to the most shattering of experiences. Brought up to idealistic notions of patriotism and honour, he had trailed around with his sick father seeing the Army he venerated turning into a rabble and the country he loved deriding that name of Bonaparte which he carried proudly (and without blemish) to the end.

Meanwhile the Emperor plumbed the depths of human misery. The piercing pain of his physical illness was not of the kind to annihilate mental suffering. Stoic, silent, still considerate for others, he remained in his saddle all day at Sedan "praying for death in a hail of shells". The long day drew to its end and the Emperor still breathed.

The Prussians who captured Napoleon III treated him gently. His resignation and despair created a mute respect. He had not led his country into war, he had struggled as far as he dared to dampen popular fervour. And now, when the flower of the French Army lay in bleeding heaps, when its frontier had been lost, the country turned to upbraid the one man who had striven to keep them out of war, and who was brave enough to lower the standard personally when defeat had come.

Louis Napoleon must have been glad to be alone among strangers, among courteous indifferent foes, this pallid, haunted Emperor, this little man of courage and goodwill, this unromantic, most gallant failure.

28

ALL Deauville overflowed with Imperial refugees bemoaning lost luggage and lost battles. Hatless, maidless, governessless, the Jerome ladies wondered where in the world to go next.

After a miserable September they accepted with docility Leonard's cable from New York ordering them to depart for England. As the German ring closed around Paris Mr. Jerome had been frantic with worry. For days he did not know that his family had escaped to the coast, or where he could find them if he took the first available passage back across the Atlantic.

With difficulty Clara Jerome and her daughters obtained places on a cross-Channel boat, and they sailed away sadly seeing France melt into a line in the distance. On arrival in England they could not decide where to go. For a time they lodged in the Norfolk Hotel in Brighton, hating the grey stone beach, the grey autumn sky, the brisk winds and above all hating "exile".

When their father reached England the girls clung to him as their one remaining rock in a dissolving world, but his practical approach to the summer's disasters disturbed them. He stated bluntly there was no possibility of returning to France. Then Mr. Jerome took his family to London and settled them in Brown's Hotel off Piccadilly.

"We may have to spend the Winter here so the girls must pick up the threads of their studies and forget about the treasures they've left in Paris."

"But Papa, the Republic can't *last*?"

"It might . . ." said Mr. Jerome.

Their faces grew long. Mid-winter came and the siege of Paris continued. Leonard brought them new frocks but still they hung their heads. Lessons had to be improvised and a special room taken for piano practice. The girls played for hours every day, hammering their moods of tearful anger into the ivory keys.

It was not long before the Duc de Persigny came to call.

"Your last visitor in Paris. Your first in London I fear!"

Leonard welcomed him with open arms. "If it were not for you my wife and daughters might yet be caught in a starving city." Persigny brought all the latest Imperial refugee gossip. There was much talk of the Emperor (a prisoner at Wilhelmshöhe) abdicating in favour of his son. They thought the King of Prussia could hardly treat with a Republican Government. A royal restoration either Imperial or Orléanist could be taken for granted. The girls pouted, *they* did not want a Bourbon back on the throne, they wanted a Bonaparte.

Then as Persigny called often, each time more forlorn and a little hungrier, it dawned upon them that "broken hearted, ill and penniless, our poor friend was put to many straits to eke out a living, selling his plate and the little he had been able to bring away with him". Having served as ambassador in London during much of the sixties he had many friends who should have been eager to help, but this made him all the more ashamed of letting people know his plight. They might have guessed his predicament but the rich seldom correctly assess the financial troubles of others. Leonard, rendered sharp and sensitive by the financial difficulties of his own youth, was the only person who came to the rescue in practical fashion. He insisted on taking a room for the Duc at Brown's Hotel and paying all his bills.

This exactly suited the Misses Jerome who, thoroughly homesick for Paris, wished to see only those French friends with whom they might discuss a speedy return of the Empire. Jennie could not get over the Prussian affront. The most scintillating of Courts had disappeared like a mirage just as she was preparing to step into it. Now she found herself ordered back to school books and music lessons with inadequate English teachers. Girls were not intensively educated in England as on the continent; Jennie and Leonie scorned the tutoring now offered. Every day they walked in Hyde Park with a German governess (German, *not* Prussian) making dull conversation. However they both wished to become expert in this tongue if only to be able to appreciate Wagner's great operas which Princess Metternich had been thrusting on baffled Parisian audiences for the last nine years. The three girls were from early years worshippers of *Tannhäuser*, and even Mrs. Jerome, like many unmusical people, could grasp Wagner's tremendous recurring motifs.

Jennie wrote:

"A winter spent in the gloom and fogs of London did not tend to dispel the melancholy which we felt. Our friends scattered, fighting or killed at the front; debarred as we were from our bright little house and our household goods it was indeed a sad time."

Her mother could not help a certain relief at having her girls in a Protestant country for she had always feared a Catholic marriage however exalted. During the first year however they made few English friends. Young Clara was very quiet during these days, being still in love with the Marquis de Tamisier who, caught in besieged Paris, was managing to send her messages by balloon. But even the thought of the hunger and danger that young man must be enduring did not soften Mrs. Jerome's views. Under the formidable pressure of her mama's displeasure Clara grew forlorn and sickened as if purposely. Finally she developed a fever which was called typhoid but which forever after she insisted had been due to frustrated love.

Leonard saw his hotel suite a rallying point for Imperialists, and grew weary of his daughters' sighs. He had good reason to try to reach Paris for he carried some private proposals from Washington to mitigate suffering. Moreover he wished to discover the fate of his best pictures. After some delay he received a diplomatic passport to visit Paris with Generals Sheridan and Burnside who were going as military observers.

They were all led blindfold through the Prussian lines to the American Minister Washbourne who had remained in Paris throughout its ordeal. Washbourne received them warmly and spoke with emotion of the individual acts of human courage and despair he had witnessed. The Washington proposals were unofficial but important enough for General Burnside to accompany Leonard to Bismarck who was quartered in the neighbourhood of Paris. Unfortunately Leonard kept no diary, and Bismarck's secretary merely recorded the visit of the American gentleman dressed "as if hurriedly in a flannel shirt with paper cuffs". (All the soap of Paris had been eaten up.) Shortly afterwards, the city capitulated and the Parisians who a year before had been shouting "*à Berlin*" retreated behind shuttered windows while the victorious Prussian columns strutted up the Champs-Elysées. Even Leonard and the American generals writhed with a sense of insult as they watched.

> "The masses of infantry, most of them wearing spectacles, marched by the Arc de Triomphe, which was barricaded, and through the deserted streets of the once gay city singing '*die Wacht am Rhein*'."

Had Leonard's daughters been present they would have wept.

With some trepidation Mr. Jerome examined his house in the Boulevard Haussman. Its cellar had been blown open by a shell but his art collection remained untouched. And Marie, the faithful maid, still waited with her mistress's packed trunks. Horrid scraps and minced rats had been her fare during the siege.

On his return to London Leonard found his daughters continued to mope at the tragedy of France. Clara, languid on a sofa recovering from her fever, could not bear to hear the stories of suffering which had come his way.

Only one pastime restored her spirits. For Christmas Persigny had presented her with an autograph book, a fine volume, bound in green leather with her name in silver letters. His courtly note accompanying it read:

> "London Xmas Day 1870.
> Dear Miss Jerome,
>   Knowing that you desire to form a collection of autographs of distinguished persons whom you have known in France I am sending you this volume which is suitable for receiving autographs. I am adding a certain number of letters, from which you can choose those you wish for your collection. Dear Miss Clara, this modest Christmas present brings the best wishes of your old friend.
>
> Persigny."

Dear Miss Clara got busy with her paste-pot. The first entry was a note from the Prince Imperial:

> "Will you please forgive my negligence in the last few days? I am suffering from a slight indisposition. I got measles from a young lady with whom I danced a mazurka and I really should not dance with any other girl."

In the hopes of stimulating Clara's return to health "the dear Duke" added various other letters: his own correspondence with Bismarck concerning the possible establishment of the Prince Imperial on the throne if the Emperor would consent to abdicate. Clara, as guileless as her old admirer, showed the collection to all and sundry with the result that a mysterious envoy from the Emperor arrived at the hotel and asked for an interview with Mr. Jerome. Leonard then learnt to his surprise that the girls he had left innocently poring over their scrap books were playing with papers "dangerous to the Imperial dynasty".

Leonard was half-amused, half-annoyed. The autograph phase had seemed impeccable as a young lady's pastime. He strode off into his dove-cote and demanded the indiscreet letters be torn out of the book and handed to his perturbed visitor who vanished forthwith. Clara remained pouting with her collection spoiled.

The Duc de Persigny then received a personal rebuke from the Emperor who, from his secretary *le petit Piétri*, had obtained a full account of the contents of Miss Jerome's album but he offered other less compromising letters to replace these confiscated. Such was his infatuation with the Jerome household that he actually handed over the Emperor's letter scolding him for unauthorized attempts to come to an understanding with Bismarck. Written on fine paper with the Imperial crown over a large N this letter survives with its envelope covered with German stamps on which the humiliating postmark *Wilhelmshöhe* is plainly visible:

> "Wilhelmshöhe,
> le 7 Janvier 1871.
>
> My dear Persigny,
> I have received your letter of the first of January, and thank you for the prayers you offer for a better future. Without desiring to enter into a discussion of the ideas you express, I will say to you that nothing good can come from the confusion which is the result of individual efforts, made without discretion, and without authority. In fact I find it somewhat singular that any one should busy himself with the future of my son, without taking account of my own intentions.
> I know you have written to M. de Bismarck, who naturally has asked me if you have done so with my authority and in full accord with me. I have answered him that I have authorized nobody to busy himself with my interests, or those of my son, without first obtaining my consent.
> Believe, my dear Persigny, in my friendship.
> Napoleon."

Another slip of paper in the Emperor's handwriting showed a rough copy of the surrender at Sedan. Clara had learnt prudence. She never showed any more letters, not even a few harmless notes from personages of the day such as the Queen of Holland and Prince Napoleon (Plonplon had safely reached Claridge's Hotel). On September 23rd, 1870, Sophie of Holland had written:

> "My dear Duke,
> During the crushing events of the last days I have constantly been thinking of you and asking for news of you. I only learnt your address two days ago from our friend Baillette. Write me a word. No one suffers with you more than I. The world that I loved has crumbled away. Nothing remains save ruins. Those who understand should hold out hands to each other. Believe in my constant friendship.
> Sophie."

Most of the letters to which Clara clung were embossed with crowns and coronets and *all* took an Imperial restoration for granted. Without expressing admiration for, or even interest in, their Emperor the *émigrés* whispered and scribbled that all would "come right". And of course no ears listened more sympathetically than those of the Mesdemoiselles Jerome. On December 19th, 1870, Plonplon wrote:

"My dear Monsieur Beaulieu (de Persigny's pseudonym),
      I wrote you yesterday and I write again to-day to share with you the news I have received from the Centre and the Midi of France. Dated December 6th to 11th it is very favourable to us. I choose this letter from a republican . . . a very serious man personally attached to me: 'Here at Marseilles there is inclination for a restoration . . . etc.' Other letters say the same thing. One from Lyon reads: 'a Bonaparte restoration is considered by all as *inevitable*.' Such information has a certain value without giving me illusions. One must then, agitate! Why are we so led and so badly led? Anyway I await news *of you know what*. . . .

Affectionately,
Moncalieri."

Throughout October 1870 Plonplon under the name of Comte de Moncalieri buzzed around Brook Street seeking to make himself important to whoever would listen. The unhappy Duc de Persigny devolving rapidly into a sick old man was summoned to Claridges and made to listen to all the Plonplonian plots when he would far rather have been sitting in the Jerome *salon* at Brown's Hotel.

"I could not set foot in France, especially when represented by republicans of such a type . . . we must not abandon each other, we must remain ready for anything." These sentiments are repeated steadily in various elegant spidery hand-writings. One long letter from Persigny's brother-in-law the Prince de la Moskowa, dated September 10th, 1870, spoke hopefully of the King of Prussia's antipathy to any republican government and also to the Orléans party:

"I know the King to be anti-republican and I hope that he will thrust aside the present government and only treat with the head of the Army. If there is a siege, I doubt if it will last long; with an army pushed on to a strong point such as Paris, one could make a fine defence but I know only too well those 4th Battalions which are nevertheless the best they have there. I do not believe therefore in a serious defence; Paris will be obliged to surrender after a short bombardment . . . the present government should soon fall . . . we can then reclaim our rights, as the Emperor, although prisoner, is none the less Sovereign as Francois I was after Pavia;

there is for him only the material difficulty of speaking to the nation, of reclaiming his rights, for his son rather than for himself, as, though I do not believe the Emperor will ever regain the throne and I doubt if he desires to, the country awaits."

So they ramble on, the gentlemen with their crested notepaper, their wishful thinking and their absolute *sureness* concerning an ultimate restoration. The King of Prussia might bring France to her knees but he couldn't be cad enough to allow a *republican* government to remain in power!

Perhaps the most interesting letter which Clara retained for her scrapbook is one from General de Paliakao, whom Eugenie had made head of her government and who had consistently given her bad advice.

"Ostend, Oct. 21, 1870.

My dear Duke,

I arrived in Ostend four days ago, and found your address.

Since our separation on the 7th I have remained in Belgium, and should have asked for news of you during that time if I had known where to send a letter.

Being threatened with arrest on September 4, I departed that evening, and sought refuge first at Namur where twenty-four hours later I was joined by my wife and daughters.

My chief aim in journeying to Namur was to be near Sedan, that I might learn the fate of my son, for whom I had great anxiety. After several days of inquiry, I at last learned that my son, after having been wounded at Sedan (a horse having been killed under him), was a prisoner at Cologne, as he would not accept the capitulation.

I left Namur for Spa, and a sojourn there not being very comfortable in the winter, I established myself at Ostend, where I await events, the issue of which I cannot foresee.

How I wish, my dear Duke, that my pen were clever enough to convey to you all the impressions I have received since the fatal Sedan. I have come to the point of asking myself how a disaster of such dimensions could be produced without the principal author of this lugubrious drama being buried under the corpses of his army.

I had thought that it was easier to die than to suffer dishonour.

The death of the Emperor at Sedan would have saved France, as well as his son: the capitulation has lost everything.

Now that France has become the prey of foreign and domestic Vandals, how can this desolation of our unhappy country be brought to an end?

Unless there should be a general war creating a division in Prussian politics, I do not see what side we can turn to. England appears to have abandoned us, and even if our alliance of 1856 could be reproduced, even then she could not count on our help, we have fallen so low.

I had offered my services to the government of the National Defence, but I withdrew my offer as soon as I saw the government, to the eternal shame of France, call a Garibaldi to defend her.

Accusations of treason reach all the generals who have served the Empire, and I am not willing to have my name bandied among all these ignominies.

Adieu, my dear Duke. If you will be so good as to send me your news I will be happy indeed . . . for our hearts are full of gratitude.

Ever yours,
General de Paliakao."[1]

This came from a fire-brand who had led the cry for war and been among those directly responsible for the *débâcle*. Having sent out an impossible order for MacMahon's army to join hands with that of Bazaine, and insulted the Emperor's new governor of Paris who alone had hope of keeping order, Paliakao had in August 1870 been the first to decide it would be expedient if the Emperor "died at the head of his troops". No one realized that sombre fact more clearly than Louis Napoleon himself and no one could have tried harder. But inconvenient as it might be, the Emperor of the French still breathed.

The Jerome girls felt strongly about this letter, and Jennie took care to quote with it General Changier who, although hostile to Napoleon III, said:

"And he has been called 'Coward'. When I remember that this man, tortured by a horrible disease, remained on horseback at Sedan an entire day, watching disappear the prestige of France, his throne, his dynasty, and all the glory reaped at Sebastopol and in Lombardy, I cannot control myself."

Poor Emperor and poor heart-broken Prince Imperial. History had discarded them.

[1] The title of Paliakao was derived from a town in China. The general had presented Eugénie with a string of black pearls from the Summer Palace.

29

IN LONDON the summer of 1871 was a season of sighs emanating from the Imperial refugees: "last year when the chestnuts came to flower we were at St. Cloud; if one could have foreseen . . ." A few of the fugitives scandalized Victorian society. The Duchesse de Carracciolo and the Countesse de Bechevet took a country house and to the horror of local squires went shooting dressed in kilts and smoking cigarettes. When Comte de Bechevet suffered an indisposition, one of his guests dressed as a priest arrived to hear his last confession while the remainder of the party hid behind the bedroom curtains to listen in. As their host's sins were recounted bursts of hysterical laughter broke out until the poor man realized he was but 'making the party go'.

Mrs. Jerome pursed her lips when these ladies visited Brown's Hotel, but nevertheless her small suite became a base for fruitless gossip.

Meanwhile France passed through a period of feverish bitterness. Civil war flared in the ashes of defeat. The peasants and bourgeoisie moaned for peace and termination of chaos, but the Parisians exasperated by the hunger, cold and suffering they had been forced to endure wanted a *real* revolution, which would allow them to revenge themselves on the generals responsible for their incompetent defence. From fear and lack of understanding between capital and country grew up the sinister episodes of the Commune. The hysterical element of Paris tried to salve its own wounds by practising massacre and pillage. Revolutionaries turned overnight into thieves and incendiaries. Leonard hurried back to Paris in order to pack up those Italian pictures which he had been collecting ever since Trieste. Clara insisted on accompanying him and together they sorted their favourites which were shipped to New York just before the riots of May 23rd when a crowd set fire to the Tuileries. On the following day Clara hurried forth in bonnet and shawl to see with her own eyes if the rumours she had heard were true. The old palace where she had attended so many balls crumbled in smoke and flame while a rough crowd threw furniture out of the windows and held auctions on the lawn. To her amazement Clara saw Napoleon's dining service in white porcelain with the golden N surmounted by an Imperial crown being sold in lots to the highest bidder. Without a moment's hesitation she joined the fray, and raised her voice for one pile of plates after another. *Ah ces Américains*—they had more money than anyone else. Who could bid against them? The crowd let her have them. There were better bargains than these old plates in any case . . . look there were bolsters and feather beds being thrown from the top floor . . . and blankets and fine eiderdowns!

Clara was left alone with her purchases lying around on the grass. Cinders floated through the air, blinding her eyes, and crash after crash marked the end of those old walls which had housed so many generations of French kings. The mob ran and roared in its hunt for household goods. For a time she watched the frenzy. So this was the Commune . . . a scramble for bargains! Then she looked around for some practical method of transporting the china back to her house. Men with hand barrows were in much demand: hiring one of these she stacked the Imperial dinner service on board and turned her back wistfully on the smouldering ruins. She would never dance there again. Better not to look.

Meanwhile Leonard, in the Boulevard Haussman, anxiously awaited her return. To his surprise she finally appeared in a state of disarray, blackened by cinders and accompanied by a small man pushing a large barrow from which stacks of plates seemed about to topple.

"What on *earth* have you been doing?"

"Look," she said, "the poor dear Emperor's best dinner set, handed out of the window, auctioned in the garden. . . . I got it but do not ask me how."

She'd got it and she kept it. Leonard felt it would be embarrassing to allow the Imperial monogram to appear at his table but years later the set came into the possession of a grandson who had no need to entertain such scruples. French ministers and generals could not help evincing curiosity when they saw the unmistakable 'N' on the dinner plates.

"How did these come into your possession?" they would inevitably ask. They could hardly have guessed the story.[1]

Returning to London, the Jeromes cheered their family with promises for the following year, and when the heat grew intense in August Leonard took them all out of town. He chose a charming seaside village where he had long intended to spend a summer. This was Cowes, that yachting base in the Isle of Wight, where the *Henrietta* had been received after her noble drive across the Atlantic.

The Jeromes took a cottage and proceeded to enjoy expeditions to

[1] This dinner service is used today by Sir Winston Churchill at Chartwell. The golden crowns remain hardly scratched.

Shanklin Bay and Freshwater. One day a gentleman called when they were all out and left a card saying he would come again. "Le Comte de Pierrefonds" they read. Who could it be? Next day the Emperor's secretary informed them that Napoleon and Eugénie had come to the Isle of Wight on a visit. Pierrefonds was the Emperor's pseudonym which he had used ever since the Germans released him. Only at Chislehurst was Imperial grandeur kept up.

"Shortly afterwards (wrote Jennie) we were asked by their Majesties to go for an expedition around the Island. The party consisted of the Emperor and Empress, the Prince Imperial, the Empress's nieces the Mesdemoiselles d'Albe, Prince Joachim Murat, the Duc d'Albe, a few Spaniards, and the suite, which was composed of one or two faithful followers. The expedition was rather a failure owing to the roughness of the sea, most of the party seeking 'the seclusion that the cabin grants'. The Mesdemoiselles d'Albe were desperately ill, and lay in a state of coma. But the Empress enjoyed the breeze. The Prince Imperial, full of life and spirits, chaffed everyone, some of his jokes falling rather flat on the Spaniards, who were feeling anything but bright, and evidently thought it no laughing matter. I can see now the Emperor leaning against the mast, looking old, ill, and sad. His thoughts could not have been other than sorrowful, and even in my young eyes, he seemed to have nothing to live for."

After Sedan nothing indeed, except the precious future of his gallant little son; for him whose fourteen years were bright with honour and love of France, for him alone he would struggle a little longer.

The Empress Eugénie enjoyed a gale. While pea-green followers wilted and drooped, she would be sure to show the best of spirits. And the young Prince recovered for a few hours from the terrible brooding knowledge of his country's failure. He had charm and wit and dash. Leonie, three years younger, fell desperately in love.

Before returning to Chislehurst, his Majesty again called on the Jeromes. After this visit, with pity and distress, the three girls watched him walking away down their garden path, a stumpy little man with a big head who walked with a halting step as if in pain. "But he was so kind and so brave."

They never saw him again.

30

IN THE autumn of 1871 tension in Paris eased sufficiently for Leonard to bring his wife and two elder daughters back to the Boulevard Haussman while little Leonie (to her marked displeasure) departed to school at Wiesbaden.

Amidst funereal exclamations the two Claras delved through their luggage which had been packed up eighteen months previously. Out of date were the tulle ball gowns and the flowered bonnets intended for garden parties at Compiègne. . . ! It would be months before their interest in clothes could be revived. Meanwhile Jennie finished off her education with an intensive study of music and languages in the continental fashion. Leonard repaired and restocked his bombarded wine cellar and opened his house to dispense what hospitality he could to racing friends of pre-war days, but French people were too weary and bruised to show much interest in sport. Persigny, their 'dear old duke' (who was to die of depression and disappointment within the next year), also returned to Paris and spent long hours commiserating with his friends in the Jerome *salon*. To tell the truth he was becoming rather a bore as people do when obsessed with a vanished past, but he had saved them from a most unpleasant experience in the siege and the Jeromes were loyal friends even if they no longer ran quite so eagerly to meet his carriage at the door. They all found life extremely 'triste'. Jennie wrote:

"Ruins everywhere: the sight of the Tuileries and the Hôtel de Ville made me cry. St. Cloud the scene of many pleasant expeditions was a thing of the past, the lovely château razed to the ground. And if material Paris was damaged, the social fabric was even more so. In vain we tried to pick up the threads. Some of our friends were killed, others ruined or in mourning, and all broken-hearted and miserable, hiding in their houses and refusing to be comforted."

Jennie who had dreamed of playing a star part at the Imperial Court now stood in the Place de la Concorde where the statue of the lost city of

American schooner *Dauntless*

The opening of the four-in-hand season

Leonie and John Leslie riding Leonard's horses

Sketch done in a London sporting club by John Leslie for Leonard Jerome,
1885

Strasbourg was swathed in crape and felt the melancholy of baffled youth surge through her heart. Clara's attempts to renew her romance with the Marquis de Tamisier were still frustrated by Mrs. Jerome and the only interesting visit paid seems to have been to the Duc de Praslin at his beautiful Château de Vaux-Praslin.

"Our host took us all over the huge building, pointing out everything of historical interest, until we came to an ornamented door, before which he paused, but did not enter. '*La chambre du feu Duc de Praslin*,' he said in a grim voice, and then passed on. This was the room of the late Duke his father, who had murdered his wife. . . . The Duchess's unfounded jealousy of the governess drove the Duke to this terrible act. On the way home we discussed the details with bated breath . . . how the Duchess had been first stabbed, then smothered under the canopy of the bed, which the Duke pulled down on her; how the Duke was tried by his peers and sentenced to death, but the night before the execution, was found dead in his cell, friends having smuggled poison to him."[1]

When in the early summer Leonard swept his daughters back to the carefree atmosphere of Cowes they could not but rejoice at leaving their once loved Paris in her period of gloom and disillusion.

Having established his family in their 'sweet little cottage', with its trim garden facing the sea, Leonard departed for New York. He travelled by steam-boat now and was teaching himself to use the weeks spent each year on the Atlantic as work periods in which he could study and invent new schemes. His energy remained, but the effort to make money bored him more and more. Only the fight to keep horse-racing on a high level held his interest. He had to withstand attacks from the dishonest, who were eager to make a racket out of the sport, and from anti-gambling Puritan and Quaker elements. "I fight one side with my right hand, and the other more persuasively with my left."

When he was lonely or wearied with business Leonard went off with James Gordon Bennett and Lawrence to hunt buffalo in the western plains. Commodore Vanderbilt always lent them his private railcar from Rochester westwards.

Meanwhile the New York *Times* was reaching the climax of its battle

[1] It has since been established that he was smuggled out of his cell and lived for years in England supported by his family. Greater fame fell on the governess than on the much pitied Duke, for at the trial she pleaded her cause so eloquently that she left the court a brave attractive figure without the slightest aspersion on her character. Eighty years later she was brilliantly portrayed in *All This and Heaven Too*. The Praslin descendants suffered severely, however, from this scandal. For eighty years they were, a Frenchman told me, "depreciated" and no big families would marry them.

with the Tweed Ring. Powerful people, long considered invincible, were being harpooned.

Briefly events had run thus. Throughout 1870 and 1871 a consecutive attack had been maintained. Tweed was openly accused of using his official position to loot the citizens of New York. In October 1870, just before the Elections, President Grant had, in response to a Republican demand that polling booths be protected, ordered several regiments to be quartered in the city forts. If the *Times* had truly affected public opinion Boss Tweed might find votes turning against him. As he owned the metropolitan police, he would not hesitate to use force to alter the tide. The presence of Federal troops to ensure fair voting might do him much harm. But Tweed, as well as running the Democrats, had bought so many of the lesser Republican politicians that the President's precautions left him unruffled. When the day arrived he was so sure of victory that he did not consider it necessary to break up polling boxes. While fifty-thousand of his red-shirted supporters marched through the streets carrying torches, Tweed spoke unctuously to a cheering crowd in Tammany Hall. The fact that he had lured August Belmont, the grandee of Wall Street, to sit on one side of him while fat diamond-studded Jim Fisk supported him from the other, in itself showed an astonishing victory, for Belmont would not normally have graced any committe to which the dubious-moralled Fisk belonged. Belmont had always supported the Democratic party. Fisk was a new convert, having been a Republican until President Grant let him down, disgracefully, so he thought, by refusing to aid his and Gould's gold-cornering schemes. Jim Fisk determined to revenge himself on the President, intended to announce that all employees of the *Erie* Railway would henceforth switch and vote Democrat.

Tweed answered the *Times's* allegations that he had scraped some fifty million dollars into the Ring's private money-box by arranging for six well-known New Yorkers to undertake an enquiry and make a public report. This eventually read: "We have come to the conclusion and certify, that the financial affairs of the city under the charge of the Comptroller are administered in a correct and faithful manner." John Jacob Astor III, supposedly the richest heir in America, headed the committee and added his name to the impressive signatures at the foot of this document.

It then looked as if Tweed must remain established in power and piety forever. Six months later, in July 1871, just at the time when Leonard was sailing back across the Atlantic in the yacht *Dauntless*, a small revolt occurred in Tammany Hall. One Sheriff O'Brian was refused his expenses, and after an unsuccessful attempt to dislodge Tweed from leadership, O'Brian deserted into the enemy's camp. He delivered to the *Times* a mass of transcripts from the account books of the Comptroller which flatly contradicted the Astor report and finally revealed that the Tweed Ring had embezzled not fifty, but about seventy, million dollars. The figures were so vast that all the chartered accountants in New York city could hardly work them out.

At Tweed's trial the jury disagreed. They argued that one man could not be responsible for such huge-scale cheating. Thousands of respectable New Yorkers must have tolerated, if not condoned, the 'Ring' or it could hardly have reached such dimensions but no names were published. At a second trial Tweed was sentenced to twelve years in prison. One million dollars of the vanished seventy was retrieved, and returned to New York City. The *Times* knew it had won the greatest victory in newspaper history. August Belmont never blinked an eyelid or said a word concerning his appearance on the Tammany platform. It was better, perhaps, to forget such associates when Tweed had been placed in jail, and Jim Fisk shot to death publicly in the Grand Central Hotel by the lover of his beautiful faithless mistress. Mr. Belmont found more pleasurable memories in his artistic collections, in the patronage of opera, the triumphs of his horses and the surveillance of that famous chef whom he commanded to cook a splendid meal every single day to keep the fellow's hand adroit.

Leonard had not been able to put his full energies into the Tweed battle but he felt proud that he had quarter-owned the *Times* for over ten years.

A final commentary on the affair has been written by Lloyd Morris:[1]

". . . it could be surmised that John Jacob Astor III's acquaintance with accounting had merely suffered a temporary lapse when, with his distinguished associates, he certified to the sound condition of the city's finances. The death of his father, William Astor in 1875, left him the wealthiest man in the United States. He often rewrote telegrams to save one word, and in many other ways was known to keep his vast fortune in excellent repair."

Ways which, alas, were unknown to Leonard Jerome.

31

LEONARD had reached the age of fifty-four, his financial flair remained, but the taste for money-making was leaving him. The big rackets which had grown out of the first exciting expansion of America had become unsavoury. President Grant, lumbering too late, was unable to prevent Jay Gould and Jim Fisk from misappropriating millions when they cornered the Gold Market, and the disaster of Black Friday 1869 had left slurs right through Congress. The reputation of the White House itself was injured. "Let everyone carry out his own corpse," grinned Fisk to President Grant's committee of investigation. Half of Wall Street suffered ruin, but although crowds of speculators set out to hang Gould and Fisk they never managed to lay hands on them. "Nothing is lost save honour," explained fat Jim, and a year later he could dare to appear once more in Broadway restaurants with flashy actresses.

Leonard allowed no hint of financial troubles to reach his family. Their happy summer days remained intact. The solemn frivolities of outdoor life in the seventies are described by Jennie's pen. She found Cowes

"delightfully small and peaceful . . . the Royal Yacht Squadron did not resemble a perpetual garden party, or the roadstead a perpetual regatta. Yachts went in and out without fear of losing their moorings. . . . People all seemed to know one another. The Prince and Princess of Wales could walk about and amuse themselves . . . like ordinary mortals."

It was in fact "delightfully small and peaceful" in the manner most likely to please Mrs. Jerome who, since the fall of Paris, had taken to behaving in somewhat the manner of an exiled queen. Her lovely elder daughters were presented to the Prince and Princess of Wales at the Royal Yacht Squadron Ball during regatta week and allowed to go to a few exclusive parties. They took it for granted they should head the *élite* in any country where they chose to alight.

In those days it was usual, when invited out to dinner, for young ladies to take their music with them so that during the evening they could be asked by inwardly groaning guests to play their 'piece'. After a few coy refusals they would relent sufficiently to sing a ditty or pick out the tune which some old governess had drummed into their rhythmless fingers for such occasions. English girls brought up backstairs in country houses with the dogs and horses, were usually painfully shy and the series of tremulous encores necessitated by politeness conveyed their anguish to the already squirming audience only too adequately.

Human nature being as it is, Clara and Jennie could hardly have been expected not to glow with satisfaction when asked for *their* 'piece'. During the last year they had been concentrating on the mastery of piano duets so that without a trace of nervousness they would sit down side by side, look at each other for a moment and with expert precision start on *Schumann à quatre mains.*

"Such a lovely sight it made, those two young heads one blonde and one dark bent raptly over the keys," remembered an admirer years later. And the inevitable triumph of the next half-hour might have elated any mama save Mrs. Jerome who wondered if it was ladylike to play *quite* so well!

No such thoughts entered the minds of the guests who had arranged themselves as comfortably as possible for the customary period of pain. The musical remained riveted; the unmusical (and there were many among English gentlemen) listened open-mouthed, unavoidably aware that with all that pounding and so many notes being hit at the same time some kind of jolly good show must be going on at the piano.

At any rate it seemed impossible not to *notice* the Misses Jerome. Their American vitality allied with continental culture created 'quite an atmosphere' at every party they attended. Clara and Jennie regarded themselves as no mean artists but so arduous had been the training leading to this standard that they accepted ovation as merely being their due for having practised four hours a day. Music had become part of the air they breathed for all Leonard's daughters. He rejoiced in their gifts but Mrs. Jerome listened less to chords and trills than to the gasps and exclamations which her girls' performance elicited. Jennie worried her in particular, she played with such fire and abandon . . . was it really becoming?

Having sought by cold baths and rigorous exercise to impart even greater health to her daughters than they already inherited, Mrs. Jerome had to admit she had succeeded beyond expectations. They now chafed like race-horses in training. Every hour of the day had to be crammed with activities. "The girls are just like Leonard," she wrote, "never, never tired . . . what does one do about it?" Perhaps Clara and Jennie became conceited despite their mother's constant efforts to restrain. Certainly these two exotic young creatures did not notice anything extraordinary in their easy entry into that hide-bound English society whose portals had so far remained closed to all not born and brought up within its ranks. Taking their social popularity for granted neither daughter dreamed that the key which opened this narrow world to them might be Leonard Jerome's reputation as a sportsman. His sailing exploits and his efforts to establish horse-racing in America had given him renown in sporting circles throughout the world, but few men receive fair due in their own home.

He had sufficient philosophy not to be hurt by the evaluation of youth, and did not eat his heart out because now he was simply regarded as a provider of pretty dresses and presents. To the end he could laugh at his daughters' sense of their own importance.

He let them frolic through the summer along with those poor hounded royalties all so "eager to throw off ceremony". No hint of his private struggle must reach Clara's ears. "She hates money or thinks she does," he remarked jokingly. "I've never discussed business matters with her." He had long ago settled various trusts in her name so that she could not be too seriously affected by his own speculations. But these gruelling days in Wall Street left him tired, and hungry for family news. He longed for letters which his daughters with the selfishness of their years were too engrossed with their own pleasures to compose. Alone in his large empty town house Leonard grew lonely. An exhortation penned on August 7th, 1873, used the family pet names pleadingly:

"Mrs. Clit, Miss Clarita and Miss Jennie.

Dearly beloved, It is nearly two weeks since I had a letter. You must be sure to write me particulars of all that is going on. I have no doubt you will see many nice people and will have Cowes all to yourselves as far as Americans are concerned. Did you get the tent from London? And do you make it lively and have you secured the Villa Rosetta for another year? etc. I rather like the idea of Cowes next summer and a yacht. Don't forget while sitting under your own vine and eating up your own fig tree that I am awfully disappointed if I don't get my weekly letters."

He needed affection to supplement his nervous energy but only little Leonie remained a diligent if rather mournful correspondent from her school in Wiesbaden and even her pages complained of lack of news from Cowes and guilelessly expressed a hope that her birthday on August 15th would not pass unnoticed.

Leonard of course remembered and sent a gift. He longed for her now, for her funny little face and impish expressions and quaint remarks. But he had to banish even the image of her from his mind for a hundred dreary papers lay on his desk and must be read. The monopolistic avenues of finance invented by Vanderbilt did not allow time for European holidays, and in any case the Flash Age was ending. Owing to mad speculation and the over-building of railways a commercial depression was setting in.

After the Civil War, Henry Clews had wholeheartedly proclaimed the importance of helping the South to recover its lost wealth by diverting foreign capital into Southern investments. He built up schemes for regenerating and revivifying the agricultural and manufacturing interests of the beaten states. Leonard, sharing these views, invested heavily. Now a sudden panic had revealed Georgia securities as worthless. The immense losses which resulted caused the failure of Henry Clews' firm and after months of protest and accusation the whole Southern relief plan seemed to be a fiasco. Jerome had to add this loss to a $600,000 he had invested in Indiana Bonds. Mr. Hudson the official agent had sometime previously obtained the State's official stamp and used it dishonestly. Eventually Indiana disowned its own agent and Jerome's $600,000 regarded as a gilt-edged investment disappeared.[1]

Amidst the turbulent roundabouts and swings of the seventies Leonard reckoned a man of his standing must be able to stand blows even on this scale without altering his way of life. He was still seen at the clubs and at his racecourses, laughing, talking to all, quick with flippant repartee, but a description has been preserved of the arrival of final disastrous news:

> "At last, one evening, while he was entertaining some friends at dinner, a telegram was brought to him, which he opened, read, and laid by the side of his plate. When the dinner was over he rose and asked pardon for the impoliteness of reading the telegram, 'but gentlemen,' he continued, 'it is a message in which you are all interested. The bottom has fallen out of stocks and I am a ruined man. But your dinner is paid for and I did not want to disturb you while you were eating it.' There was a babble of questions; then a sudden scattering, and Mr. Jerome was left with his telegram. He has chosen to remain alone ever since. Only a very few persons are now admitted to his companionship and fewer still to his intimacy.

Ruined as he called himself, Mr. Jerome was still a wealthy man. He had settled a large fortune upon his wife; he recovered a fortune from the

---

[1] A newspaper clipping states: "In 1862 the agent of the State of Indiana swindled Jerome out of $600,000 by the unauthorized issue of Indiana 5 per cent bonds. The agent of the State, duly appointed by the Governor and Senate, having his office at 20 Wall Street, was entrusted with these bonds. The State repudiated the acts of its agent and as an individual is not allowed to sue a State, Mr. Jerome was, and still is, unable to collect the debt."

wreck of his speculations; he has made a fortune since by his investments. But in Wall Street he no longer ruled, and that to him meant ruin."[1]

One can visualize the darkened room as guest after guest left the dining-table, the candles flickering out and waiters hovering around uncertainly clearing the half-emptied wine glasses. *Mr. Jerome was left alone with his telegram*; none can read his thoughts. Only Clara his wife far away in the Isle of Wight might guess how little he cared for his own, but how much for his daughters' sakes.

Leonard Jerome did not speak for a long while, then he dropped the crumpled message on the floor, bid the waiters good night and walked home. They knew him well and noticed that he moved a little more slowly than before but with a back as stiff as a ramrod. "Like a military gentleman", they say. At last Leonard Jerome had to realize that his career as a financier was over. Long ago he had ceased to take the game seriously and yet the irrevocable knowledge came hard. Jerome the Sportsman remained.

In the house where he now lived alone the gas lamps were burning brightly. A letter from his wife lay on the hall table. He took it up to read in bed as a sedative. But the pages covered with tremulous spidery writing contained no soothing good-night message. His tired eyes deciphered the words: "hasty . . . rash . . . headstrong . . . unconsidered . . . impulsive. You must return to England by the next boat."

They had only known each other three days. The young man had not yet started any career and there were other reasons to be written later underlining the general unwisdom of this impetuous decision.

Jennie, his precious beautiful Jennie, was engaged to be married.

---

[1] *Eminent New Yorkers*, 1887, by Stephen Fiske.

32

THE person whose advent on the Jerome horizon had spread this sudden conflagration of feeling has been described by the most adequate filial pen:

"Behold him now at twenty-three, a man grown, markedly reserved in his manner to acquaintances, utterly unguarded to his intimate friends, something of a dandy in his dress, an earnest sportsman, an omnivorous reader, moving with a jaunty step through what were, in those days, the very select circles of fashion and clubland, seeking the pleasures of the Turf and town."[1]

Lord Randolph Churchill had, up to this date, made no particular imprint beyond that of the ardent sportsman admired by his caste.

The younger son of the seventh Duke of Marlborough by Lady Frances Vane, eldest daughter of the third Marquis of Londonderry, he had been brought up in the fashion traditional for boys of the English aristocracy.

The splendour of Blenheim Palace was his background, a nursery wing in that vast structure meant 'home', and the park with its oak trees, which had witnessed the hunting of Plantagenet kings, was his playground. Educated at boarding-school since the age of eight, he had, on leaving Eton, made a continental tour before entering Merton College, Oxford. The university lay only a few miles from Blenheim, so that he could often bring his friends home and offer them the sporting delights of an enormous estate. "His nature responded to the glory and romance of Oxford; and in its cloistered courts, so rich in youth and history, he found a scheme of life more varied, tolerant, and real than any he had ever known." For three years he had sudied moderately, hunted zealously and made some lasting friends "not many in number but staunch and true". His Eton acquaintance Lord Dalmeny[2] often accompanied him on visits to Blenheim where, among other Conservative statesmen, the boys met the Prime Minister Disraeli who took a particular interest in the young. Dizzy would talk and joke with them by the hour. In such an environment, with this company

---

[1] *Lord Randolph Churchill*, by Winston S. Churchill.
[2] Afterwards Lord Rosebery, Liberal Prime Minister.

during formative years, it seems hardly strange that both youths developed almost casually a natural brilliance of expression. These boyhoods contrasted severely with that of Leonard Jerome. Within the precincts of Blenheim Palace no inkling could have arisen of the hard inducements of that American system which encouraged a poor boy to labour his way through college ignoring social status. In England a classical education was dealt out automatically to boys of the upper class. Often they loathed it, and scorned scholarship and its fruits forever, but Latin and Greek remained a class privilege. The duke's son was not likely to find his waiter sitting next him at lectures.

In the serenity of Blenheim Park studded by thousand-year-old oak trees, amidst its legends and its history the children of the Dukes of Marlborough were raised in consciousness of their heritage. In that vast palace presented to his illustrious ancestor by the English nation, at the table of his parents who formally entertained the eminent Conservative politicians of the day, young Randolph felt the ease of his birthright. A seat in Parliament waited ready for him if he wished. Woodstock, lying practically within his father's demesne, would be his whenever he cared to stand. His name alone assured that. Against a Churchill no outsider ever had a chance. To the working and middle classes the path of young Lord Randolph must have looked golden; his forbears had nobly fought for England, he inherited the glory of John Churchill's name and unless he did "something dreadful", such as turning Liberal, he could rest assured his world would automatically regard him as an interesting, distinguished person. He ought to have been happy. But contrary impulses shadowed his mind.

The Duke had determined that Randolph *must* stand for Parliament because it would ensure Woodstock being held for the Conservatives.

> "No one could possibly have so good a chance as the young cadet, born and bred on the soil, who knew half the farmers and local magnates personally, whose excursions with the harriers had made him familiar with all parts of the constituency and whose gay and stormy attractiveness had won him a host of sworn allies.
>
> Yet he had often in words and in letters expressed a disinclination for public life. It is curious to notice, how even in the days of buoyant unconquered youth, moods of depression cast their shadows across his path."

Such was the situation and state of Lord Randolph Churchill when in August, 1873, he went to Cowes for the pleasures of sea and sailing then so much in vogue. Among the "little balls" which Mrs. Jerome allowed her daughters to grace with their presence was one in honour of the Czarevitch and the Czarevna, given by the officers of the cruiser *Ariadne*, then lying as guard-ship in the Roads. To this festivity not unnaturally "all the pleasure seekers who frequent the Solent at this season of year made haste to go in boats and launches from the shore and from the fleet". Merriest and loveliest of the butterflies who flitted out to the cruiser that evening were the Jerome sisters in their white tulle frocks adorned with fresh flowers. Both loved to dance and were expert in every step, having been schooled nearly as carefully in this line as at the piano. Their ease and grace, their vivacity and shining eyes made them the cynosure of the crowded ship's ballroom. Lord Randolph Churchill, usually bored at dances, took one look and began to search for a friend who could arrange an introduction. Jennie's dark eyes smiled at him from a host of admirers. He detested dancing of all kinds but his only chance to further their acquaintance lay in some kind of terpsichorean effort. He led her boldly to the floor.

After a formal quadrille in which he was not quite sure of the steps, Jennie could hardly express sorrow when he asked her to sit out. She soon discovered that he talked better than he danced and, though her eager feet hated to miss one moment of a waltz, some vibrant quality in this young man with the prominent eyes and changeable expressions held her interest. Discovering that Lord Randolph was not shy and made no secret of his feelings she began to sparkle in the effort to parry his wit with her own. Until this evening men had merely been dancing partners. She welcomed one who was not. That night as casually as possible she asked Mama to invite Lord Randolph to dinner on the following evening and Mrs. Jerome sent a note, though not without a look of interrogation. She had not seen that expression in Jennie's face before.

"The dinner was good, the company gay and attractive, and with the two young ladies chatting and playing duets at the piano the evening passed very pleasantly. . . . That very night Miss Jerome told her laughing and incredulous sister of a presentiment that their new friend was the man she would marry; and Lord Randolph confided to Colonel Edgcumbe, who was of the party, that he admired the two sisters, and meant, if he could, to make 'the dark one' his wife."

On the following day they met again, according to their own account 'by accident', and went for a walk. Once more Mrs. Jerome was asked by her daughter to proffer an invitation to dinner. "Are we not inviting that young gentleman rather often?" she queried. But he came.

"That night—the third of their acquaintance—was a beautiful night, warm and still, with the lights of the yachts shining on the water and the sky bright with stars. After dinner they found themselves alone together in the garden, and brief courtship notwithstanding, he proposed and was accepted."

The tiny garden bathed in moonlight, the sea, the stars, Jennie with her flushed cheeks and curved red lips and deep eyes, even more beautiful now that she was in love than before . . . amidst these intoxications young Randolph lost his head completely. He returned to Blenheim

"shaken by alternating emotions of joy and despondency. He had never been in love before and the force and volume of the tide swept him altogether off his feet. At one moment he could have been preferred; the next he trembled lest all his hopes should be shattered by circumstances unforeseen. Nor indeed was his anxiety without reason; for many and serious obstacles had yet to be encountered."

In a letter written on August 20th from Blenheim Palace he sought somewhat lengthily to explain to his father the amazing feelings which beset him and which he was quite sure lovers had never known before.

"You won't feel any annoyance with me for not having consulted you before saying anything to her. I really meant to have done so; but the night before I was leaving Cowes (Friday) my feelings of sorrow at parting from her were more than I could restrain, and I told her all. I did not say anything to her mother, but I believe that she did after I was gone: for she wrote to me just as I was starting (I did not, after all, leave Cowes till the Monday) and she said in her letter that her mother could not hear of it. That I am at a loss to understand.

I told Mama when I got here and should have written at once to tell you; but I was so wretched and miserable at leaving thus, I was quite incapable of writing quietly.

I now write to tell you of it all, and to ask you whether you will be able to increase my allowance to some extent to put me in the position to ask Mrs. Jerome to let me become her daughter's future husband. I enclose you her photograph, and will only say about her that she is as good as she is beautiful, and that by her education and bringing-up she is in every way qualified to fill any position.

She has an elder sister, and one younger, who is not yet out. Mr. Jerome is a gentleman who is obliged to live in New York to look after his business. I do not know what it is. He is reputed to be very well off, and his daughters, I believe, have very good fortunes, but I do not know anything for certain. He generally comes over for three or four months every year. Mrs. Jerome has lived in Paris for several years and has educated her daughters there. They go out in Society there and are very well known.

I have told you all I know about them at present. You have always been very good to me, and done as much and more for me always than I had any right to expect; and with any arrangement that you may at any time make for me I shall be perfectly contented and happy. I see before me now a very happy future, almost in one's grasp. In the last year or so I feel I have lost a great deal of what energy and ambition I possessed, and an idle and comparatively useless life has at times appeared to me to be the pleasantest; but if I were married to her whom I have told you about, if I had a companion, such as she would be, I feel sure, to take an interest in one's prospects and career, and to encourage me to exertions and to doing something towards making a name for myself, I think that I might become, with the help of Providence, all and perhaps more than you had ever wished and hoped for me. On the other hand, if anything should occur to prevent my fondest hopes and wishes being realized (a possibility which I dare not and cannot bring myself to think of), how dreary and uninteresting would life become to me. No one goes through what I have lately gone through without its leaving a strong impress and bias on their character and future. Time might, of course, partially efface the impression and recollection of feelings so strong as those I have tried to describe to you but in the interval the best years of one's life would be going, and one's energies and hopes would become blunted and deadened.

I will not allude to her. I believe and am convinced that she loves me as fully, and as strongly if possible, as I do her; and when two people feel towards each other what we do, it becomes, I know, a great responsibility for anyone to assist in either bringing about or thwarting a union so closely desired by each.

Good-bye. I have written to you all I have done, all I feel, and all I know.

Anxiously wishing for an answer from you,
   I remain,
     Ever your most affectionate son,
       Randolph."

"The Duke was very seriously disturbed at the news of his son's intention and declined to commit himself to any expression of approval until he had made searching inquiry into the standing and circumstances of the Jerome family. He deplored the precipitancy with which the decision had been taken. 'It is not likely,' he wrote upon August 31, 'that at present you can look at anything except from your own point of view; but persons from the outside cannot but be struck with the unwisdom of your proceedings, and the uncontrolled state of your feelings which completely paralyses your judgment.' His rebuke was supported by his wife, who urged affectionate counsels of caution, patience and self-restraint, and was pointed by a set of witty and satirical verses from his brother, Lord Blandford, setting forth the unhappy fate of those who marry in haste and repent at leisure."[1]

Meanwhile Jennie contended with the difficulties raised by her own family. Randolph's surprise that Mrs. Jerome "would not hear of it" sprang from his ignorance of that lady's character. Quite as firmly as the Duke and Duchess of Marlborough she distrusted love at first sight and the violence with which these two young people had, after three days, affirmed the *eternal* aspect of their feelings only caused her to fear the opposite. Concerning marriage proposals she had always maintained a most cautious outlook. No one seemed good enough for *her* daughters, and as a younger son Lord Randolph did not appear a tremendous 'catch' when the peers of France had circled around her eldest girl. He was at least a Protestant, but for the moment neither party appeared able to express an idea with any clarity except a pathetic hope of 'allowances' from fond parents which would permit the marriage to take place soon.

Mrs. Jerome did all she could to cool her hot-headed daughter, but when she realized the Duke and Duchess were hesitating to give consent to their son's marriage her indignation knew no bounds. She wrote furiously to Leonard, and her letter crossed one of his giving a conditional assent to Jennie's engagement. Leonard had long experience of human nature. He deplored the daily scenes and storms and tears which he knew must now be engulfing the previously contented little household at Villa Rosetta. Not daring to leave New York for financial reasons he had sat back and given the matter that calm consideration of which mothers are often incapable in matrimonial matters. He wrote advising her to soothe Jennie and let things take a slow course. But the moment he heard of the Duke's opposition he angrily cabled "My consent withdrawn".

In the midst of his scattered fortune, with long days of work necessary to retrieve a few hundred thousands, Leonard Jerome rose up in fury. *He* might put questions to a future son-in-law but none had the right to query his daughter. The great name of Marlborough left him cold. Leonard had in his time known many European dukes and duchesses and on the whole found they impressed him less than they impressed themselves. While the pride of a haughty Yankee flared in New York, chill bewilderment descended in Blenheim Palace. What exactly *were* Americans? Rebels against the British crown? And did one *marry* them?

Lord Randolph Churchill, by Winston S. Churchill.

33

AT THE end of August 1873 Mrs. Jerome shut down the Villa Rosetta and took her daughters back to Paris. She forbade Jennie to answer any letters she might receive from Randolph and the Marlboroughs learnt that American mothers can be very fierce. As a result of her high-handed action Randolph went for two weeks without news and created an atmosphere of tension so intolerable to his own parents that the Duke was soon only too glad to acquiesce to a formal engagement of one year. At Randolph's request he wrote a soothing letter to Mrs. Jerome and she, holding smelling-salts in one hand and writing cables with the other, relented sufficiently to ask Leonard to cancel his cancellation of the original conditional assent.

During these complicated and highly emotional manœuvres Jennie had been threatening to lose her looks and Randolph his mind. As soon as they gained their own way they became normal or almost normal people. With the superiority of triumphant lovers, they took up pens.

"In this field the young lady had a great advantage. The placid succession of the duties and amusements of country life, the round of shooting parties, the varying totals of slaughtered hares and pheasants, the mornings on the Woodstock bench, and descriptions of relations and county folk, however vivacious, were inadequate materials to set against days spent in Paris during the autumn of 1873, when the gossip of the world was reviving after the gag of the war, when Bazaine was on trial for his life, when Gambetta declaimed in the Assembly, and when the drawing rooms, even of foreigners, were full of Royalist and Bona-partist whisperings. For the most part, his letters were strictly confined to the subject of main importance. They told over and over again, in the forcible, homely English of which he was a natural master, the oldest story in the world. Indeed, but for the contributions of Miss Jerome, the correspondence would certainly have lacked variety."[1]

On September 23rd, 1873, Randolph wrote joyously from Blenheim:

[1] *Lord Randolph Churchill*, by Winston S. Churchill.

"I cannot tell you what pleasure and happiness your letter gives me: it makes me feel quite a different being, so you really must not threaten me with a long silence. You certainly have great powers of perception, and I cannot but own that there is a good deal of truth in what you say about my being one moment very despairing and another moment very sanguine. I cannot help it: I was made so.

My father has been away for a few days, and yesterday I got a 'piece' from him on the subject of his consent. After a good deal of unnecessary rigmarole and verbosity he says:

'The great question is still unsolved, whether you and the young lady who has gained your affections are, or can be, after a few days' acquaintance, sufficiently aware of your own minds to venture on the step which is to bind you together for life. What I have now to say is that if I am to believe that your future is really bound up in your marriage with Miss Jerome you must show me the proof of it by bringing it to the test of time. I will say no more to you on this subject for the present, but if this time next year you come and tell me that you are both of the same mind we will receive Miss Jerome as a daughter, and, I need not say, in the affection you could desire for your wife.'

Now these are his words, but I do not mind telling you that it is all humbug about waiting a year. I could, and would, wait a good deal more than a year, but I do not mean to, as it is not the least necessary; for though we have only known each other a short time, I know we both know our own minds well enough, and I wrote a very long and diplomatic letter to my father yesterday, doing what I have done before, contradicting him and arguing with him, and I hope, persuading him that he has got very wrong and foolish ideas in his head. You see, both he and my mother have set their hearts on my being member for Woodstock. It is a family borough, and for years and years a member of the family has sat for it. The present member is a stranger, though a Conservative, and is so unpopular that he is almost sure to be beaten if he were to stand; and the fact of a Radical sitting for Woodstock is perfectly insupportable to my family. It is for this that they have kept me idle ever since I left Oxford, waiting for a dissolution. Well, as I told you the other day, a dissolution is sure to come almost before the end of the year. I have two courses open to me: either to refuse to stand altogether unless they consent to my being married immediately afterwards; or else, and this is still more Machiavellian and deep, to stand, but at the last moment to

The Jerome Sisters

Lord Randolph Churchill

threaten to withdraw and leave the Radical to walk over. All tricks are fair in love and war."

A month later he was writing to Miss Jerome with still more confidence:

"I was so happy to see your handwriting again; it is the next best thing to seeing you. As you will have seen from my letter of Friday, we have no cause now to be disappointed or to be in bad spirits; everything goes on as favourably as we could expect, and my father does not wish for a moment to prevent my seeing you as often as I can, and has promised to give his consent to our marriage when he is sure we are fond of each other. As to the year, I have every right to say that I do not think they will insist on it. . . .

The clouds have all cleared away, and the sky is bluer than I have ever seen it since I first met you at Cowes. It is exactly six weeks tomorrow since we met on board the *Ariadne*, and I am sure I seem to have lived six years. How I do bless that day, in spite of all the worry and bother that has come since; and I am sure you will not regret it. I have not had a further conversation with my father since I wrote to you, for I think it is best to leave things for the present as they are. Our early golden dreams of being married in December won't quite become realized, but still it won't be very long to wait; and I shall be able to see you from time to time, and write as often as I like; in fact, we can be regularly engaged, and all the world may know it. . . .

It is curious what an effect books have on me; I have two old favourites. When I feel very cross and angry I read Gibbon whose profound philosophy and easy though majestic writing soon quiets me down, and in an hour I feel at peace with all the world. When I feel very low and desponding I read Horace, whose thorough epicureanism, quiet maxims, and beautiful verse are most tranquillizing. Of late I have had to have frequent recourse to my two friends, and they have never failed me. I strongly recommend you to read some great works or histories; they pass the time, and prevent you from worrying or thinking too much about the future. Novels, or even travels, are rather unsatisfactory, and do one no good, because they create an unhealthy excitement, which is bad for anyone. I wonder whether you will understand all this, or only think me rather odd.

There are three new elections to come off, owing to death vacancies; and if they go against the Government, as they very probably will, we are sure to have a dissolution, and then I shall become member for Woodstock. But, after all, public life has no great charms for me, as I am naturally very quiet, and hate bother and publicity, which, after all, is full of vanity and vexation of spirit. Still, it will all have greater attractions for me if I think it will encourage me to keep up to the mark.

I hope your sister is quite well, comforts you, and sticks up for me when you abuse me to her or doubt me."

Meanwhile the Jerome sisters followed their intent and interesting life. Together they went to the trial of Marshal Bazaine at Versailles which took place in

"a long low room filled to suffocation with a curious crowd many of whom were women. A raised platform, a table covered with green baize and holding a bottle of water, a few chairs arranged in semi-circles, completed the *mise-en-scène*, which seemed rather a poor one for the trial for life or death of a Marshal of France."

Clara had not set eyes on Bazaine since that far-off country house party at Compiègne three years before, when his wife's red gown had caused deeper sensation than the rumours of war with Prussia. Now she saw him, a disgraced Commander-in-Chief, led in to face the Duc d'Aumale, president of the accusing court. Jennie writes:

"All eyes turned on him, and some of the women jumped on their chairs, levelling their opera-glasses at the unfortunate man. This was promptly put a stop to by the gendarmes present, who pulled the offenders down unceremoniously by their skirts. '*Fi donc!*' I heard a gendarme say, '*C'est pas gentil;*' nor was it."

Bazaine sat impassive, even while Maître Lachaud his advocate, making a curious defence at one moment, pointed with a dramatic gesture to the accused, exclaiming: "*Mais, regardez-le donc! Ce n'est pas un traître, c'est un imbécile!*"

The trial lacked the elements of reality. France was but chasing the most obvious scapegoat. Bazaine, found guilty, received a death sentence which was commuted to twenty years' imprisonment, and the authorities permitted him to escape some months later. It seemed unbelievable he had ever been a real Marshal or commanded a real Army. But perhaps the dead slept better in the knowledge that a fool had led them, rather than a traitor. The trial gave sharpness to Jennie's facile pen, and soon she received a scolding for using the verb "to prorogue" incorrectly. Instead of submitting with meekness to this reprimand, she hurried to a young friend, Count de Fénelon, whose name should have made him an authority on word usage, and secured his backing.

This was not the manner in which Lord Randolph, hot from the chase of foxes over Oxfordshire fences, expected his future wife to receive literary instruction.

". . . Hang *le petit Fénelon*," he wrote, ". . . little idiot! What do I care for him? He may be a very good authority about his own beastly language, but I cannot for a moment submit to him about English. . . . To prorogue, means to suspend something for a definite time to be resumed again in exactly the same state, condition, and circumstances. Therefore to talk about proroguing the Marshal's powers, would mean that they were to be suspended for a certain time and then resumed again exactly as before. Parliament is prorogued, L'Assemblée is prorogued; that does not in the least mean that the powers of either are lengthened or increased in any way, but that they are temporarily suspended."

"What a very English letter!" commented Mrs. Jerome, while Jennie, confused but valiant, maintained her point and continued to quote the Count.

By December, Randolph had obtained consent from both sides to visit his betrothed. He ended a letter with:

"I am looking forward particularly to utterly suppressing and crushing *le petit Fénelon*. We must really, tho', drop this argument when I am with you, as it is likely to become a heated one, I fear. We will therefore 'prorogue' it."

Lord Randolph had won. He intended to arrive in Paris with a ring, not a dictionary.

34

DURING the months of Jennie's courtship Leonard remained glued to his responsibilities in New York. The times were bad for speculators. The Vice-President of the United States, cabinet officers and a future President had been involved in the misappropriation of forty-four million dollars from the Union Pacific Railroad through a set-up called the *Crédit Mobilier*. As the Union Pacific was sponsored and financed by the United States the whole country suffered from the crash of its stocks. Five thousand other commercial enterprises collapsed and panic rocked the people. All financiers lost heavily during 1873, and Leonard Jerome was among them. President Grant summoned a conference of great business brains to give him advice. "Building railroads from nowhere to nowhere is not a legitimate business," remarked the old Commodore. Five bleak years followed.

After long deliberation Leonard had decided to pack up the picture collection and ship it back to his wife, who appeared to be permanently settled in Paris. He could not run the house in Madison Square without her, nor did he wish to. The Raphael and small masters they had bought during the 'fifties in Italy were crated and dispatched back to Europe. On November 22nd, 1873, the *Ville de Havre*, in which they had been consigned, met with a collision at sea off the Azores. The ship went down with large loss of life and no treasures could be salvaged. The Jerome Collection, which had received scant appreciation in New York, sank uncatalogued and uninsured. Clara had been longing for her pictures: "They were like old friends but one must think only of the poor people who died."

Leonard wrote sadly, but the girls were immersed in other interests, in music and politics.

Jennie showed her capacity for maintaining that urgent pace which had once been a characteristic of her father. She kept up her studies, attended concerts, read avidly in three languages and as Leonard said, formed her own "original, if a trifle arrogant opinions".

"Oh dear, with what haste Jennie does things," complained her mother. "I do not mind her practising from eight until eleven every morning, but one would think all those other activities would wear her out. They wear *me* out."

Only Jennie's elders, however, suffered from a depletion of nervous energy in her proximity. To the younger generation, she imparted her own enthusiasm and vitality. Lord Randolph Churchill had a taut, rapier-like mind and brittle nerves.

"Although possessed of unusual nervous energy his whole life was a struggle against ill-health. Excitement fretted him cruelly. He smoked cigarettes till his tongue was sore, to soothe himself. Capable upon emergency of prolonged and vehement exertion, of manifold activities and pugnacities, of leaps and heaves beyond the common strength of men, he suffered by reaction fits of utter exhaustion and despondency. Most people grow tired before they are over-tired, but Lord Randolph Churchill was of the temper that gallops till it falls. An instinct warned him of the perils which threatened him in a life of effort."[1]

Instinct led him towards Jennie. The stamina and strength he lacked would be her gift to him.

Two unexpected impediments prevented Randolph's December visit to Paris. First, he had to spend a month in Ireland awaiting the death of his aunt, Lady Ely, and then Mr. Gladstone suddenly dissolved Parliament. This latter event placed a weapon of considerable power in the ardent suitor's hands. The Duke regarded the local borough of Woodstock as his family heritage. He had himself, when Marquis of Blandford,[2] been its M.P. until his defence of the Corn Laws brought him into collision with his father, who forced his retirement. In 1847 when this issue had been decided, he was again elected and sat in Parliament until 1857, when he succeeded as seventh Duke. His brother, Lord Alfred Churchill, was then elected but two years later created a horrible commotion by swerving from the Conservative ranks and condoning the Liberals' policy. The Duke, his brother, now developed into a high Tory, issued a sharp reprimand, and an acrimonious correspondence ensued, until the next General Election, when Lord Alfred was dismissed and a new more obedient candidate selected. Politics brought into family life can prove a mixed blessing. In this case

"so embittered were the relations between the brothers that, when the departing Lord Alfred was entertained by his constituents in Woodstock

[1] *Lord Randolph Churchill*, by Winston S. Churchill.
[2] The elder son of a Duke may carry a courtesy title but not being a peer is eligible to sit in the House of Commons.

in 1864, the Duke would not attend the dinner but sent Lord Randolph in his place; and this schoolboy of fifteen, with impressive gravity and unfaltering utterance, delivered or rather, indeed, recited the necessary speeches, and so made, under rather a lowering sky, his first embarkation upon the uncertain waters of party politics."

Now, nearly ten years later, the Conservative member wished to resign and who but the Duke's younger son was the candidate most likely to succeed? Marlborough did not fear his boy's political views. He did fear losing the seat to a Liberal. If Randolph could be persuaded to stand, a Conservative win would be certain. The Duke had always wished to see this talented son embark into public life and Randolph, knowing his father's hopes, could rejoice that the moment had arrived to strike a bargain.

"All tricks are fair in love and war," he had written Jennie three months before. The noble Duke learnt this with rapidity for when the General Election dealt Randolph the ace of trumps he did not hesitate to use it. Rather than risk thwarting his son, just as the Conservative electors of Woodstock were dispatching a formal entreaty to him, Marlborough agreed that the marriage might take place "within less than a year".

Having gained this point, Randolph showed no small alacrity in carrying out his side of the bargain. No longer intent on fighting his own family, all effort could be diverted against the Liberal opponent. Although loath to cancel again that visit to Paris he hurried back to Blenheim where the annual coursing meeting happened to be taking place in the Great Park. To Jennie he wrote:

"Blenheim. Monday.

. . . all the farmers were there, and as they had a day's sport were all in great spirits. I took the chair at their dinner at the Bear Hotel, and you cannot imagine how enthusiastic they were for me. They all go as one man. I hear nothing certain as to any opposition; there are no end of rumours, but no one as yet has appeared publicly; I suppose we shall know for certain to-morrow.

I am now off to a part of the borough four miles distant to see more people, and have a large meeting of my committee at four in Woodstock. I think I may say that for the present everything is satisfactory. There are 1,071 voters, and I do not think more than 800 will poll; out of these I calculate at least on 460, which will be enough. But this is, of course, mere guess-work; it is still very uncertain, and I am glad I lost no time in arriving."

"Blenheim. Tuesday.

"The Radical candidate, Mr. Brodrick, arrived this morning; I made his acquaintance, and we shook hands and were very friendly. The contest will be a hard one and the result doubtful; it is impossible to say how the labourers will go. However, I have made a very good start, and have nothing to complain of as yet."

"Blenheim. Saturday.

I am sure it is not necessary for me to excuse myself for not writing to you; you would not believe what work it is. We had a great meeting last night, which was very successful; we had a good speaker down from London, and I made a speech. How I have been longing for you to have been with me? If we had only been married before this! I think the reception you would have got, would have astonished you. . . . My head is in a whirl of voters, committee meetings and goodness knows what. I am glad it is drawing to an end, as I could not stand it very long; I cannot eat or sleep.

I am now off again, 10 a.m. to see more people."

"Blenheim. Sunday.

At last I have a pretty quiet day; but I have been very busy this afternoon, and, in spite of its being Sunday, I have been active among several little odd fellows whom it is important to pick up. How this election is going I really can form no opinion, and the excitement and uncertainty of it make me quite ill. Yesterday I was canvassing all day in Woodstock itself. People that I think know better than anybody, tell me it will be very close. You see, with the ballot one can tell nothing, one can only trust to promises, and I have no doubt a good many will be broken. Our organization and preparations for Tuesday are very perfect, and the old borough has never been worked in such a way before. You have no idea how this election gets hold of me. One can positively think of nothing else except voters and committees, &c., till one's brain gets quite addled and in a whirl. I have a presentiment that it will go wrong. I am such a fool to care so much about it. I hate all this excitement. . . . I saw my opponent to-day in church. He looks awfully harassed. I feel quite sorry for him, as all his friends here are such a dreadfully disreputable lot; and as I have got the three principal hotels in the town, he had nothing except a wretched, low, miserable pot-house to stay in."

Unfortunate Mr. Brodrick! The result of the election in no way belied the quality of his accommodation.

"Ever since I met you everything goes well with me, too well; I am getting afraid of a Nemesis. I always hoped I should win the election, but that under the ballot and against a man like Brodrick I should have that crushing overwhelming majority (of 165 out of 973 voters) never entered into my wildest dreams. It was a great victory; we shall never have a contest again. The last two contests '65 and '68 were won by 17 and 21 majorities; so just conceive the blow it is to the other side. You never heard such cheering in all your life. The poll was not declared till eleven, and the hours of suspense were most trying; but when it was known, there was such a burst of cheers that must have made the old Dukes in the vault jump. I addressed a few words to the committee and so did Blandford and was immensely cheered; and then they accompanied us, the whole crowd of them, through the town and up to Blenheim, shouting and cheering all the way. Oh, it was a great triumph and that you were not there to witness it will always be a source of great regret to me. . . .

There is nothing more to be done except to pay the bill, and that I have left to my father."

Never could a new Member of Parliament have felt more triumphant. Not only had he won his seat, he was free to marry the girl he loved.

The Duke, admitting himself out-played, travelled to Paris to meet the Jerome ladies and succumbed completely to their charm. He had to acknowledge that his son had chosen a very talented as well as beautiful bride. Randolph appeared serene. He had in a few months won over his own parents and his prospective mother-in-law. Only Mr. Jerome had yet to be conquered.

35

AFTER a harassing winter in New York, Leonard sailed for France determined to see Jennie's emotional predicament for himself.

A storm of excitement met him. It was all settled. Mrs. Jerome found the Duke of Marlborough a 'perfect dear', and Jennie had taken to holding forth with astonishing confidence on English party politics. All that Papa need do was to settle a dowry and the marriage could take place.

Lord Randolph had never troubled about money. Having written glibly that his political bill would be paid by his father, presumably he expected a large allowance to follow. In England, gentlemen did not 'earn' money. If they inherited no estates, they served the State or the Army. Younger sons had to be endowed, or they left the country.

Leonard hesitated. He was an American. He wished his daughter to be well provided for, but in his view her husband was the proper man to do it.

In his own struggling youth, he had felt it unchivalrous to marry until he could support his wife in the manner accustomed. The material inefficiency of European nobles seemed to him supine, even despicable. No one could call the English aristocracy effete; their boys were brought up hard, but to be leaders, not workers. Randolph would be given a suitable house in London, and an income sufficient to carry him along on his career, but there would be little left over to deck one of the most spectacular beauties in Europe. No way could ever be open to him of "making money". Jennie would have to dress and entertain on the settlement made by her father.

"Mr. Jerome had strong and, it would seem, not unreasonable views, suggested by American usage, about married women's property and made some propositions which Lord Randolph considered derogatory to him."

Once again the house in Paris reverberated with heated discussions. The 'padded' furniture proved itself more useful than ever when Clara fell into vapours (she was secretly strong as an ox), or Jennie wished to succumb to those tears so particularly becoming to long dark lashes.

Meanwhile Lord Randolph, walking on clouds, amidst the flowering chestnut trees which have intoxicated many a lover, announced a firm determination to earn his own living "in England or out of it". And Jennie romantically acquiesced. Back in his Palace, the Duke read an exalted letter concerning his son's new chosen course "in which I am bound to say she thoroughly agrees with me", while Mr. Leonard Jerome found himself faced with an ultimatum. Together Randolph and Jennie were a formidable pair: their very faults of impetuous youth and exuberance making them the more wininng.

Randolph's temperament allowed him to suffer moments of painful despondency. Not so his lady. She possessed an optimism which no parental opposition could daunt. Despite her feminine beauty, Jennie alone had caused her father to say "she ought to have been a boy. . . ." Now she allied her vibrant physical energy to a man far more highly-strung than herself, imparting an immunity to fear of defeat which had been his only lack. Dear dear kind Papa! He soon capitulated. The daily torrent of verbiage on the nobility of impecunious love, capped by a vision of these two scintillating innocents setting forth hand-in-hand "to earn a living anywhere . . . any country would do", was more than he could stand.

Randolph offered his name, a parliamentary career, a town house and a couple of fine horses (carriages could probably be borrowed unnoticed from Blenheim). Jennie should have £6,000 a year settled on her without delay. Mr. Jerome hoped it would prove sufficient. He could certainly afford no more.

Randolph, growing hourly more impetuous and prolific in arguments, now insisted he had waited long enough. Life was short, and parliamentary duties loomed ahead. If the marriage did not take place soon, there would hardly be time for a honeymoon. Romance triumphed. Melted by a veritable pandemonium of emotion, his elders and betters ceased to offer unheeded advice. It was announced that on April 15th, 1874, Lord Randolph Churchill and Miss Jennie Jerome should be married at the British Embassy in Paris. The Duke could not leave England but he sent a blessing, and the Duchess rejoiced that her favourite son had chosen her birthday for his wedding.

Fifteen-year-old Leonie left Wiesbaden to be a bridesmaid with Clara. In careful schoolgirl script she listed the wedding presents, beginning with the gold Russian *coffre* and a locket of pearls and turquoise which arrived from the Prince and Princess of Wales. This list and a letter describing the wedding, which she evidently thought too interesting to post, were tucked away in her desk and discovered some eighty years later.

Randolph's three sisters, his brother Lord Blandford, and his aunt Lady Camden arrived in Paris with Francis Knollys, the Prince of Wales's Private

Secretary, who was to be best man. After a large family dinner, came an inspection of Jennie's trousseau of "twenty-three very pretty dresses; six or seven bonnets and some very fine linen".

On the following morning, Clara and Leonie in pale blue silk with white embroidery, wearing crystal bridesmaids' lockets around their necks, attended their sister. The bride's dress was of white satin, with a long train and flounces of Alençon lace. A long tulle veil "covered her entirely".

Leonard clasped a pearl necklace around his daughter's neck, and drove her to the ceremony. Mrs. Jerome in "a grey silk dress with street trimmings" followed with the girls in another carriage.

During the wedding breakfast, Randolph and Jennie ate in a little drawing-room by themselves. Then after a brief visit to the guests, Jennie changed into "a very pretty dark blue and white striped dress for travelling, and a white hat with a white feather".

It was a fine day, and an open carriage with four grey horses and two postilions waited at the door. When his daughter left the house, Leonard gave her a second present, a parasol of Alençon lace mounted on a delicate gold and tortoiseshell handle. "It's the loveliest thing I've ever seen," said Jennie. Her father felt his heart melt.

As the carriage moved off through the spring sunshine, the young couple turned to wave good-bye. Jennie looked unbelievably lovely clutching the parasol, her eyes sparkling against its foam of lace. Dear, dear Papa. Why, Mama, don't cry. Life is going to be perfect . . . always. Leonie and Clara were busy throwing old slippers with the guests. After four, they both departed on a country visit and that evening Leonard and his wife sat alone in their house in the Rue du Roi de Rome. They found the rooms unexpectedly sad, and the piano "terribly silent".

36

THE Continental honeymoon lasted only two weeks, for Lord Randolph wished "to return in triumph with his bride to receive the dutiful laudations of the borough of Woodstock". In early May the pair arrived at Blenheim; cheering tenants unharnessed their horses and insisted on dragging the carriage from station to palace. The old oak trees of the park were in fresh foliage. As they passed the entrance archway, Randolph cried out with that adoration which Englishmen develop for their family homes: "This is the finest view in England!" Jennie admitted herself impressed, but being an American, at the sight of Vanbrugh's immense pile she gathered her wits sufficiently, or says she did, to tease her spouse with Pope's famous lines on Blenheim Palace:

> " 'See, sir, here's the grand approach;
> This way is for his grace's coach:
> There lies the bridge, and here's the clock,
> Observe the lion and the cock,
> The spacious court, the colonnade,
> And mark how wide the hall is made!
> The chimneys are so well design'd
> They never smoke in any wind.
> This gallery's contrived for walking,
> The windows to retire and talk in;
> The council chamber for debate,
> And all the rest are rooms of state.'
> 'Thanks, sir,' cried I, ' 'tis very fine,
> But where d'ye sleep, or where d'ye dine?
> I find by all you have been telling,
> That 'tis a house, but not a dwelling.' "

The Duke and Duchess were waiting on the wide steps to greet her with kindness, slightly tinged by condescension. She felt them watching closely to see what an American daughter-in-law could be like. In this house criticism would always be easy to arouse. Jennie soon enjoyed the small

malice of showing herself better educated than their own daughters reared
in the background by elderly governesses. In vain had Leonard tried to teach
this ebullient daughter not to show off; she found the temptation irresistible.
And for a pupil of Stephen Heller who had been Chopin's own pupil it was
only too easy. She trilled on the piano until the Churchills were prostrate,
she played the great silver-piped organ (this she had studied in St. Sulpice)
until their ears rang. And then she wrote mischievous mocking notes to
Mama. The Marlboroughs knew nothing of fashion! They used funny
frumpy old table mats, and kept water decanters with ordinary thick
tumblers "the kind we use in bedrooms" before each place at dinner, and
their shoes were the wrong shape. "How strange life in a big country house
seemed to one who, until then, had been accustomed only to towns!" she
wrote. Every day followed a formal routine. Even breakfast proved cere-
monious, the ladies appearing in long velvet or silk trains, while at luncheon
the Duke and Duchess themselves carved up joints for the entire family,
including tutors and governesses, and the remains were carried off to poor
cottagers by the children on afternoon walks. Jennie took in every detail
concerning the great house which would henceforth be her continual background, but apart from the splendid architecture nothing impressed her.
She fidgeted to be off to the small house in Curzon Street which the Duke
was providing.

> "The London season of thirty [now eighty] years ago was far more
> prolonged and its glories more apparent than they are now. It was
> looked upon as a very serious matter which no self-respecting persons
> who considered themselves 'in society' would forego, nor of which a
> votary of fashion would willingly miss a week or a day."

Certainly not the young Lady Randolph who, according to the fashion
of the day, appeared appropriately clad on Gold Cup Day at Ascot in that
exquisite wedding-dress of white satin and point lace. She wore a bonnet of
nodding roses and Papa's parasol created a filmy cobweb behind her head.
Jennie's deep eyes flickered around the Royal Enclosure and made quite a
sensation.

At that time newly married couples seldom appeared at large gatherings
for two months at least, but the Season had opened on May 1st and the
young Churchills could not resist attending a ball in honour of the Czar
Alexander II, at Stafford House.

When Jennie was presented and the Czar learned she had only been
married a few weeks he fixed a cold grey eye on her remarking:

"*Et ici déjà!*"

What trivialities occupied the minds of the powerful! A man who held the destinies of All the Russias in his sway could be troubled to express disapproval because a bride went dancing a few days earlier than was usual.

On May 22nd Randolph delivered his maiden speech in the House of Commons and Disraeli wrote to compliment the Duchess on her son's successful debut. "But the course of the session, and of the years that followed, offered few opportunities to young members for winning Parliamentary distinction. The waters of politics flowed smoothly and even sluggishly."

For the moment Randolph had time to accompany his glamorous wife to every function she wished to attend.

With frankness Jennie writes of that first season which she enjoyed

"with all the vigour and unjaded appetite of youth. After the comparatively quiet life of Paris, we seemed to live in a whirl of gaieties and excitement. Many were the delightful balls I went to which, unlike those of the present day, invariably lasted to five o'clock in the morning. Masked balls were much the vogue. Holland House, with its wonderful historical associations and beautiful gardens, was a fitting frame for such entertainments, and I remember enjoying myself immensely at one given there. Disguised in a painted mask and in yellow wig, I mystified everyone. My sister [Clara] who was staying with us, had been walking in the garden with young Lord ——, who was a *parti*, and much run after by designing mothers with marriageable daughters. Introducing him to me, she pretended I was her mother. Later in the evening I attacked him, saying that my daughter had just confided to me that he had proposed to her, and that she had accepted him. To this day I can see his face of horror and bewilderment. Vehemently he assured me that it was not so. But I kept up the farce, declaring that my husband would call on him next day and reveal our identity, and that meanwhile I should consider him engaged to my charming daughter. Deficient in humour and not over-burdened with brains, he could not take the joke, and left the house a miserable man.

Generally speaking, there is no doubt that English people are dull-witted at a masked ball, and do not understand or enter into the spirit of intrigue which is all-important on such occasions. One reason may be that both sexes are masked in England, whereas abroad this is not the practice, nor would it be understood. The licence a man might take if his identity were to remain unknown would never be tolerated. Besides, it stands to reason that unless one of the two remains unmasked there cannot be much mystifying. Some women refuse to say anything but

'Yes' and 'No' in a falsetto voice, and think they have had a glorious time as long as their disguise is not discovered. 'You don't know me. You don't know me,' was the parrot cry of one lady. 'And I don't want to,' said Lord Charles Beresford, fleeing from her, 'if you've nothing else to say.' "

Randolph was particularly intolerant of bores, a trait which did not add to his popularity. On one occasion when button-holed at his club he listened half-way through an interminable story and then rang the bell for a footman whom he instructed to "Listen until his lordship finishes," while he himself slipped away.

The Conservative Party had been swept to power with a majority of fifty which allowed Disraeli to be generous towards the Liberal Opposition. While Randolph steered a quiet course through the new Government's first uneventful year, his wife impressed society as "the most beautiful dark woman anyone had set eyes on". The first American to enter the portals of this small exclusive world, she took all bastions by storm. The side of fashionable London which amused her most was Rotten Row, where she rode or walked from twelve to two every day. "It was a brilliant and animated scene which filled the foreigner with admiration and envy, no capital in Europe being able to compete with it. . . ."

Clara soon came to stay, and after their afternoon of piano practice together (when lesser spirits were resting on chaise longues), the sisters ventured into the Belgravia of Disraeli's novels. In the freshly-painted flower-bedecked mansions which English gentry threw open each spring

"dinners, balls and parties succeeded one another without intermission till the end of July, the only respite being at the Whitsun recess. A few of the racing people might go to Newmarket for a week, but the fashionable world flocked only to the classic races, the Derby, Ascot and Goodwood. . . . We used to drive down on coaches in Ascot frocks and feathered hats, and stay to dinner, driving back by moonlight."

A July letter from Clara to her mother describes the end of the season when too many parties had caused tempers to get slightly frayed.

"Curzon Street.
Thursday.

My darling Mama,

What a letter I got from you this morning. Such a sermon! However you will be happy to hear that we had already thrown over the Murietta's dance.

Jennie got a letter from [Oliver] Montagu yesterday saying that he

191

was charged to arrange the Quadrille for the Fancy Dress Ball and that H.R.H. [the Prince of Wales] wanted Jennie and I very much to dance in it. Jennie is to be Queen of Clubs according to H.R.H. and will dance with the King of Diamonds being the Duke of Atholl, and I the Seven of Hearts to dance with Lord MacDuff as Seven of Spades, but Randolph is furious that the Prince should send us word through Montagu and not Francis Knollys, besides which he says it will be a great expense as the dresses can't cost less than £15 apiece. R. says he won't let us go. I think it is too bad as it will be very lovely. Only 24 ladies had he asked. My quadrille is M., Princess Christian and Pcess. Louise. I do hope R. will change his mind but he is so obstinate. The Duchess is going to have a small party at Blenheim for the last week in July, and had asked Jennie and I and Randolph. I think it is to bring on the de Grey affair but I don't know. We went with the Duchess to pay some visits yesterday, to Mme de Bulow and Mme de Brilaccias who has asked us on Saturday to meet the Prince and Princess. To-morrow night we are all dining at Lady de Rothschild's, a grand dinner. To-night dinner at the Square [the Marl-boroughs] and going to Lady Carnarvon's afterwards. And there is a charming garden party at Hatfield, two hours from London. R. is going to ask for an invitation for me, and as the Duchess of Buccleuch is a great friend of his, I am sure to go. We are to make a nice party to go down there together. They say there are going to be 3 other fancy balls, but if we don't go to Marlborough House we shan't be able to go to any. Jennie and R. have quite decided to come to Deauville after Blenheim, and R. after depositing Jennie and I with you, will go off for a cruise with the Duke in his new yacht. It wd be very nice if you could be at Deauville 3 days before us to get the rooms. Do bring dear Leonie, I don't think Deauville will be too gay for her, will it? You will feel as if you still had three daughters to look after. You must not think that we are at all fast. In fact we are very humdrum and stay a great deal at-home. Jennie, you see, can't go out really very much. Goodbye my darling mama, you will soon have us again to bother and worry you!

Yr. loving,

Clara.

I have seen some charming little tables for 5 pounds *dans le genre* of those *l'impératrice* had only much prettier. I do think you shd. let me get a few things for the house, dear Mama. It would make my blue Salon look so pretty, and the things here are fascinating."

August and September were devoted to yachting or stalking. Then the gentry dispersed to their country homes where they hunted the fox, shot game and entertained the statesmen and sportsmen of all lands. Big London houses closed down from October until February when the Winter Session brought members of parliament back to town. Scanning Jennie's memoirs, this country respite seems perhaps fortunate, or a small Churchill might have arrived with scant dignity in Rotten Row or during a moonlit coach ride. Events were to prove sufficiently inconvenient as it was. Jennie, with her health and prowess undiminished, was actually dancing at a small party at Blenheim Palace when she had to hurry away past the endless suite of drawing-rooms, through the library, "the longest room in England", towards the longest corridor in the world, the quarter-mile of dark red carpet which led to her bedroom.

She never got there.

Next morning the bells of Woodstock Church rang a peal to celebrate the arrival of a possible heir;[1] and soon after *The Times* printed among birth notices: "On the 30th of November at Blenheim Palace, the Lady Randolph Churchill, of a son".

The baby had been born in a small room on the ground floor, a room which had once belonged to the first Duke's Chaplain and retained the name of Dean Jones. It was not even a bedroom, but had been converted for the evening into a ladies' attiring room and was strewn with velvet capes and feather boas which made a merry, gipsy-like setting for the new arrival. "Most unconventional," said the Duchess.

Leonard and Clara telegraphed their delight from Paris. The first grandchild! A little boy, who would be called Winston Leonard Spencer-Churchill; Winston after an ancestor, Sir Winston Churchill, father of the great Duke; Leonard after a grandfather from the new world.

---

[1] He remained an heir presumptive until 1897 when Consuelo, grand-daughter of the famous old Commodore Vanderbilt, produced a son for the 9th Duke.

37

THE parliamentary sessions of the next few years were uneventful. Lord Randolph and his wife moved to a larger house in Charles Street and there began entertaining their own political circle. At first Jennie, whose up-bringing had been artistic and unpractical, could not realize that food did not grow on trees exactly as her mother's French cook had always produced it. She found housekeeping terrifying. Happily Mr. Disraeli and Randolph's college friend, Lord Rosebery, who often came to dine, were too busy talking to notice if the entrée had been dumped in the soup or the toast served as a course on its own.

Mr. Disraeli possessed a singular flow of effusive language quite peculiar to himself. One evening he refused Randolph's offer of liquors with, "My dear Randolph, I have sipped your excellent champagne, I have drunk your good claret, I have tasted your delicious port, I will have no more." Jennie, sitting next him at dinner, could not help being amused, for she had noticed he drank nothing except weak brandy and water.

Before long, the Randolph Churchills had become the most sought-after young couple in England. They set each other off and turned every party they attended into a success. From the first moment he saw them, the Prince of Wales coveted the company of the Jerome sisters to enlighten the heavy snobbish boredom of his famous "set".

Jennie learnt from her husband to use her ready wit as an adornment rather than a torment; and Randolph prepared himself quietly, amidst the company of older statesmen, for that career which he had needed such persuasion to enter.

Every house party which included the young Churchills proved a success. Although Randolph read continuously and deeply, cooling his fevered nerves and easily-ruffled mind with the classics, he could, within two minutes of shutting a volume, flippantly amuse any drawing-room. His shafts of wit cut through the dull atmosphere of Victorian house parties, lighting small fires of laughter and dispersing the tedium which so often grows amongst those who eat too much and have not enough to do.

One evening when 'thought-reading' had become the rage pretty Lady de Clifford insisted on dragging Randolph, who was reading in a corner, to join the general game. Snatched from the cool depths of Gibbon, he found himself blindfolded in the middle of the drawing-room. Lady de Clifford made passes with her hands saying, "Don't resist any thought which comes into your head; do exactly as you feel." Without hesitation he embraced her before the whole company. To her remonstrances he replied, "You told me to do what I felt like doing, so I did it."

Henceforth Randolph was left in peace.

Several months each year were spent with the Marlboroughs, and Jennie tried to live in harmony with her austere mother-in-law, at the rustle of whose silken skirt the household trembled.

"When the family were alone at Blenheim, everything went on with the regularity of clockwork. So assiduously did I practise my piano, read or paint, that I began to imagine myself back in the schoolroom. In the morning, an hour or so was devoted to the reading of newspapers, which was a necessity if one wanted to show an intelligent interest in the questions of the day, for at dinner conversation invariably turned to politics. In the afternoon a drive to pay a visit to some neighbour or a walk in the gardens would help to while away some part of the day. After dinner, which was a rather solemn full-dress affair, we all repaired to what was called the Vandyke room. There one might read one's book or play for love a mild game of whist. Many a glance would be cast at the clock, which sometimes would be surreptitiously advanced a quarter of an hour by some sleepy member of the family. No one dared suggest bed until the sacred hour of eleven had struck. Then we would all troop out into a small ante-room, and, lighting our candles, each in turn would kiss the Duke and Duchess and depart to our own rooms."

There is scarcely any mention of young members of the family. Victorian châtelaines did not keep their children to the forefront of their (extra-ordinarily childish) lives. Jennie luckily procured a wonderful nurse for Winston. Dear fat kind Mrs. Everest created an atmosphere of cosiness and affection which 'the grownups' in their tail coats and boned silks were too busy to know about. The Summer Session, the Winter Session, the Hunting Season, the London Season, Cowes Week, the house parties in beautiful old mansions . . . all this routine, which it was imperative to follow, left little time for the upper classes to pay even fleeting visits to the nursery.

In the following spring, a very plump Mrs. Jerome came to stay in

Charles Street. Crackling in stiff dark silks, and wearing a bonnet, she inspected baby Winston, listened to Randolph rehearsing a short sharp speech on the release of Irish State prisoners, outlined the Parisian trends to Jennie, and departed "quite exhausted".

Young Clara spent the London season of 1875 with Jennie. A first letter to her mother after leaving France survives in its heavy monogrammed envelope:

> "Monday morning,
> 48 Charles St.
>
> My darling Mama,
>
> I never had such a nasty drizzling odious crossing! It was so rough, and we never got to London till half past 8!
>
> Jennie and R. just going off to a charming little dinner at Lady Dufferin's which had been arranged for *me*, but I was so tired that, after having a little something to eat, I went straight to bed. I just got your letter this minute and am so sorry about the bonnets but I can get on with some old ones until they come. R. has got my invitation for this Court ball next Thursday at Buckingham Palace through Francis Knollys which will be very jolly; and also one, he thinks, for the Dudleys for Wednesday. To-morrow Jennie thinks I ought to wear the white crepe with sequins as it will be my very first appearance, and it is everything to look well.
>
> Poor Rosamond is ill in bed to-day with a feverish cold, but they hope it won't be anything serious and that she will manage to get up to-morrow for the ball. We have just come from the Row where we walked with Col. Edgcumbe and Mr. Farquhair. I got up so late that I had no time to write first. However, I will do my best to write every day and tell you everything. R. is in very good humour as he made two hundred pounds at the Derby, and Jennie £20 on her own book.
>
> Goodbye my own darling Mama. I love you so much, but I hope you don't miss me much as you have Leonie. I will soon be home again. Love to Leonie.
>
> Clara."

Apparently Mrs. Jerome must remain in Paris studying bonnets for her daughters, who considered Parisian modes more beguiling than those of London, while Mr. Jerome's role was to earn sufficient in New York to pay for extensive wardrobes. In return the loving parents were to receive plenty of news.

A letter dated June 16th, 1875, reads:

"Darling Mama,

    I got your cross note this morning, and cannot understand how it is that you have not got my Saturday letter at least. Really my darling Mama if you had known what a hurry and bustle it was, and how tired I was too at Ascot you wd not be so cross about it. Besides you say it is 10 days since you heard from me and that cannot be as I wrote the minute I got home. We had a most charming dinner last night. I wore the blue chosen by Leonie and Jennie her black gauze and Mrs. Standish her black. Vogüé[1] gave me a most charming bouquet. Blount gave one to Jennie and then we went to the play where Vogüé *would* sit next to me. And then dressed and went to the Marjoribanks ball. Jennie wants me so much to be nice to Sir William Gordon-Cumming and wants him to make up to me. I think *entre nous* that it wd take very little to make him devoted to me, although he is a young man who never speaks to a young girl and only flirts with married ladies. He began *très sérieusement à faire la cour* to Jennie but last night he would not leave me in the hall. But I could not think of him at all as he is very poor[2] and awfully conceited and not *sympathique*. I don't think I could really like a man like that. Vogüé has just asked us to dine at his house in John St., Berkeley Square should I stay longer, but he leaves the end of the week for Switzerland and he told me he would come back by way of Germany and look us up at Ems, but Frenchmen have such a way of saying things they don't mean.

    To-night there is this dreadful dinner at the Square, [the Marlboroughs] which will be such a bore. Rosamond [Randolph's younger sister] has been a week at Brighton and is looking very well so perhaps they will ask some 'choice young men' for her. I can't tell you how jealous Randolph says the Duchess is of Jennie and I. She is always very kind and amiable but *une certaine aigreur* in the way she talks. Poor Jennie doesn't know what to do while we are at Ems as she thinks it very expensive to come with us and it would be considered very fast for her to stay here by herself without Randolph. What a pity it is she has not more money. . . ."

Leonard could hardly allow his daughter to make the "fast" choice which happened also to be the economical one and stay alone in her London house. A cheque arrived by the next post.

    Clara's digs at the unfortunate Rosamond continued in most uncharit-

[1] Comte de Vogüé, a charming and erudite Frenchman, well known in racing circles and a friend of the Prince of Wales.

[2] Not at all. Sir William Gordon-Cumming, Bt., was a rich Scots landowner famous for shooting tigers on foot in the Indian jungle. Other indictments probably true.

able form as relays of exquisite tulle gowns were dispatched from Paris. We hear of her flaunting pale cream lace with rose-buds, white satin and chiffon with blue bows and forget-me-nots while Rosamond looks 'rather pasty' and the Duchess frowns. This may have been a telling method of adding to her list of proposals but it did not gain invitations to houses where there were marriageable daughters. And a whispering campaign that the Jerome sisters *'painted'* soon caused considerable distress to Jennie and Clara.[1]

The "lost letter" of which Mrs. Jerome complained eventually reached her and was placed in a trunk of family papers.

"Saturday June 12th 1875.

"My darling Mama,

We have just come home and I sit down immediately to write you *with my hat on*. I wrote you from Ascot a tremendously long account of all we were doing but I found out afterwards the servant preferred going to the races and never posted it at all. We were a cheery party. Although the men were not particularly *sympathique*, but every day there were a crowd of outsiders to tea and dinner. My party consisted of Sir William Gordon-Cumming (who is charming), Captain Oliphant, Davidoff etc. The first day we all were down to breakfast at ten, then played lawn tennis in the garden, then dressed for the Races which were awfully jolly as the Prince and Princess were there. I never saw such wonderful *toilettes* and the Royal Enclosure was very swell and select. Lord Hartington took me to lunch in a private room with the royalties, the Prince himself giving his arm to Jennie and altogether the day was *très réussi!* Vogüe and Halley Blount were a great addition as of course they were all devoted to us and as Halley and Castlereagh etc. were stopping with the Prince they were considered big swells. I can't tell you how much I like Vogüé. I always thought I would if I ever knew him and I think he likes me. All the Frenchmen came home with us piled up on the coach and had tea on the lawn. Hardwicke also making his effect in his wonderful Master of Buckhounds costume. Each lady found a charming little bouquet every night at dinner, the men boutonniers and afterwards some of them played billiards and the rest of us danced! *Voila Mardi!*

Everyone dragged in one after the other for breakfast, then we dressed for the races. I wore Leonie's blue silk which was thought very pretty. The Princess was not there, but the Prince flourished and won

---

[1] Forty-five years later I overheard Jennie and Clara still refuting the charge. They were saying to my grandmother: "You know we really never did use rouge. It was just our circulation."

a lot of money and did like the other day. I walked about with all the men and then took lunch with Mr. Delane editor of *The Times*. He has a charming house on the other side of the course and we only had chic people. Mrs. and Miss Stephens[1] were there, and Mrs. Stephens told Mrs. Farquhar it seems that she 'hoped little Lady Randolph had better manners than she had last year'. Such a common vulgar creature she is. Vogüé, Hardwicke and Blount came to dine. I wore my white muslin and pink roses and Jennie wore her dark blue low dress. Lady Dudley kept seats for us every day at the races and was most kind so handsome too. Lord B—— walked a little with me but he was very distrait throughout the meeting as he had horses running every day. Jennie took her Sir William Cumming all to herself, he being the swell of the party and does not let anyone else talk to him but I don't think him as nice as Carrington and Vogüé who are my *cavaliers particuliers*! The Prince is very kind to us and takes us for a little walk every day. Thursday was Gold Cup Day. Jennie wore her wedding dress with new crêpe de Chine trimmings and I my pale blue with marguerites *au corsage* and my new marguerite bonnet, which is very pretty. We managed to have lots of fun after the races as Oliver Montagu invited us to take tea at the "barracks of the Blues" at Windsor. So we all crowded on top of the coach and Oliver and Col. Williams (Col. of the regiment) received us in grand state with tea on the lawn, the band playing. Oliver felt fine with his uniform on. He *has* been kind to me and I hear he goes about telling everyone how nice I am! We got home tired after a long dusty drive and gay although some of the men who had lost were rather cross. *Friday*. A bad day but I never enjoyed myself so much. I wore my pink foulard and Jennie her dark blue and the men were all *very* nice to us. After the Races Hardwicke took us all with the coach to see the Queen's hounds in their Kenels (which I don't know how to spell), and then we went home and as more of the men have won back their money the dinner was more cheerful. Jennie wore her pale blue tulle with silver and I my white tulle with jet and then went to the Ball at Chiswick (the Prince and Princess's place) which was a great success. Carrington and Vogüé were there and looked particularly dashing. I never enjoyed a dance so much although I think Lord E. a humbug. The Princess had on a brown tulle and looked very well and we did not get home till 5 o'c. Old Lord Westmoreland (that is he is about 45) took a great fancy to me, but he is a bore I think although he is considering something wonderful this evening. We all made a point of being down to breakfast together and then all came down to London by the 2 o'c. train . . . then on to Windsor for the cricket match and

[1] Americans of large fortune. Miss Stephens became Lady Paget.

danced on the lawn in tents, the Prince and Princess being there but she gave it up. I ran up to see Baby Winston a minute and here I am writing you my journal. . . . Jennie sends her love and is writing too. Kiss Leonie.

Your loving,

Clara."

What eons of time these great ones had to waste, and how important the 'dressing' seems. They were being pulled in and out of their clothes all day. A lady could not go to the play except in black or dark blue; this accounted for the scampers home at 11 p.m. to 'dress' for a ball. And breakfast! That solitary tray of coffee and orange juice which is our luxury, then consisted of two hours' conversation in velvets, while in formal houses the men had to don morning coats before re-attiring themselves in shooting jackets.

Our heads spin, and yet the frivolity of these letters rings so true a note. After all her expensive education, Clara can't spell *kennels* but she knows how to dress, quote French and German, and play the piano. Her mother has taught her correct tactics with that mob she refers to as "the men"; these she used to show in dumb pantomime as a coy beckoning, followed by hands held up in shocked reproach.

Evidently she still preferred Frenchmen, and lucky it was for her that Sir William Gordon-Cumming failed to please or her name might have been tarnished with his at Tranby Croft a few years later.[1]

[1] Sir William's friendship with the Prince of Wales combined with his Colonelcy of the Scots Guards seems to have made him odiously conceited and rude. His contemptuous remarks to ladies in particular made him enemies who rejoiced in his final downfall. When Gordon-Cumming was introduced to my grandmother Leonie, then a lively sensitive girl of nineteen enjoying her first walk in Hyde Park at the fashionable hour, he snapped: "Over here husband-hunting I suppose?" Even more unforgivable was his remark in a drawing-room to Louisa, Duchess of Manchester before she married Lord Hartington (later Duke of Devonshire): "When is Harty-tarty going to make an honest woman of you?" Louisa turned pale and bided her time. When Gordon-Cumming was eventually accused of cheating at Mrs. Arthur Wilson's famous country house party given for the Prince of Wales at Tranby Croft, Louisa Devonshire made certain that every club in London knew. A party of men had in fact previously noticed Cumming's play in Jennie's own house where he had flared up at poor Leonie, snapping, "Why do you stand behind my chair?" but Randolph refused to allow a scandal to break under his roof and merely desisted from ever inviting him again. The Wilson sons suspected Cumming and unwisely laid a trap during the royal visit. When challenged he was led to the Prince's bedroom by General Williams, where he signed a paper swearing never to play cards again. H.R.H. kept the paper and secrecy was assured him. But the men of the party had wives and lady loves who could not resist blatting at Doncaster Races next day. When Cumming returned to London he drove straight to his club. As he entered, every man there deliberately turned his back. Shame forced him to bring an action; the newspapers took it up and sensational publicity resulted. Not only did Cumming have to resign his regiment and accept exile in Scotland for ever, but tension reached such a pitch when the Prince of Wales appeared in the witness-box to give evidence, that Queen Victoria suggested to her son that he had better consider relinquishing his succession to the throne. The Kaiser leapt at this chance of wounding his royal uncle by a letter expressing horror that the Honorary Colonel of a German regiment should be involved in a gaming case. For a generation the name of Tranby Croft signified not a house but England's greatest social scandal.

Jennie's letters of the seventies are unfortunately brief; she merely mentions the Prime Minister to dine or Lord Rosebery and Lord Salisbury as accompanying her at the Opening of Parliament. Knowing the clear forceful mind she showed in later years, and her powers of expression, knowing her to have been surrounded by interesting personalities, by ambassadors and statesmen and kings, one regrets that in the only surviving epistle of length to darling mama she delineates but a single person and him in strokes inadequate if unforgettable: "I do like him, Mama. He has such a lovely moustache."

Back we turn to Clara's ingenuous prattle:

"Sat. 19th June 1875.

My darling Mama,

    I slept to-day till 1 o'c. and found Sydney and Col. Edgcumbe in the Salon waiting for Jennie and R. to come to lunch and to talk of the Ball last night. It was a great success and I enjoyed myself immensely. I danced with Ld. Carrington, Ld. Henry Somerset, Gordon-Cumming etc. and the Cotillion with Col. Edgcumbe. The Prince gave me his bouquet in the flower figure and I saw Rosamond and Miss Stephens *green* with jealousy. He (the Pce.) was very civil to Jennie and I talked to the Princess so taking it all in all it was most satisfactory. I will write a long letter to-morrow morning. . . .

Kiss Leonie,
Yr. loving,
Clara."

Clara's agreement that not a day must pass without a line being written is honourably fulfilled. The letters are to be posted on to Papa in New York. She can't get it on paper a second time. It is hard enough writing with her hat on as it is.

"Thursday.

My darling Mama,

    Jennie's last night!

    Dined out and then went to the Duchess of Wellington's a very small party and then came home, dressed again and we went off to the Duchess of Westminster's. It was a beautiful ball but the house I think is *too* big for a small ball as everyone was lost and could not find each other again. I must say although one admits it is a fine *coup d'œil* I enjoy myself more in a small house. The Prince was very good to me and asked me for a dance and I think it was because I looked well. Everyone told me my dress was the prettiest. The Duchess and Rosamond looked so jealous when Jennie and I appeared in our new dresses.

To-day Constance and Henry came to lunch and in the afternoon we went out in the brougham to leave some cards. Poor Mrs. and Miss Stephens have been robbed of all their jewels by a servant whom they took without references. I feel rather sorry for her, as she does not seem to enjoy herself much. Chiswick (the Prince of Wales house rented from Duke of Devonshire) has been put off on account of bad weather. I am sure the dinner there next Sunday will be awfully stiff . . . Count Schovaloff the Russian Ambassador has invited us for *Dimanche la nuit* to dine with him and meet the Russian Grand Duke and the Prince and Princess. I don't know why but people seem to always ask us whenever H.R.H. goes to them. I suppose it is because Jennie is so pretty and you have no idea how charming Randolph can be when *il fait des frais*! And I don't want to be conceited but I think I make myself agreeable too as they could easily ask them without me. If you could only see what sticks English women are and how badly most of them dress. To-night we are going to the Duchess of Sutherland's, a very small dance, only 150 people at Stafford House and I am going to wear again my crêpe. . . . I suppose Leonie practises all day? what fingers she must have. . . .

Your loving,
Clara."

Leonie indeed, with furrowed brow and smouldering ardour, was practising longer hours than either of her sisters had ever known. She hated being the younger sister, chained to governesses while Jennie and Clara enjoyed the gay world. Music was her only compensation, and under the tuition of Stephen Heller (Chopin's friend and pupil) she became the best pianist of the three sisters. Mrs. Jerome fussed because she was not going to be pretty like the others, but Leonard called her his 'funny little thing' and she began to be his favourite.

<p style="text-align:center">~~~~~~~~~~~ 38 ~~~~~~~~~~~</p>

THE following years invoked a continuation of hard work for Leonard Jerome. Because of his daughters' manner of life, a diligent concentration on financial matters became increasingly essential. Being more interested in horses and yachts than in royalty, the doings of Jennie and Clara could not enthrall him to the extent they enthralled the American newspaper readers. Jennie's beauty had a quality which could "knock you for six". She became for countless hardworking housewives the idolized symbol of what an American girl could achieve.

Meanwhile Mrs. Jerome had, in plump middle age, developed into a patroness of cultivated unfortunates. Unpublished poets, ousted prime ministers and sacked diplomats stumbled amidst the out-moded inlaid 18th-century French furniture of her *salon* in the Rue du Roi de Rome. Her sympathy, withheld from the 'fast set' of the Prince of Wales, into which her daughters ventured with trepidation and delight, flowed lavishly towards 'the poor dear Empress', that 'unfortunate archduke' and those minor ex-kings who strolled Europe in search of good dinners and consoling phrases.

From Leonard's point of view the most companionable member of his family had become the sixteen-year-old Leonie, whom he noticed practising the piano with grimy fingers and iron will up to eight hours a day. Stephen Heller taught her to play Chopin with extraordinary charm, but much of her time was spent at that 'hateful finishing school at Wiesbaden', the smartest in Europe, where the girls, polished within an ace of their lives, were given an education suitable for the curator of a Museum. The pupils who issued forth made spectacular high-class marriages and remained impractical intellectuals all their lives. (Leonie's best friend there, Sophie Chotek, was to marry the Archduke Ferdinand and be assassinated beside him at Sarajevo in 1914.)

In 1875, Leonard decided to spend the winter at Pau with his unmarried daughters, and in the spring he snatched a couple of months to visit Ems and Bayreuth. Leonie had discovered Wagner and made Papa take her to the first production of the *Nibelungen-Ring*, and in Budapest Leonard heard Minnie Hauk rehearsing the roles of Senta (*Flying Dutchman*) and Elsa (*Lohengrin*) at the Royal Court Theatre.

Once or twice Mr. Jerome paid a visit to London, met the Duke and Duchess of Marlborough, played with the little grandson, and observed what he could of the activities of his busy, breathless daughters. The storm of preparation and entertainment which took place daily in Charles Street ('boxes of hats and gowns seem to arrive every hour'), drove him out to clubs and racing stables. He visited once more his old friend Mrs. Ronalds. Having spent a period improving her delicate lungs as a guest of the Bey of Algiers who regarded her as a 'divine being', Fanny had now settled permanently in London. Her musical *salon* in Cadogan Place offered something quite new to English society. Visitors came to tea, made highbrow conversation, and listened to those struggling musicians whom Mrs. Ronalds considered worthy of launching. For the unmusical who disliked long hours on hard gilt chairs, a snobbish consolation might be scraped from meeting His Royal Highness the Duke of Edinburgh, a violinist of no small merit, for whom Fanny played accompaniments. The love of her life "dear, dear Sir Arthur Sullivan" was nearly always present. One day his bars of music engraved on her tombstone in Fulham Cemetery would give a clue to the conventional epitaph "Forever thine". And those who possessed a score would know to whom Fanny finally left her heart.

Leonard accompanied "sweet Mrs. R." to Covent Garden Opera, where she owned a box. She glanced at him sideways with those brown eyes which so many men apoplectic with emotion had tried to describe. "Your daughters must marry Englishmen," she said, "and bring their children to my tea parties to learn to care for music." (They did, but owing to the imprint of tone-deaf English sires none of Leonard's grand-children had a note in them.)

With distressing frequency Mr. Jerome had to break off amusing commitments in Europe, sail back to New York and earn sufficient for the upkeep of the several large houses which now devolved entirely on his pocket.

If he grew lonely during these family separations no trace showed in speech or letter. He wrote: "the strict old Union Club, although shabby and sombre, remains my favourite haunt". Here gentlemen of leisure could discuss horses, *prima donnas* and yachts in solemn whispers, and now James Gordon Bennett was planning to introduce polo to America. Having learned this Indian sport from retired army officers in England, he had just shipped the first polo mallets, balls and ponies to New York. With Frank Griswold he began to teach the rules to teams of oddly mounted friends in a riding academy. August Belmont, ageing but still game, joined in, and Leonard cursed the old strain suffered in that weight-lifting contest which made it impossible for him to attempt this new game. The first American polo match was played at Jerome Park in 1876, Bennett's and Jerome's coaches transporting the players. The sport proved such good value to spectators that it was decided to inaugurate matches after the Races, and Polo began to flourish under the selective influence of a smart Club. Nothing could be called a real success unless a number of people who were dying to 'get in' were 'kept out'.

While Leonard, aged fifty-eight, fretted at his inability to participate in the matches, he received a letter from which fell the spark of a new idea. Jennie wrote that Randolph's brother, the Marquis of Blandford, was driving his own coach as a public vehicle between London and Dorking. Leonard roared with laughter: "If I can't earn indoors in Wall Street, I'll earn outdoors as a coachman."

He had already founded the Coaching Club along with Colonel William Jay and De Lancey Kane who were brilliant masters of four-in-hand driving, and now he started excursions to all the taverns and inns within fifty miles of New York City. The first public parade of the Coaching Club had taken place in Fifth Avenue during the spring of 1876. Horns blew, and Colonel Jay, in bottle-green coat, yellow-striped waistcoat, and silk topper and *boutonnière*, led the smartest array of turnouts New York had ever seen. Rules had to be strict; every horse must have artificial flowers on its throat-latch, the driver's apron must be folded outside when not in use, and only the most elegant ladies were invited to perch behind the driver. Their feathered hats and lacy parasols caused almost as many gasps of interest as the beribboned horses. A newspaper article of April 29, 1876, states that "Mr. Leonard Jerome, one of our most experienced whips, came next [fourth], handling a good-looking bay team, hitched to a dark coach with red wheels, built by Jacobs, of Guilford."

Minnie Hauk and her mother returned briefly during this summer, and let him listen to excerpts from Bizet's *Carmen*. "What do you think of it?" she asked, and he replied, "I like it but will the public accept anything so new?"

"I'll make them," said Minnie, "the dull fools, I'll make them like it."

L'amour est un oiseau rebelle carolled Minnie in her strange voice with its thrilling range. The refrain had hardly faded when Jennie and Randolph arrived with a long breathless story. Randolph and his brother had quarrelled with the Prince of Wales, and split London society into warring factions. Queen Victoria was sore distressed and an unprecedented number of people could never speak to each other again.

Jennie noted that her father alone seemed able to listen without becoming ruffled. Walking to the windows that overlooked Madison Square, he pulled back the red plush and white lace curtains to let what little breeze there was blow into the room.

"Tell me quietly," he ordered.

The tale poured forth. Randolph's brother Lord Blandford (he who had written those sarcastic lines on hasty marriages), had himself wedded a daughter of the Duke of Abercorn and become the father of several children. Despite a propensity to describe in verse how marriage ought to go, he did not prove a model husband, but Lady Blandford never noticed anything, and when he openly courted the pretty Countess of Aylesford she merely copied that lady's dresses.

Lord Aylesford was a famous man to hounds, a heavyweight who made a brilliant reputation for cross-country riding in the Shires. Eventually the Prince of Wales (himself entranced by Edith Aylesford), went to India taking "sporting Jo Aylesford" in his company. Lord Blandford indiscreetly seized this moment to move his horses to a hunting inn adjacent to Lady Aylesford's country house.

When Lord Aylesford returned he started a case which caused the whole structure of society to tremble. The Prince of Wales insisted that, having compromised the lady, Blandford should ask for a divorce and marry her. This Lord Blandford refused to do. Meanwhile the only person in England who knew nothing of her husband's predicament was Lady Blandford. She had always enjoyed practical jokes, and one morning when Blandford came down to breakfast late and lugubrious, reflecting on the recent arrival of a child for the Countess of Aylesford, she innocently devised a joke which by coincidence excelled all the others. While awaiting her husband's arrival, she replaced his poached egg by a small pink baby doll. She thought it would be such a surprise when he lifted the cover! It was. Lord Blandford choked, fled the room and disappeared abroad for several weeks. His wife could not think why.

Meanwhile Randolph furiously championed his brother against the Prince, and actually threatened to reveal certain love letters written by the Prince which Lady Aylesford had for some reason allowed him to read. Hot words flew and finally H.R.H. sent Lord Knollys to challenge Randolph to a duel, suggesting Rotterdam as a suitable place. Even Jennie's iron nerves began to grow frayed. She passed sleepless nights until Randolph appointed Lord Falmouth as his second and dispatched him with a message to say he would fight any nominee, but could not lift a sword against his future Sovereign.

At this stage Queen Victoria expressed grave displeasure. Society divided, and the London season broke up amidst acrimonious argument.

Such was the tension that as Jennie tactfully put it, "Randolph felt in need of solace and distraction." This had been sought in a hasty trip through Canada with Lord Ilchester which may have cooled tempers, but so pitiless a heatwave was in progress that "we seemed to spend most of the time eating melons and having cold baths".

Leonard listened carefully.

"Forget it," he said. "It was really your brother's affair. And now we will all go to Newport to sail and drive and see what I have got left in the way of horses."

Off they went to the haven of Jennie's childhood which was throwing up a plague of Roman temples and Loire Châteaux in place of the country villas she had known. The August Belmonts entertained them with ten-course dinners while liveried footmen held candelabra up the stairs and young Mrs. Henry Clews, "Newport's best dressed lady", confided that each year she set aside $10,000 for "mistakes in clothes".

At Saratoga, where Leonard took them to the Races, "the beauty of the ladies and gorgeousness of their dresses astonished the Englishmen of the party". Lawrence Jerome arrived. "For heaven's sake keep them diverted," begged his brother. Lawrence suggested a visit to the Philadelphia Exhibition. Jennie describes her uncle as one of the wittiest men of his day who kept them in transports of laughter. Stopping at various stalls, he would accost the rest of the party as though they were strangers and, taking up some new invention, would produce such a comic flow of salesman talk that crowds collected to buy the article while a delighted shop assistant tried to slip Lawrence a "commission". Soon Randolph ceased to brood over the injustices of royal personages, and according to Jennie they all returned to England "refreshed".

Randolph now took an increasing dislike to the vapid society portrayed by Clara's guileless pen. As his son has written, without this trouble over Blandford he might have "wasted a dozen years in the frivolous and expensive pursuits of the silly world of fashion".

Disraeli had often asked the Duke of Marlborough to accept the appointment of Viceroy to Ireland. Now that his two sons had quarrelled with so august a person as the Prince of Wales, the Duke acquiesced. Blenheim Palace was to be closed down and its entire household transported to Dublin Castle.

In December 1876, the Viceroy made his State Entry riding in uniform amidst a glittering Staff. The family, including Randolph and Jennie with baby Winston, followed in carriages with postilions and outriders.

All official entertaining had to be conducted in the sombre old Castle, but the Viceregal Lodge, a Georgian house in Phoenix Park, was put at the

Duke's disposal as private residence. For Randolph, who was to act as un-official private secretary to his father, there was a charming little white house five minutes' walk from the Lodge.

The Viceroy's son and daughter-in-law naturally assisted at all official functions. Jennie's presence threw a curious glamour over the most formal and austere of ceremonies. Lord D'Abernon (then considered England's most handsome young man) has paid no mean tribute to her especial quality:

> "I have the clearest recollection of seeing her for the first time. It was at the Viceregal Lodge, Dublin. She stood at one side to the left of the entrance. The Duke was on a dais at the farther end of the room, sur-rounded by a brilliant staff, but eyes were not turned on him or his con-sort, but on a dark lithe figure standing somewhat apart and appearing to be of another texture to those around her, radiant, translucent, intense. A diamond star in her hair, her favourite ornament—its lustre dimmed by the flashing glory of her eyes. More of the panther than of the woman in her look but with a cultivated intelligence unknown to the jungle. Her courage not less great than that of her husband —fit mother for descendants of the great Duke, with all these attributes of brilliancy such kindliness and high spirits that she was universally popular. Her desire to please, her delight in life and the genuine wish that all should share her joyous faith in it, made her the centre of a devoted circle."[1]

Lord Justice Fitzgibbon, the 'Law Adviser' to Dublin Castle, describes his first meeting with Randolph after the presentations in the throne room. Lord Randolph hurried in hot-headed, to ask legal advice regarding the sacking of a disgruntled footman. The Lord Justice dispelled Randolph's illusions regarding possible methods of dealing with those servants who "did not like the look of the Castle". And there began, so Fitzgibbon wrote later: "a friendship which, although full of constant anxiety and appre-hension, is one of the dearest memoirs of my life. How it grew so fast I can hardly tell. I suppose electricity came in somewhere. . . ."

When a panther is married to a gentleman emitting electric sparks their dinner table is likely to be stimulating. During the four years that she lived in Ireland, Jennie has said she never met one really dull man. Mr. Butt (leader of the Irish party in the House of Commons, and tame forerunner of Parnell), Professor Mahaffy the most erudite wit in Dublin and famed Father James Healy, dined frequently in the miniature lodge hurling forth

[1] *An Ambassador of Peace:* Viscount D'Abernon.

Little Winston with his Aunt Leonie
Dublin, 1880

"She shone for me like the Evening Star"

W.S.C.

My dear mama
I am so glad
you are coming
to see us I had
such a nice
bathe in the
sea to day.
love to papa
your loving
winston

Winston's first letter

argument and anecdote. Venturing away from Dublin, Jennie studied with amazement the strange poetical peasantry. She accompanied Randolph on shooting, fishing and hunting expeditions and knew great happiness for the natural charm of the Irish people hung like a smoke-screen over a country simmering with bitterness. Each autumn the Duke rented a sporting home, Lord Sligo's in Mayo where the snipe shooting led to fantastic walks through Connemara or Knockdrin Castle in Westmeath where the foxes were as wild as the people. Now Jennie's prowess as a horsewoman could be shown to advantage. "Hands, hands! light hands!" Leonard had drummed into her; insisting the greatest sin for a woman (except singing a false note), was to jerk a good horse in the mouth. She wrote:

"Hunting became our ruling passion. Whenever I could beg, borrow or steal a horse, I did so. We had a few hunters of our own which we rode indiscriminately, being both of us light weights. Some of my best days with the Meath and Kildare Hounds I owed to a little brown mare I bought at Oxford, who negotiated the 'trappy' fences of the Kildare country and the banks and narrow doubles of Meath, as though to the manner born. Many were the 'tosses' I took, as the Irish papers used to describe them, but it was glorious sport, and to my mind, even hunting in Leicestershire later could not compare with it. With the exception of the Ward Union Staghounds and the Galway Blazers, I think we hunted with nearly every pack of hounds in Ireland."

Leonard's mail reaching him in New York or Paris or Pau or Ems (for he lived in trains and ships these days), regaled him with descriptions of his daughter's long runs, of how she and Randolph and Colonel Forster the Master of the Horse, had ridden proudly forth on their best horses and *all* three met disaster before noon, how she had galloped fourteen miles, crawled from a ditch, leapt a 'gap', negotiated an old iron bed used in lieu of a gate. And she told of the driver of a jaunting car taking Colonel Forster to a meet. They passed an elegant young man admiring his own boots and patting his waistcoat. "Who is it?" asked Forster.

"Bedad, Colonel, I'm thinking that maybe he is not knowing it rightly himself by the way he is looking."

The Empress Elizabeth of Austria took a place in Meath for the hunting, and cut a daring figure over the fields, wheedling her horse with precision over banks and ditches, galloping her brave, unhappy spirit to some sort of peace. Jennie remembered her father's descriptions of the Austrian Empire, and of young Elizabeth's efforts to humanize the Emperor's directive. The Duke of Marlborough issued an invitation to the Viceregal Lodge but her

Majesty pleaded inability to spare one moment from her hunting and the attendant preparations.

In view of later happenings it may be of interest to record Jennie's impressions of the west of Ireland:

> "In our walks we had many opportunities of seeing the heart-rending poverty of the peasantry, who lived in their wretched mud-hovels, more like animals than human beings. Alas! I fear these deplorable conditions must ever prevail in Ireland, where neglect and misery have rooted the people in their shiftless and improvident habits."

During these four years of tramping the bogs and galloping after hounds a firm conviction was forming behind her husband's pointed, steel-hard brain. Lord Randolph Churchill appears to have been one of the few Englishmen in the 19th century who realized that an Ireland, misgoverned for five centuries and burning to revolt, might prove the most urgent problem, indeed the greatest danger the British Empire could face in calamity's hour.[1]

Mr. Disraeli it is true, in a letter to the Duke of Marlborough as Viceroy, was to state that

> "nevertheless, a danger, in its ultimate results scarcely less disastrous than pestilence and famine and which now engages your Excellency's anxious attention, distracts that country. A portion of its population is attempting to sever the constitutional tie which unites it to Britain in that bond which has favoured the power and prosperity of both. It is to be hoped that all men of light and leading will resist this destructive doctrine."

But he, as Prime Minister, had consistently ignored every serious plea for new Irish legislation. Every Irish bill of importance was cast out, especially those dealing with the vital questions of land and education. "The power and prosperity" had been England's only. In 1877, Lord Randolph still a minor member of the Tory party, though no longer an uncritical admirer of his chief, made a speech which created considerable consternation:

> "I have no hesitation in saying that it is inattention to Irish legislation that has produced obstruction. There are great and crying Irish questions which the Government have not attended to, and as long as these matters are neglected, so long will the Government have to deal with obstruction from Ireland."

[1] Neither he nor any other statesman of that century could have foreseen the day when lack of the Irish ports would almost lose Britain a war against Germany.

The Press gave much publicity to these unconventional utterances, the *Morning Post* observing in its leader:

"It is no exaggeration to say that neither Mr. Parnell nor Mr. Butt could have used stronger language in support of their respective lines of action. But it is not an Irish Home Ruler, or Irish Obstructive, who has used it. It is the Conservative representative of an English borough and the son of the Lord Lieutenant of Ireland."

Sir Michael Hicks Beach deplored Randolph's outburst to his father, and the Duke (who may have been excused for thinking he had suffered enough from his sons for one year) replied:

"Guisachan: September 25, 1877.

My dear Beach,
The only excuse I can find for Randolph is that he must either be mad or have been singularly affected with local champagne or claret. I can only say that the sentiments he has indulged in are purely his own; and, more than this, I was as much amazed as you in reading them, and had no conception that he entertained such opinions. The conjuncture is most unfortunate and ill-timed; but at the same time it must be remembered that though my son, and occupying by leave P. Bernard's house, he is not in any way officially connected with me, and the assumption therefore that he represented my opinions would be both unwarranted and unfair. I quite appreciate your consideration in making no allusion to his remarks, and perhaps, unless it should be absolutely required, the less notice drawn to them the better. Should you, however, feel it to be necessary to correct misapprehensions consequent on his speech, I conceive you are perfectly entitled to do so. I can only repeat that I am extremely annoyed at the folly of his utterance, which I believe on reflection he will regret himself. Perhaps, if I might suggest, a letter from yourself to him in your official position and responsible for Irish business in parliament might be the best way of dealing with the occurrence.
Yours very sincerely,
Marlborough."

Tension between the Viceregal Lodge and the white doll's house at its garden gate grew acute. Jennie distracted herself by planting rose trees and playing with her son on the tiny lawn. When the Duke and Duchess strolled along to ask her to remonstrate with this uncontrollable rebel whom all of them loved so dearly, she assumed evasive tactics. Randolph knew his own mind, she countered, he could not be persuaded to admire a Conservative policy he found wanting, and who was she to scold him for having Radical and Liberal friends? Surely it was unwise for wives to argue with their husbands?

Then came the famine of 1879. The Duchess of Marlborough issued an appeal for the starving poor in their wet hovels and collected £150,000 for food, fuel and clothing. Jennie and Randolph hurled themselves into the work and grew appalled at the nightmare problem of this ill-treated angry unbowed nation. But after four hundred years of harsh and stupid rule, how could it suddenly be changed? The Duchess's charitable efforts were only a palliative; blankets and soup kitchens would not affect the tragedy of many thousands of evictions in the following year, and the retributions wrought by desperate peasants, turned out of their squalid cabins because they could not pay the rent. No personal contribution, not even £500 from the Queen of England, altered the hard fact that grain was being exported from a country suffering 'famine'. And the efforts of certain land-owners who helped their tenants in the time of distress proved negligible in the general misery.

One of these landlords, a Sir John Leslie of Glaslough in Monaghan, brought his son to the Viceregal Lodge at about this time and held discussions with the Duke concerning measures which could be taken for the protection of tenants in these hard days. During the previous famine of 1847 a five-mile wall had been built around his own demesne as a temporary method of giving employment and now food was being distributed. Sir John's four daughters drove out daily in dog-carts to bring help to far-flung bog cottages, unchaperoned and unfearing in a land where hate and ambush and murder was becoming rife. Sir John's son, a quiet blue-eyed youth of twenty, stayed to dinner and was invited to attend the small dance being held in the Viceregal ballroom. Being the youngest guest he naturally danced several times with the debutante of the house, Miss Leonie Jerome, just out of the super-schoolrooms of Wiesbaden and Paris, a connoisseur of things artistic, an arbitrator on things fashionable, with no knowledge at all of the woes of bogland. He sat out with her behind a pillar, and in the precipitate fashion of those days, as if fearing he might never see her again, suggested marriage. The lady reacted according to the books on etiquette. She was shocked rather than flattered, and delivered a pretty little sermon.

Then Jennie descended: "What *are* you two talking about so seriously? Politics, I'm sure." And the conference was broken up, or 'prorogued', to use a favourite family word, for young Leslie did not take 'no' for an answer (if indeed he really got 'no'), and four years later, having at intervals resumed the subject, he succeeded in obtaining a different reply.

In the spring of 1880, when the hunger had abated but the evictions were about to begin, the Duke of Marlborough resigned his Viceroyalty and returned to Blenheim, where many complaints awaited concerning the running of his estates during his absence. A General Election took place just before his return and Randolph, who had spent March touring his constituency and listening to the labourers' grumbles, managed to keep Woodstock for the Conservatives. But Disraeli's government was 'out'. Old Gladstone had rumbled forth from retirement and been once again returned to power with a large majority.

Describing Lord Randolph at this time, his son has written:

"Starting with many advantages, he was still at thirty-one obscure. ... His party was now humbled in the dust. ... Grave and violent dangers beset the State, and no one troubled to think about an undistinguished sprig of the nobility. Nevertheless his hour had come."

39

THE fact that life would always be exciting in the proximity of Lord Randolph Churchill grew more apparent every day. He had set London society sizzling and left it because hostesses had to choose between him and the Prince of Wales at every smart party, at every dinner and ball and gathering. He had ventured an independent political opinion, and already his father and the excellent Sir Michael Hicks Beach, a family friend, appeared to reel from shock. Jennie realized that a buzz of criticism and indignant comment would arise whenever her husband showed signs of activity. She rather liked the turmoil. Yet when she had married him she had not realized he was a fighter of genius.

Ireland had given her that peace which accompanies cross-country riding. She had seldom accompanied her husband to London on his political visits, for the strain of bearing the Prince's anger drained pleasure from all social outings, but Randolph insisted she come over for the famous 'Peace with Honour Banquet' (peace with Russia over the Dardanelles being the issue), where she heard Disraeli accuse Gladstone of being "inebriated with the exuberance of his own verbosity". Later she attended a reception given for Dizzy at Stratford House[1] by Lady Constance Leslie, the mother of John Leslie, the shy Grenadier Guards officer who would follow Leonie around and then just "stand and turn pink". As she went up the stairs Disraeli was bowing low and making fulsome compliments to Lady Constance regarding her brocade dress. "From Damascus, I presume?" Then, turning to observe the drawing-rooms lit with flickering chandeliers, he continued in that strange flamboyant manner which intrigued the reticent English: "What vistas!"

His hostess beamed until she noticed John hurrying towards Jennie. Inarticulate, but desperate, he whispered, "Is your sister over?" "No," answered Jennie curtly, for she knew the Leslies were planning a grand English marriage for their only son. And Mrs. Jerome was planning an even grander French one.

Meanwhile Leonard shepherded his protégée Minnie Hauk. At last she had succeeded in inducing a Manager to present *Carmen* in London. She left

[1] Now Hutchinson House.

New York full of Leonard's encouragement, for she had sung it over till he knew each bar by heart. One of her few surviving letters to him reads:

> "Langham Hotel, London.
>
> April 22nd 1879.
>
> My Dearest Friend!
>
> The first to whom I write is you after arriving on the old side of the Ocean again. For somehow I have not ceased to think of you during the whole voyage. I cannot tell you my friend how disappointed I was in not seeing you again before leaving New York. I made so sure you would call the last day of my stay that only late in the evening after I found you had not come, I wrote you a hasty line.
>
> We had a miserable time of it crossing for we were sick the whole way, it being so stormy and rough.
>
> I longed so to thank you with viva voce for your more than friendly interest and advice given to me as from a father to his daughter—which to my utmost ability I followed and obeyed.
>
> I hope you will not disappoint me by not coming to London for you said you would, and I am looking forward to this with great pleasure. We arrived on Sunday at Liverpool and came to London. I am announced to open Her Majesty's on Saturday April 26th with 'Carmen' so you see not much rest for me.
>
> Please give my very sincere regards to your dear family—and for yourself my most affectionate love and esteem.
>
> Please write to me,
>
> Yours
>
> Minnie Hauk.

When the controversial new opera opened the three Jerome sisters were in a box together, and for days after they were leading the arguments aroused by hammering out phrases on their pianos in London, Dublin and Paris. When Leonard did arrive in Europe he grew somewhat tired of *Carmen*.

Randolph's letters to Jennie at this time are almost entirely concerned with politics. He had abandoned for ever that dream of a country gentleman's existence. It was a mirage. He did not carry within himself the possibility of quiet living.

"I am sure the debate will be very stormy," said one letter. "I am in great doubt what to do. I think I could make a telling speech against the Government, but old Bentinck got hold of me to-day and gave me a tremendous lecture. Of course I have my future to think of, and I also have strong opinions against the Government policy. It is very difficult.

I shan't decide till the last night of debate, which won't be till next Monday or Tuesday, so my departure for Ireland will be postponed.

Northcote made a very feeble speech to-night, and the country every day gets more and more against the Government. Russia's terms of peace are monstrous, but after all it concerns Austria so much more than us, and if she won't move we are practically powerless.

I had a pleasant evening last night at Dilke's. . . . Harcourt, G. Trevelyan, Dicey, editor of the *Observer*, and Sir Henry Maine. Harcourt was very amusing. You need not be afraid of these Radicals, they have no influence on me farther than I like to go, but I hate the Government. . . ."

And another written casually enough:

"I dined with Lord Wharncliffe last night, and took in to dinner a Mrs. Langtry, a most beautiful creature quite unknown, very poor, and they say has but one black dress."

Jennie little guessed that a rival in the history of beautiful women had been heralded upon the scene. A year or so later crowds were standing perilously on chairs to catch one glimpse of the 'Jersey Lily' as she walked through Hyde Park.

Furniture removal cost little in those days, and it was with pleasure that Jennie established herself in a London house while large horse drays unloaded what Randolph called "the stage props" on the doorstep. Inheriting her mother's unrestrainable impulses to buy "18th century junk" quite *démodé*, in dusty antique shops, Jennie had enjoyed 'slumming' in Dublin, where the perpetual 'selling up' of the large houses of improvident Irish gentry brought Georgian furniture on the market at low prices. A clutter of "horrid old-fashioned bits and pieces" going off to furnish the new house aroused sniffs among the housemaids and footmen who thought they knew what was what in *English* households.

While waiting for the decorators to finish Jennie wrote her mother an illuminating account from a London hotel. The whole family had been worried over Leonie's beau Charlie Fitzwilliam.

"July 12th 1880,
London.

Dearest Mama,

I owe you all letters but the time flies and life here in London is such a 'hurry scurry' that even when I have a quiet moment it is with difficulty that I settle down. Old Everest got a cold and I had to give her a holiday—and she is still away. Luckily I found a very good monthly nurse who looks after the Baby. Winston is a very good boy, and is getting on with his lessons, but he is a most difficult child to manage—So much for the infants! You will be glad to hear that R. has been covering himself with glory and I'm told he has made himself a wonderfully good position in the House. Last Monday he spoke on an Irish Question which interests all the landlords at the moment, and he made a *really* splendid speech—everyone says so—and Gladstone got up and answered him for an hour. I am sending you *Vanity Fair*. It is a capital caricature I think. When this Govt. goes out (which they say will be soon) I fancy R. and his boon companion Sir Henry Drummond Wolff must be given something. I am only so afraid of R. getting spoilt—he wd lose half his talent if he did. I keep reminding him of it. London is very gay just now. I haven't been to many balls; as I simply cannot afford to get dresses and one can't wear always the same thing. Besides I was not bidden to the one I want to go to [because of the Prince] and I did not care about the others. This week I am going out every night, to-morrow to the opera; I was sent a box so I called Natica and Johnny Kaye.[1] We were thinking of going to Dinard for August but they say Parliament will not be up till September. I shall send Winston and John to Ventnor for a month. Money is such a hateful subject to me just now don't let us talk about it. So glad to hear the Races had come off so successfully but I agree with you in everything you say about Fitzwilliam. I never thought it was a good match in a money point of view but if they had as much to live on as we have they wd do well enough. As far as position goes nothing cld be better, and last but not least Leonie cld *never* find a nicer man. At the same time I clearly see all the objections and no one feels more than I do all you say of her being worthy of something better from the worldly point of view—but when I look around here it seems to me the chances for *any* girl, are very small—there are so few *partis*, and when I see a girl like Georgie,[2] with everything that money, dress and position can do for her, hanging on year after year! and she is not the only one—there is one of the Duchess of Newcastle's daughters Lady Beatrix Clinton a nice looking girl, very well educated, and with a large fortune, they say £12,000 a year. Well this is her first season, and she insists on marrying Johnny Kaye's brother, Mr. Cecil Kaye a sick tiresome youth. I'm only telling you this to show you what nonsense it is trying to arrange marriages and how difficult it is to marry *at all*.

[1] Sir John Lister-Kaye, Bt., engaged to Natica Yznaga of New York.
[2] Lord Randolph's fifth sister. She married Lord Curzon, son of the 4th Earl Howe in 1883.

. . . Of course if you ask me not to encourage Fitzwilliam I won't. At the same time I am *dreadfully* prejudiced in his favour. . . . Give my best love to Papa and Randolph's who wants me to say that he is delighted at the success of the Races he takes the *greatest* interest in it all.

Ever yr. loving,
Jennie."

Leonard disapproved of the European aristocrat's habit of looking for heiresses instead of for opportunities to earn, but his wife had caught the *parti* fever. The period in England which Jennie described was curious in that it stopped natural pairing of the species. Primogeniture had always prevailed in England but during the 19th century a new snobbism arose which prevented the younger sons from going into trade or striking out independently as normal men. Although obsessed by the importance of money they could take no action to rectify their own situation. Hanging around on allowances they were only able to better themselves along the narrow paths of Army, Navy or Diplomatic Service. Naturally they tended to eschew marriage and its responsibilities.

While each noble family was only able to produce *one* elder son it usually furnished a bevy of husband-hungry daughters, not necessarily as well-endowed as the Duke's daughters quoted by Jennie but nevertheless reared in a great mansion and accustomed to the grand style. If unable to catch an heir these girls had to decide between remaining on their high shelf or stepping down to share the frustrations of a younger son, thus slipping from the titled heights of the nobility into a vacuum of landless gentry. After nerve-racking intrigues and long waiting Randolph's five sisters did eventually manage to procure *eldest* sons, four of whom were peers. The 'upper class' seemed to be mentally paralysed by its own snobbery. It took an American to bluntly state the situation. It was as Jennie said, "extremely difficult for a girl to get married at all".

The Churchills' new house in St. James Street lay next door to that of Sir Stafford Northcote who had inherited the Conservative Party from the failing Disraeli. He was a bland inoffensive old gentleman, unsuited to lead an Opposition, and Randolph, a fighter to the core, writhed at the ineffectual manner in which Conservative affairs were conducted. Combustive force enabled him to form that extraordinary Fourth Party which for five years was to outrage, delight, goad into action and reduce to impotent exhaustion the Whigs and the Tories in turn.

Meanwhile Jennie hung her new drawing-room with silk panels, and wept when the winter fogs destroyed them. But thick walls were more important than inner hangings. Old Northcote grew puzzled and then furious when he learnt of the four self-assertive men who were preparing their independent political stings in 'the house next door'.

The other members of the Fourth Party, Sir Henry Drummond Wolff, a witty and respected older member, Mr. John Gorst, an eminent lawyer, and young, charming, incalculable Mr. Arthur Balfour had already been accustomed to sit on the Front Bench in the House of Commons. Lord Randolph joined them when an elderly Conservative vacated a seat beside them muttering, "This is getting too hot for me."

The industry of this band in moving amendments and preparing devastating speeches aroused groans among the Liberals, who after their victory at the polls had thought to ride easily. It seemed hardly believable that only four men could conduct such sustained and co-ordinated attacks. At first the older members of the Tory party, too hidebound and cautious to render constructive criticism or spirited opposition themselves, were delighted to find the job done for them. But when they noticed the Radical tendencies of the Fourth Party in regard to the Workmen's Compensation Bill and the like, frowns spread over elderly brows. They realized that the unforgivable sin of original thought was infesting Conservative ranks.

In August 1880, five months after the Election, the Liberals solemnly rebuked the Fourth Party for 'obstruction'. During this short period its four lively members were accused (amidst laughter), of having made between them 247 speeches and asked 73 questions! Randolph retaliated by quoting from an old article written by Gladstone himself:

"Now if a great party may obstruct, it is hazardous to award narrower limits to the small ones, for it is precisely in the class of cases where the party is small, and the conviction strong, that the best instances of warrantable obstruction may be found."

"This," he cried, "will be our charter!"

In September when a hot summer and long hours had reduced remaining members to ill-tempered exhaustion the session closed, and Randolph and his friends in the best of form joined Jennie in the country, where she had retreated with six-year-old Winston and the new baby son named John.

Jennie knew that her husband's star was rising fast, his brain and wit and clarity of expression had no rival in Parliament, but what a pathetic side of her existence is revealed by a letter written at the beginning of winter from Blenheim. Leonard was sending her all he could afford to ease the burden of Randolph's career, but the path of a beauty in an alien country is not necessarily strewn with roses. This is the first American version of life in a ducal palace:

Dearest Mama,

I was so pleased to get your letter. You know you don't treat me very often to one! I'm so delighted to think that you are coming over in March. It will be great fun going over to Paris together. It is such ages since I've seen you. It is really too long. I quite forget what it is like to be with people who love me. I do so long sometimes to have someone to whom I could go and talk to. Of course Randolph is awfully good to me and always takes my part in everything, but how can I always be abusing his mother to him, when she is devoted to him, and wd do anything for him—The fact is I *loathe* living here. It is not on account of its dullness, *that* I don't mind, but it is gall and wormwood to me to accept anything or to be living on anyone I hate. It is no use disguising it, the Duchess hates me simply for what I am—perhaps a little prettier and more attractive than her daughters. Everything I do or say or wear is found fault with. We are always studiously polite to each other, but it is rather like a volcano, ready to burst out at any moment. Clara and Leonie both know what her ways are like. So it is no use describing *les petites misères* that make up the total of one's existence here. What one can laugh at in the abstract is most bitter when one is living with a person and accepting their hospitality. We've been here more than a month. The children have got charming nurseries and are well looked after. I've got a very nice room and sitting room on the ground floor; I paint and do pretty much what I like. Well! You can believe me when I say that I wd be happier living quite alone in our little house without seeing a soul. However it is not for long, only a fortnight more. I know I am very foolish to mind what can't be changed but it is trying! Now to talk of something cheerier you will be glad to hear R. made a capital speech at Portsmouth. I wish I cd send you the *Morning Post* but I couldn't get it. Of course the Liberal press is furious at his attacks on the Govt. but their spiteful articles are rather flattering than otherwise. How I wish the Conservatives might come in. We could then have a chance. Meanwhile our money affairs are pretty much like everyone else's it seems to me, hard up notwithstanding Papa's most generous "tips".

Randolph is obliged to spend so much in a political way, going to these meetings etc. and this big public dinner in Woodstock will cost a lot . . . the building alone costing £120. . . . But this demonstration is of great importance to R. and the thing must be well done with Ld. Salisbury and a lot of big swells coming. You don't know how economical we try to be. I've not bought but one winter dress, and that was bought in Woodstock for twenty-five shillings and made by my maid—dark red thin flannel. Clara and Leonie would cry fi! of my wardrobe. There is no one here but Ld. Portarlington and Lady Londonderry—the Dowager. They both asked after Clara and said nice things. I've heard no amusing gossip, only a few letters from sporting friends. Best love to all dear Mama.

Ever,
Yr. loving,
Jennie.

P.S.—R. sends his best love—By the bye couldn't you send a barrel of American eating apples to St. James Place? I'm so fond of them."

Fi! is the word I fear for a lady who receives £6,000 a year, and only has one red flannel dress and must beg Mama for apples!

40

WHILE her husband developed into the most notorious, as well as most fascinating character in London, Jennie revelled in his political tumults. From breakfast until dinner, plots were hatched around her dining-table. The Duke of Marlborough, accustomed to entertain only Conservative leaders, suffered a fresh shock on learning that the more brilliant members of the Liberal party were frequently invited to his son's house. But he chided Jennie in vain. She enjoyed sharp repartee even if of Liberal origin. Envious London society abandoned the old whisper that she 'rouged' and charged her instead with the red tinges of Radicalism!

Joseph Chamberlain, Sir Charles Dilke and Sir William Harcourt were the friends whom the Duke found most pernicious. All three begged Jennie to do their portraits. She had taken up oil painting with her usual impetuosity, starting off with huge canvases and dozens of tubes of paint. "It is such fun to let oneself go," she explained to the dubious friend who had mistaken one of her pictures for a brilliant piece of wool work. But she refused to immortalize these Liberals saying, "I couldn't paint you black enough to suit my father-in-law."

It had not yet become fashionable for young pretty women to attend debates, but Jennie spent many successive evenings in the Ladies' Gallery. "As we could not yet enter the same house as the Prince of Wales much of the vain and foolish excitement of London society was closed to us, and politics became in fact our entire and all-absorbing interest." Mrs. Ronalds came to practise with her and recounted the small anecdotes concerning the Prince of Wales' set which were considered of such vital interest. She had been to the Duke of Portland's first great week-end at Welbeck where the Prince had been 'kept amused' (they always seem to have found this exceeding difficult) by Fanny's accounts of her adventures in many lands. Other guests present were the Duke and Duchess of Manchester and Lord Hartington "who looked often at Louisa Manchester". No one missed a trick. They had nothing else to do.

Years later the Duke of Portland tentatively described Mrs. Ronalds as "a remarkable woman, not only for her glorious soprano voice, but also for her great beauty".

A letter from Jennie, written after her sisters had just returned to New York, shows a cool view on matrimony:

"29 St. James Place. S.W.

May 30th 1880.

Dearest Leonie,

I was so glad to see the arrival of the *Bothnia* last week and to know that you were all safe. I have been very dissipated of late, there seems to be so many things going on. I lunched with Lady Lonsdale such an extraordinary set she has about her, Consuelo and Natica,[1] Bertie Balfour, Tyrvoliss (*et v'là un nom*), and the youngest Lowther. The house is charming, full of beautiful pictures and tapestry, but she has no taste. Last Sunday R. and I dined with Philip C—— at his little house on Clapham Common. He made himself so agreeable and gave us such a capital dinner, his house was full of pretty things, and he had *violet* silk curtains and yellow walls in his drawing room! He talked a great deal about Clara and kept asking me 50 times when she was coming over. Tell her, that if Papa agrees, she had much better take him. He is as good-looking as ever—and *so* agreeable and clever. R—— swears by him.

Randolph made a speech the other night about 'Bradlaugh'[2] which was a tremendous success. Everyone was full of it and rushed up and congratulated me to such an extent that I felt as tho' I had made it. I'm told that Tumtum[3] expresses himself highly pleased and the result is that we have been asked to meet both him and the Princess to-morrow, at a dance Lord Fife is to give. I suppose he must have been told to do it as he is about the court officially. Friday I went to two balls both very good.

Such an absurd thing happened yesterday. The Star man[4] was here having tea when a very smart carriage drove up powdered footmen, wigs, silk stockings and inside a very fat old trump. "Who on earth is this old demon?" I said. "Why it's my mother!" the Star confessed. *Tableau!* There are 2 such pretty girls going out now, the Duchess of Newcastle's daughters, they dress so well. The other night they had mauve satin ball dresses, the skirts tulle with little plisses.

Winston and I went yesterday to the Horse Guards for the Queen's

---

[1] The beautiful Yznaga sisters from New York. Consuelo had married Lord Mandeville (Louisa's son) who was to become 8th Duke of Manchester. Natica was engaged to Sir John Lister-Kaye.

[2] The famous renegade of the House of Commons who refused to take the oath.

[3] The Prince of Wales. Queen Victoria was ordering courtiers to effect a reconciliation.

[4] Lord Falmouth who had acted as Lord Randolph's second in the intended duel.

birthday and nearly came to grief in the crowd, had it not been for Lord Valentia who came to the rescue and pulled us out. I've seen nothing of Johnny Kaye of late. I'm told that Mrs. Candy is in love with him and much to his ennui rushed about after him. The other day she heard him asking me if he might come to tea—and to my astonishment *she* appeared! I'm glad to say he did not turn up so she was sold! Consuelo proposed herself to dinner the other night. We had old Chancellor Ball and Lord Portarlington and she being *en veine*, insisted on telling 'roguey poguey' stories, which I think astonished them—they did me! Quite between ourselves I think it *du plus mauvais goût* to talk like that before men.

Best love *et à bientot*.

Yr. loving,
Jennie."

The members of the Fourth Party were naturally Jennie's closest friends. Sir Henry Wolff had admired the Jerome girls since their early days in Cowes, and John Gorst, as well as Arthur Balfour, possessed musical tastes, so that when the House allowed, she swept "half the Fourth party" off to concerts. Balfour could play Beethoven and Schumann with her, and she kept a letter of his dated 1883:

"House of Commons.

My dear Lady Randolph,

I am groaning and swearing on this beastly bench: while you are listening to Wagnerian discords, I am listening to Irish grumblings, there is a great deal of brass in both of them; otherwise there is not much resemblance! I am sitting next ——, I might be sitting next you! I am an unhappy victim. However, there is no choice. Monday night is a most unlucky one for Richter: the Irish have a talent for turning everything into an Irish debate; and when the Irish speak I must answer, as I have just been endeavouring to do!

Your miserable servant,
Arthur James Balfour."

Gladstone's Government vainly sought to shelve the stark Irish Question, while the peasants grew more desperate, the crops failed more regularly and amid scenes of riot and misery evictions continued.

It was upon the subject of evictions that "Lord Randolph delivered the first of those Irish speeches which, in the course of the next three years, were to win him acceptance as an authority upon the Irish question". His years in Ireland had equipped him "for the discussion of the one vast and pre-

Winston with his younger brother John
1884

The Leonard Jeromes
1887

dominant question of the day. He took rank almost at once among those to whom Parliament would most gladly or most gravely listen upon Irish affairs".

After the terrible winter of 1880–81, Parnell, himself a landlord, had invented the process of "boycotting". Any man who evicted peasants unable to pay their rents was to be 'segregated'. No Irish person would speak to him, serve him in a shop, or work on his fields. The method first tried out on Captain Boycott, a landlord's agent, proved effective and stemmed a number of thoughtless evictions.

General Gordon who visited the west of Ireland at the time has left an impartial Englishman's impression:

"I must say that the state of our fellow countrymen in the parts I have named, is worse than that of any people in the world, let alone Europe. I believe that these people are made as we are; that they are patient beyond belief; loyal, but broken spirted and desperate; lying on the verge of starvation in places where we would not keep cattle."

In the spring of 1882 Randolph became ill, and Jennie took him to America for a few months' rest. Leonard assessed his son-in-law as "frail but fiery", and told Clara: "I think Jennie is wonderful for him, he draws on her strength. I love having them here. I believe completely in R."

All through the following winter Randolph assailed Mr. Gladstone on the questions of Ireland and Egypt, but he fought almost as hard within his own party, for it had become his firm intention to force the replacement of Sir Stafford Northcote by Lord Salisbury.

Mr. Gladstone was sensitive to the terrible working conditions created by the Industrial Revolution but despite his efforts and promises factory life remained a hell on earth, and the disillusioned workers turned wildly to any new leader. 'Randy's' clear-cut views, and sense of reality, aroused roars of acclamation wherever he spoke. Only he and Mr. Gladstone could draw such crowds. Liberals and Radicals raged with fury at the sight of a young aristocrat stealing their thunder with the working men. His own party watched with raised eyebrows, and made what use they could of this "meteor whirling in our midst". But meteors are always regarded with caution and usually with distrust.

"Give it to 'em hot, Randy," was the cry of the street crowds and *The Times* and *Morning Post* began to record his speeches verbatim.

The world of rank and fashion watched with annoyance, and yet with respect, for he raised his party from oblivion when he proclaimed: "I hope before long to see Tory working men in Parliament. . . . If you want to gain the confidence of the working classes, let them have a share, and a large share, a real share, and not a sham share, in your party Councils."

Only Randolph would have used the word *sham*.

Lady Blandford had divorced her husband just before he became duke so for a time Jennie acted as châtelaine but she wrote "it is hardly a success for my American efficiency will out and they call me bossy."

In the late autumn Randolph took Jennie and little Winston abroad. They explored the Swiss and German mountains, and at Gastein had tea with the Emperor William I of Germany. Randolph wrote:

"The Emperor, I must admit, was very guarded in his conversation, which was confined to asking me how long I had been here, and whether I had come for my health. My wife, however, sat by him at tea, and had much conversation which, I have ascertained, was confined to the most frivolous topics. I have reason to believe, though it is humiliating to confess it, that the fame of the Fourth Party has not yet reached the ears of this despot. I must say he is a very fine old fellow, and the Germans seem to love him. There were several other Prussians and Austrians present; but I was rather bored on the whole and so was my wife."

Jennie was not too bored to note the Emperor's diet while on a cure: "He began with poached eggs, and went on to potted meats, and various strange German dishes, added many cups of strong tea, and ended with strawberries, ices, and sweet, tepid champagne."

41

WHEN Lord Randolph returned to London the Third Reform Bill, which was to increase the English electorate from three million to five million, had started its stormy progress through the House. Lord Randolph with the other Tories opposed this Bill, showing a strangely reactionary outlook for one who later was to appeal so deeply to the people.

He constantly tried to exact legislation which would better the Irish people's material condition, but he considered Home Rule "impossible" and certainly not beneficial to the Irish. Brilliant as Lord Randolph's speeches are they contain many sublime errors. "We owe the Irish a great deal for our bad government of them in the past," he said, and then proceeded with the remedy, "if we are not stingy, there are few injuries, however deep, which money will not cure".

The Irish care nothing for money and cherish injury.

From December 1884 until March 1885, Randolph travelled through India shooting tigers. When he returned, the excitement of the forthcoming General Election had superseded the dramas of Irish Nationalism and Russian aggression. "It is not easy to estimate, and quite impossible to explain, the personal ascendancy which he had by this time acquired in the House of Commons." "What place will you give him when the Government is formed?" a friend asked Sir Stafford Northcote. "Say rather," replied the Prime Minister presumptive, "what place will he give me?"

This passage was repeated to Randolph who was heading the movement to replace Northcote by Lord Salisbury. With unthinking cruelty he murmured, "I had no idea he had so much wit."

Randolph's assertions on the "indisposition of Sir Stafford for acute party warfare" were presumptuous. He often doubted the outcome of his stand, and fell prey to bouts of depression.

To a friend in the Turf Club he said: "I am very near the end of my tether. In the last five years I have lived twenty. I have fought Society. I have fought Mr. Gladstone at the head of a great majority. I have fought the Front Opposition Bench. Now I am fighting Lord Salisbury. I have said

I will not join the Government unless Northcote leaves the House of Commons. Lord Salisbury will never give way. I'm done."

But Northcote was persuaded to retire to the House of Lords and brilliant Sir Michael Hicks Beach became Leader of the House of Commons in his stead.

Having triumphed Randolph accepted the office of Secretary of State for India which, owing to the anxieties caused by Russian moves towards Afghanistan, could be considered the most important post after the Foreign Office.

On joining the Government, a member had to seek re-election in his constituency. Over-pressed by ministerial work of importance he allowed Jennie, who had always accompanied him on political gatherings, to fight the election for him. She bought a new bonnet, memorized necessary speeches and hurried to the Bear Hotel, Woodstock, which she and Randolph's sister Lady Georgiana Curzon made Tory Headquarters. The seat was uncertain and in some anxiety Sir Henry Wolff, Lord Curzon and Sir Frederick Milner travelled down to aid the two ladies, but Lady Randolph and Lady Georgiana, sure that none could conduct a campaign better than themselves, rose to the occasion superbly. "We were most important, and felt that the eyes of the world were upon us. Revelling in the hustle and bustle of the committee-rooms, marshalling our forces, and hearing the hourly reports of how the campaign was progressing, I felt like a general holding a council-of-war with his staff in the heat of a battle."

There were only a thousand voters in Woodstock and all could be approached personally. Lady Georgiana, a fine driver, brought down her tandem, and they decorated the horses with ribbons of pink and brown, Randolph's racing colours. Together the two ladies trotted through the countryside, smiling and waving to the folk they knew, stopping to cajole those they doubted.

Their faces were well known to all around Blenheim, and only on the very outskirts of "Marlborough territory" did jeers arise. But these Jennie turned to good account. Off on her own, out of earshot of the committee, she dared throw aside the usual political slogans and speak as she liked. Randolph might have winced had he heard her but, on the whole, she found "Please vote for my husband, I shall be so unhappy if you don't," accompanied by an appealing smile, more effective than diatribes against Gladstone's policy. It was a dour fellow indeed who could resist the spell of Jennie Churchill when she drove into the fields, climbed on a hayrick and with flushed cheeks begged for a vote.

At the end of a fortnight everyone concerned was worn out except the two ladies. Lord Randolph won by 532 to 405. Jennie's triumphant farewell speech from the Bear Hotel ended by thanking the electors "from the bottom of my heart". She returned to London in a state of elation, and wrote her father: "It must have quite gone to my head for it seemed odd the crowds in the city streets did not recognize and applaud me."

Certain people wondered if such canvassing could be deemed entirely fair. Not many members possessed a sister with a saucy tandem, and none a wife with Jennie's eyes. Jingles on the subject were printed:

> But just as I was talking
> With Neighbour Brown and walking
> To take a mug of beer at the Unicorn and Lion
> (For there's somehow a connection
> Between free beer and election),
> Who should come but Lady Churchill, with a turnout that was fine.
>
> And before me stopped her horses,
> As she marshalled all her forces,
> And before I knew what happened I had promised her my vote;
> And before I quite recovered
> From the vision that had hovered,
> 'Twas much too late to rally, and I had changed my coat.
>
> And over Woodstock darted
> On their mission brave, whole-hearted,
> The tandem and their driver and the ribbons pink and brown.
> And a smile that twinkled over,
> And that made a man most love her,
> Took the hearts and votes of all Liberals in the town.
>
> Bless my soul! that Yankee lady,
> Whether day was bright or shady,
> Dashed about the district like an oriflamme of war.
> When the voters saw her bonnet,
> With the bright pink roses on it,
> They followed as the soldiers did the Helmet of Navarre.

Sir Henry James the Attorney General wrote:

> "New Court, Temple, 1885.

My dear Lady Randolph,

    You must let me very sincerely and heartily congratulate you on the result of the election, especially as that result proceeded so very much from your personal exertions. Everybody is praising you very much.

But my gratification is slightly impaired by feeling I must introduce a new Corrupt Practices Act. Tandems must be put down, and certainly some alteration, a correspondent informs me, must be made in the means of ascent and descent therefrom; then arch looks have to be scheduled, and nothing must be said 'from my heart'. The graceful wave of a pocket handkerchief will have to be dealt with in committee.

Still, I am very glad

Yours most truly,
Henry James."

42

THE quarrel between the Prince of Wales and Lord Randolph Churchill had simmered on. An early attempt to rectify the breach ended badly. Lord Randolph received a summons to the Prince's levée; he wished to avoid it, but friends persuaded him to go. By some misunderstanding His Royal Highness had not been alerted of Randolph's presence; he stared in cold surprise at the gentleman whom he had challenged to a duel, and Randolph, considering himself insulted, returned home pale with fury saying that he had been "caddishly trapped" and then cut. The friends who had busied themselves preparing this reconciliation did not dare approach and even Jennie with nerves of iron departed to the country to recover from "such seething and fulminating".

In 1883 Queen Victoria took pains to end the feud, and Jennie attended a Drawing Room at the Queen's special wish. Aware of Randolph's white-hot pride, the Prince started to send messages suggesting that a reconciliation might lie within the dignity of both parties. For seven years society had found itself in a dilemma whenever the two antagonists approached the same house, and dramatic as this may have seemed at the beginning it had devolved into a great bore. Now, as Queen Victoria doubtless observed, it might soon prove embarrassing to have a Minister of the Crown who could not speak to his future Sovereign.

After the reconciliation had been effected, Jennie marked the event by giving a dinner party for the Prince and Princess of Wales, at which Mr. and Mrs. Gladstone and Lord Rosebery were among the guests. The conversation proved so animated there was no possibility for awkward thoughts, or looks, or even silences to occur.

In March 1886 H.R.H. took pains to be gracious to Mr. Leonard Jerome, who was staying near him in Cannes, complimenting him on what he had done to further horse-racing in America, on his sailing prowess and above all on his three remarkable daughters. Leonard copied out the terms of the big American Stakes for the Prince, who was astonished to hear of the large number of nominations in forthcoming years.

While Randolph held the India Office Queen Victoria sent for Jennie, and personally bestowed on her the Order of the Crown of India, a pretty affair of pearl and turquoise which, if it added but vaguely to her prestige, would certainly enhance any evening dress. Jennie travelled down to Windsor Castle by train. Her outfit had been decreed by a card from a lady-in-waiting:

"The Lady Randolph Churchill:
Bonnet and morning dress: grey gloves. To Kiss the Queen's hand after receiving the decoration, like the gentlemen to-day. A room will be prepared for her."

The Queen, wearing a long white veil, stood with her back to the window so that an aureole shone around her plump little figure. With a few kind words she tried to pin the Order on to Jennie, but alas the best velvet dress embroidered thickly with jet gave no hold, and after some prodding her Majesty ran the pin straight into Jennie's shoulder. With difficulty the honoured lady restrained a squeak of pain but the Queen saw her start and was much concerned at having spiked a loyal subject. Eager as Jennie was to note details concerning this seldom-seen sovereign, Queen Victoria seems to have been equally interested in the most talked-of beauty of the day. Next morning a note arrived:

"Windsor Castle, Dec. 5th.
My dear Lady Randolph,
I hope you got home quite comfortably yesterday, and took no cold. The Queen told me she thought you so handsome, and that it had all gone off so well.

Believe me ever,
Yours truly,
Jane Ely."

This note was proudly placed among the invitations on the mantelpiece of her new drawing-room. No. 2 Connaught Place, beside Marble Arch, was now the Churchills' house, and this she had decorated with panelling which the fogs could not destroy. Although on an amateur basis Jennie had, in fact, become the first interior decorator.

Shortly after the pinning episode, Lord and Lady Randolph were commanded to Windsor for the night. They dined in a small room hung with Winterhalter portraits. Jennie found the habit of conversing in whispers when in the royal presence was to put it mildly, "conducive to shyness".

When Her Majesty spoke, even the whispers ceased, and the answer to any question had to be given in a silence where one dropped fork would have clattered like castanets. Jennie felt once more the Queen's cold grey eye rove slowly over her. Fervently she hoped that her dress was not a shade too low, her colour too high or her answers too pat. "I tried hard to keep my tongue under control," she said later. "You know how I tend to rattle on, and I was terrified of saying a word too much, and arousing that dread 'We are not amused.'"

In December, when the General Election took place, Lord Randolph attacked in the Liberal stronghold of Birmingham. Jennie found the Duchess of Marlborough had now become her ally and had ceased to resent that unfair endowment of beauty. Together they tramped through miles of slums, canvassing house by house and addressing men in factories. It was the first time that women had attempted personal canvassing in industrial slums and they found the workers resentful. As both parties always seemed more interested in obtaining a majority in the House than actually bettering the wretched industrial conditions this was hardly surprising. When the Duchess, shaken by bad language, retreated from a doorway, Jennie rallied her. She had to put her own wits and courage to the test as never before. Soon she found it easier to cease argument and trade on her appeal instead. As long as Randolph was not watching she was ready to use any methods. One day she met sullen silence in a factory.

"Why are you all so cross?" she asked.

A man stood up. "We don't like being asked for our votes."

"But you have something I want. How am I to get it if I do not ask?"

They stared at her and began to laugh.

Jennie's method of approaching 'the people', her easy manners with grocer's wife and butcher's lady, permeated the Conservative Primrose League until sedate English peeresses declared themselves ready to capture votes 'by hook or by crook'. "Would it not be too vulgar?" gasped a member, when an entertainment was being discussed by the Ladies' Council. Lady Salisbury, wife of England's Conservative Prime Minister, rose up: "Vulgar? Of course it is vulgar, that is why we have got on so well."

Lord Randolph did not manage to defeat the famous John Bright in Central Birmingham, but his new Tory Democracy obtained considerable success in other working-class centres. Having altered the vote from 2 Liberals to 1 Tory to 3 Liberals to 2 Tories, Lord Randolph returned to London and was elected for South Paddington, his home district. In the House 335 Liberals were returned against 249 Conservatives and 86 Parnellites. This meant that Gladstone could not swing a majority. And the Tory resurrection was entirely due to Randolph.

The country proceeded to wait for Gladstone's decision on Home Rule, "the dream of a sun-lit Ireland, loyal because it was free, prosperous and privileged because it was loyal, the crowning glory of an old man's life, all find their place in that immense decision".

On January 26th, Lord Salisbury's "Cabinet of Caretakers" resigned and Gladstone formed his own Ministry. Throughout the spring, the confused and divided parties prepared their stand on the Irish Bill which was to be the tombstone of the Grand Old Man. In June, Gladstone brought the Home Rule debate to a close with his splendid speech, that which ended with:

". . . the ebbing tide is with you and the flowing tide is with us. Ireland stands at your bar, expectant, hopeful, almost suppliant. Her words are the words of truth and soberness. She asks a blessed oblivion of the past, and in that oblivion our interest is deeper than even hers. . . . Think I beseech you—think well, think wisely, think not a moment, but for the years that are to come, before you reject this Bill."

Protestant Ulster, the nettle which Gladstone had never really dared to grasp, roared that it would fight if the Bill went through and the huge Liberal core of industrial England expressed dissent from its own Prime Minister's view. That night the Liberal party split. Amidst tumultuous shouts, the Bill for Home Rule was rejected by 341 votes to 311, and the six-month-old Government fell. Gladstone saw that Irish Home Rule had broken his own party in two. "The Parliament so lately returned in his support had destroyed itself, almost before it had lived, rather than follow him further." Parliament was dissolved, and on July 1st the country went to the polls for the second time in six months, with only one issue in mind: to vote for or against parliamentary union with Ireland.

43

IN THE summer of 1886 came the most exciting election of the century. Life-long friends fought each other bitterly. An entirely new cleavage arose. Between Home-Rule Liberals and Liberal-Unionists arose a rift which threw the latter into the Tory camp. Sure of his London seat, Randolph spoke only in Manchester and Birmingham the enemy strongholds.

The voters of England showed their opinion sharply—Gladstone and the Home Rulers were utterly defeated. Lord Salisbury became Prime Minister and Randolph accepted the responsibility of two high offices, that of Leader of the House of Commons and that of Chancellor of the Exchequer.

"How long will your leadership last?" asked a friend.

"Six months," Lord Randolph laughed.

"And after that?"

"Westminster Abbey."

Jennie saw her husband, at the age of thirty-six, entrusted with two of the most important appointments in England. He was the natural leader of his party; the Conservatives did not love him, but they could not do without him: "the double fascination of mystery and success lent him an air of authority, which neither irreverent language nor the impulsive frankness of youth could dispel".

Happily, Randolph also possessed a serious side, for as Disraeli noticed: "An insular people subject to fogs and possessing a powerful middle class, requires grave statesmen." Lord Justice Fitzgibbon wrote:

"if I were you I would rather not be obliged to carry as Leader the financial reputation of the State, in addition to the rest of the load. The English are your sheet-anchor and finance is their pole-star; and a middle-aged commercial Chancellor would make them easy in their minds when you could not."

Tackling the Irish Question, Randolph proposed monetary drafts to help the deep-sea fishing industry, to improve railways, and to drain bogland around the great rivers. Parnell hurled back these offers of material assistance, and the Irish Nationalists listened in moody silence whenever the new Chancellor of the Exchequer rose to speak. "You must find it very hard work," said a friend, "leading the House, and at the same time being at the Exchequer."

"Not half such hard work as it was getting there," he riposted.

When the session ended Randolph kept up a continual correspondence with Lord Salisbury on the subject of Russian angling for the Dardanelles.

"If Russia attacked Constantinople," observed Salisbury, "and all the other Powers refused to intervene, I am rather disposed to the idea that we should have to act in the Dardanelles."

Randolph wrote back fretfully at the Foreign Office: "I feel sure that our present niggling, meddling, intriguing, fussy policy is gaining for us the contempt and dislike of Bismarck every day."

In October "young Churchill" aroused unprecedented feeling when he said in a speech:

"I will not conceal from you that my own special object, to which I hope to devote whatever energy and strength or influence I may possess, is to endeavour to attain some genuine and considerable reduction of public expenditure and consequent reduction of taxation."

Then he proceeded to outline England's foreign policy regarding Russia. "There are other Powers," he proclaimed in the tactful manner of the day, "who betray from time to time a regrettable tendency towards contentious and even aggressive action." It was England's duty to support the liberty-loving Powers of Europe "in whose favour our timely adhesion would probably, and without the use of force, decide the issue".

For those days it was plain speaking. Russia would not be allowed a walk-over to Constantinople. Lord Randolph Churchill's name suddenly resounded throughout Europe. No statesman had spoken so clearly for years.

Randolph's career had been swift and dazzling. The House of Commons, a hard school, had moulded him, and now it responded instinctively to his oratory. Jennie began to take it for granted that her husband would reach the post of Prime Minister. But in late December, he contradicted the Cabinet concerning the Budget.

After an emphatic disagreement with Mr. Smith the War Minister, Lord Salisbury wrote: "The Cabinet, happily not I, will have to decide the controversy between you and Smith. But it will be a serious responsibility to refuse the demands of a War Minister so little imaginative. . . ."

On December 20th, 1886, Lord Randolph was summoned to Windsor

Castle. He spent the evening with the Queen who appeared to delight in his company and kept him long in conversation. On this occasion her Chancellor seemed unusually gay and vivacious. He spoke on many topics, but never mentioned that he was ready to pledge his career on reducing armament expenditure. Late that night, on Windsor Castle note-paper, he wrote his famous letter of resignation to Lord Salisbury saying:

> "I am pledged up to the eyes to large reductions of expenditure, and I cannot change my mind on this matter. If the foreign policy of this country is conducted with skill and judgment, our present huge and increasing armaments are quite unnecessary, and the taxation which they involve, perfectly unjustifiable. . . ."

Lord Salisbury wrote back a long letter ending with

> "no one knows better than you how injurious to the public interests at this juncture your withdrawal from the Government may be.
> In the presence of your very strong and decisive language I can only again express my very profound regret."

But the Prime Minister did not communicate the matter to the Queen until a second letter arrived from Randolph, formally taking leave of the Government. This letter only reached the Prime Minister at half past one in the morning of December 23rd. He immediately sent the news to Windsor; but before midnight Lord Randolph had left the theatre, where in a box Jennie sat, gay and unguessing, to impart his information to *The Times*. The first inkling Her Majesty received of Randolph's resignation was, therefore, when she opened her morning paper. With cold fury she sent an enquiry concerning this breach of etiquette. The fact that his letter of resignation had been written on *her* notepaper seemed the last straw.

For some inscrutable reason, Randolph allowed *The Times* to inform his wife as well as his Queen. Jennie came down to breakfast stunned, with the newspaper in her hand.

"Quite a surprise for you," smiled Randolph.

Mr. Moore, a devoted official from the Treasury, rushed in, pale and distracted. "He has thrown himself from the top of the ladder, and will never reach it again!" Moore, who adored his chief, collapsed and died within a month of broken heart.

Randolph offered no explanation. He had pledged his word to economize. He was confident and had gambled all his power on one throw. Jennie felt too crushed and miserable to remonstrate or even to question.

During the next few days England spoke of nothing save 'the resignation'. Friends rushed to Connaught Place to bewail Randolph's eccentricity, and sycophants disappeared. Queen Victoria intimated her extreme displeasure, and Randolph's letter of apology to her was frigidly received.

"How well I remember my bitter feelings in those days!" wrote Jennie. "The political atmosphere round us seemed suddenly full of strife and treachery. It was gall and wormwood to me to hear Randolph abused in every quarter, often it seemed by the men who owed their political existence to him."

He certainly ruined Christmas for all his friends, especially for the Ministers who had to return from sporting holidays.

For two weeks the Government tottered and then, discovering, perhaps with a sigh of relief, that it might hold together without Churchill, appointed a Chancellor less incisive and a Leader less wayward. None possessed Randolph's brilliance, but was such brilliance necessary or really very safe? The Tories he led to victory had always feared this Radical in their midst. But they thought he was young, that he would learn from a hard lesson and come back to their fold, still with his fire but chastened.

Only Jennie watching with desperate anxiety saw the health begin to ebb from that frail taut body. She knew that, for good or for bad, he had shot his bolt, and that in his own words, "with profound regret, but without doubt or hesitation", Lord Randolph Churchill had renounced power for ever.

44

DURING the years of Randolph's rise to fame, Mr. and Mrs. Leonard Jerome had, for financial reasons, lived chiefly in New York, and Clara and Leonie had both been married there in Grace Church, where the smart set always made their nuptial pledges.

Clara married first. She had hovered between offers in France and England, while her mother, fussing like a hen, never considered any suitor quite up to standard. Yet as the years slid by Mrs. Jerome found the daily hours of chaperonage grow tedious. Whenever a gentleman called to see Miss Clara, her mama was expected to sit at the other end of the room pretending to be busy on embroidery, too far to hear what words were exchanged but "within sight". Mrs. Jerome, grown accustomed to her own little coterie of cultured Parisian admirers, found this insufferably boring. "So dull to listen to young people, but even duller to not quite be able to hear." She had always hoped for a big European marriage. With disappointment she realized the unlikelihood of this occurrence now that the girls' dowries were reduced.

No sooner had the Jeromes settled back in Madison Square than a trickle of romantic-minded Englishmen began to call. Several of them had crossed the Atlantic especially to press their suits, but the one who captured Clara appeared from the west where he had been exploring the buffalo trails of the Big Horn Mountains. Moreton Frewen strode noisily into the New York scene, talking of cattle ranches for British lords in Wyoming, of converting the American Government to different financial views, of saving the great herds of wild fauna in national parks, and various other schemes. Senator Jones of Nevada had told him, "it's no good hunting foxes with a brass band", but this was a lesson he would never learn.

Clara took one look at this tall sunburnt self-assertive sportsman and fell in love. She learnt that he came of an old Sussex family, that he was a famous shot and one of the best gentlemen riders in England. Neither she nor her parents could guess at the strange future she had accepted for herself.

The second son of a Squire who considered himself the first Commoner in Sussex, Moreton Frewen had been brought up in the grand English tradition by gamekeepers, poachers and grooms. His boyhood was spent on horseback, hunting in the shires, or riding alone over Salisbury Plain. He could catch salmon and jump double-oxers with art, and he knew every wild bird of England. He also learned to read and write and at eighteen proceeded to Trinity College, Cambridge, where he enjoyed polo, steeple-chasing, and lent a kindly hand "nursing friends back to consciousness when they crashed over timber". During an Irish holiday he rode and won the famous midnight point-to-point race in Monaghan against Lord Rossmore, but this did not prevent him being "sent down" from the University. He spent the next six years hunting in Meath and Leicestershire, or riding steeple-chasers against sporting lords. At Melton he rode in fine company with Bay Middleton, Whyte Melville and Lord Lonsdale. The *Cream of Leicestershire* shows him on its cover riding through the railway cut on the day of the great Ranksborough run of January 20th, 1877. Men say yet "ride straight as they rode it from Ranksborough Gorse".

In 1878 he had to decide between a Polar expedition in James Gordon Bennett's ill-fated yacht *Jeannette*, mastership of the Kilkenny Hounds, or the career of cattle-puncher. With £16,000 in his pocket he set out to explore Texas: "my capital was but a younger son's portion—that and some ability to ride young horses". Across the Red River he saw thousands of buffalo skeletons covering the plains. Three million of these animals had been shot by hunters in the last four years and the Southern herd was almost extinct. Moreton learnt that a 'bad man' with brown eyes need not be feared, but "the fellow with grey eyes or grey-blue, whose eyes went darker as they looked down a gun—that was the sort of man to reckon with". With a notebook containing this and various other pieces of useful information, he returned to England for the racing season. When he placed all his winnings on a horse ridden by his friend, the famous Fred Archer, "The dear handsome little horse just failed to get home," and this decided him to return finally to "the Wild West". Lord Dunmore, Lord Lonsdale and Lord Desborough were Moreton's best friends. He advised them excitedly of the wealth of Colorado and Wyoming which he was off to exploit, and suggested they follow with all their immense capital.

In his wake the "great silent places between the Yellowstone and the Peace River two thousand miles north" became alive with adventurous English gentlemen.

The Crows and the Blackfeet were growing antagonistic to white invaders but they used Moreton, who was a splendid shot, to pick out buffalo for them. Seeking to ride in winter over the Great Divide of the Rockies which had been a main buffalo trail, ". . . a trail the vast herds of old times used and by which, in their spring migrations, they got up from the prairie into the mountains for summer grazing", Moreton and his brother with two other men were caught by deep snow. All would have perished had they not been able to head off a section of a huge buffalo herd into the mountains and follow over the tightly packed snow, using the stampeding animals as a living snowplough. "At one or two deep transverse drifts the leaders plunged in and went clean out of sight, but in a few yards they bobbed out again like porpoises playing through a wave." High in the mountains the buffalo left them. But the narrow path above the canyon was now clear of snow and they rode safely down to Powder River. To south, east and north they could see two hundred miles—all virgin prairie which was to fill up with settlers and cattle in the next five years.

"Of course we had no realization that we had accomplished a journey that no man in all probability would ever attempt again—the passage of the main range of the Rockies from Camp Brown on the west, to Fort McKinney on the east, in December."

Soon indeed the attempt would have been impossible, for there were no buffalo or herds of wapiti to keep the canyon trails open.

Moreton and his brother decided the prairies around Powder River would make perfect cattle country. They built a house of pine, and then Moreton started alone on the two-hundred-mile ride to Rock Creek, the nearest railway. His horse lamed itself at 'Forty Mile Ranch' so, leaving it there, he proceeded to walk the remaining forty miles. "I was wonderfully well after five months of such conditioning as I had gone through, lean and hard and tough as pin-wire." He started at sunrise but falling into a field of breaking snow, took twenty-six hours to cover the forty miles.

"I battled through this snow field nearly all night, the temptation to go to sleep almost irresistible but at about 3 a.m. I seemed to get my 'second wind'. . . . It was truly a great escape, and it is said that old-timers out there still tell the tale of that legendary walk!"

Soon he was on the train to New York determined to save the great game herds of the Big Horn Mountains. Congress had segregated the Yellowstone Park but, as snow covered up all winter feeding there, the park was worthless for the big wild fauna. In Washington Mr. Frewen pushed forward proposals to include the whole Wind River basin in the park. This area was free of settlers and harboured fifty thousand buffalo, and twice that number of wapiti. "Had it been made a sanctuary for wild life, there would to-day have been a pleasance for the naturalist and traveller; but the fates decreed otherwise and so the great game herds rapidly disappeared."

Few listened to Mr. Frewen in Washington but he himself picked up a life-long passion for Bi-metallism, and proceeded to New York defending Free Silver as well as buffalo, with his natural gift of the gab. Such was the gentleman, lean, strong and opinionated, who caught the eye of Miss Jerome. Leonard naturally took a liking to this original adventurer.

"My predestined father-in-law Leonard Jerome, one of the kindliest of men, was the centre for a brilliant coterie to which I had the entrée. Stammering and witty Bill Travers, and equally witty Senator Evarts . . . and travelled men blew in from the uttermost ends of the earth, Lord Dunraven, Jones of Nevada, Lords Kintore and Dunmore and 'Uncle Larry'. I doubt if on the earth's surface did such a far-flung group of men ever collect round a single table."

After a brief glance at Miss Clara, and a not-too modest recital of his exploits in the Big Horn Mountains, Moreton disappeared to Wyoming, where he spent a year driving cattle. Clara returned to England and heard of his prowess as a horseman all during the following winter. She sighed, and the vision of a hard-limbed adventurer struggling through the Rocky Mountains caused her to continue refusing all marriage proposals, even those which Jennie strongly advised accepting!

In 1881, with no little excitement, the social columns of the New York Press announced the engagement of Leonard Jerome's eldest daughter to Mr. Moreton Frewen, squire of England and present owner of a pine log house on Powder River. The Frewens had inhabited Brickwall, a large Elizabethan mansion, since the days when Good Queen Bess visited them (and left a pair of satin shoes which still remain). They were one of the oldest landowning families in England but their fortunes were depleted, their sons scattering and the heritage of Brickwall was for the eldest only. Clara did not care.

Moreton spent the day before his marriage in the Union Club with Leonard and Pierre Lorillard, waiting to hear the results of the Derby. As well as racing his yacht *Vesta* (which had competed in the great Atlantic Race), Mr. Lorillard kept a stud farm in New Jersey for mares of the Glencoe-Lexington strain, so famous for stamina. "Mares they were with wonderful legs and feet; with the girth of a dray-horse and the back and loin of a short-horn cow."

Lorillard had entered *Iroquois* in the English Derby. The "ticker" was ticking. Lorillard had the tape between his fingers when there slowly spelled out—"Derby Stakes. Epsom. Won by Iroq . . ."

"Oh," he cried. "My horse!"

Moreton exploded. "The first American to win the Derby and he is not there!"

All that night Leonard and Moreton and Lorillard celebrated the great win. On the following morning, Leonard led his eldest daughter up to the altar of Grace Church. She had arrived very late—for Mrs. Jerome was in tears—and Moreton had retreated nervously to the vestry with his best man, Lord Bagot, where, to her amazement, Miss Jerome, waiting in a cloud of white tulle, heard them still heatedly discussing *Iroquois*.

After the service Leonard hung a string of diamonds around Clara's throat. Then, when the huge reception had ended, with her trousseau packed in studded trunks and her own French maid (for she was incapable of doing up her own boots), Clara set forth on a honeymoon to be spent cattle ranching! As the train roared westwards the maid's face grew steadily longer. By the time she had seen Madame's wonderful trousseau carried out at the railway point of Rock Creek and driven two hundred miles over a rough trail to that house of pine logs she was on the verge of hysteria.

"It's quite safe," comforted Mr. Frewen. The last Indian raid had taken place in the previous year when a cattle buyer had, on leaving the Frewen ranch, been killed by a band of travelling Sioux. Moreton's brother Dick had chased the Indians for weeks but never caught up with them. He found it not unnatural that the Indians should be averse to the decimation of the buffalo herds, their only food supply, by white cattle men. "They won't come again, don't worry," laughed Moreton. "If you are nervous try shooting lessons."

Clara thought it a pity that her silk gowns from Paris should have to be packed away, but any life that Moreton planned must be *marvellous*. She was in love. The maid was not.

Young Mrs. Frewen had yet to discover what fate can lie in store for those who marry bronzed Englishmen who emerge from snowdrifts.

45

CLARA transformed the log house into a "dear little hunting box". Animal skins covered the floors and walls and flowering branches were placed on rough tables. With cowboys for company, the French maid fluffed up and Buffalo Bill himself volunteered to act as scout to the dauntless Englishman who was bringing rifles to Johnson County, "a tract hitherto on lease from God to the buffalo".

One dawn shortly after arriving Clara evinced slight surprise when her spouse sat up in bed, suddenly shouted, "A buffalo at the creek!" and seizing his rifle leapt out of the window in his nightshirt. Then she grew accustomed to such occurrences.

Moreton spent all his days driving cattle, camping, fishing, exploring and hunting. After Sir Maurice de Bunsen stalked and shot their only milch cow in mistake for an emaciated buffalo, they lived entirely on fresh meat and fish.

Guests were plentiful, for Moreton's friends, the bucks and beaux of the hunting shires, arrived in droves. In the visitors' book they entered the bears, mountain sheep and puma they killed, but it was agreed not to touch buffalo or deer, except when meat was needed.

Lord Queensberry (of Boxing Code fame), Lord Manners, Lord Caledon, Lord Rodney and Lord Castletown were sportsmen who enjoyed Moreton's hospitality. Less than a day's journey from the house they could camp by Trout Creek and "catch three pounders by the bushel".

Came Lord Mayo and a typical entry reads: "Manners and M.F. killed ninety-five wild duck, mallards, shovellers, widgeon and teal, within a mile of the house." This solved housekeeping problems.

Sir Samuel Baker, a famous sportsman, liked relating his African stories over the camp fire, and discussing with Moreton "the future of our planet, Africa's place in it and our Empire's place." The talk, like the game, was always big. A bear measuring eight-feet-six by eight enters the visitors' book when he attacks a hunter named Hanna, but is killed at fifteen feet range. This day ends with: "Hanna badly mauled but will live."

Clara's life as châtelaine of Powder River ended sadly. When she needed a doctor, Moreton hurried her off to Cheyenne in Buffalo Bill's Deadwood Coach. Her still-born child was sent to New York to be buried in the Jerome family vault, and some weeks later she herself arrived in Madison Square to be nursed back to health while the French maid horrified the other servants with accounts of life on Powder River.

Meanwhile Moreton camped alone, where the lovely Tongue River flows out through its deep canyon. One day while wading about casting he suddenly came on a big bear disporting itself in a pool. He shot the animal through the head, and had resumed his fishing when a passing Englishman shouted that Sitting Bull was in camp near by. Moreton splashed to the bank, hurried off and found Sitting Bull squatting behind his camp fire gnawing a small dog's head. The great chief walked him quarter of a mile to the scene of his battle with three hundred troopers under Captain Custer whom his band had exterminated a few years before, and in sign language explained details of the fight.

Lord Desborough and another English friend, Gilbert Leigh, one of the original four explorers and now a Member of Parliament, came out to stay.

"A few days later a messenger rode in to say that Leigh was missing and asked us to send every available man to help search. By the time we reached their camp his body had been found by Bob Stuart, the trapper. Apparently in the twilight he had mistaken the tree-tops of the pine trees sticking out of a deep canyon for some cypress brush, and had walked on and fallen a hundred feet sheer."

Leonard now ordered Moreton to return to civilization. On reaching New York he found that two former acquaintances from London, Oscar Wilde and Lily Langtry, were scheduled to arrive on the scene. Moreton had been among Mrs. Langtry's many early admirers. He had given her *Redskin*, the horse she rode timorously when accompanied by the Prince of Wales, but he had ceased going to tea at her house because Prince Rudolph of Austria was an "inconveniently frequent visitor there in whose favour *les convenances* obliged me to give place". Mrs. Langtry had introduced him to Wilde, and now that the poet was entertaining New York, Moreton joined in the famous dinners where William Travers and Lawrence Jerome helped Wilde "like mid-wives to deliver his famous *bons mots*". It was Moreton who gave Wilde the famous yarn that Western audiences were requested not to shoot "well-intentioned performers".

In 1885 came the Great Cattle Disaster which wrecked ten millions of British capital. Cleveland, the new American President, ordered the instant removal of half a million cattle from the Indian Reservation of Oklahoma. Moreton's stockman advised quitting Wyoming before the Southern herds arrived. Moreton cabled the directors of his company asking leave to drive his forty-five thousand head of cattle on the hoof to Canada, but they looked at the distance on the map and refused. A kindly Duke became Chairman of the Company. "This lent confidence, though it did not improve the grazing." Two winters later the herds had been starved down to three thousand. Wyoming was eaten out!

Moreton dispatched his wife to England where a 14th-century manor house on the Frewen estates awaited her. On June 23rd, 1885, he made a final note in his ranch visitors' book:

"Am leaving to-morrow via Superior for England, and this abode of pleasant memories and good sport is to be abandoned. The pressure of settlement is driving us cattlemen northward.

It was a perfect summer morning when I left, and with quite a lump in my throat I halted my horses on the ridge, and before passing for ever out of sight took a long last look at the good black and white house which the river folk called 'The Castle'. It had proved the centre for a very short-lived social system."

Moreton strove to move his dying herds northwards. Lawrence Oliphant, the famed Victorian traveller, had long ago told him of a fine land-locked harbour at the end of Lake Superior, and here he bought and cleared a thousand acres of rough swamp and forest. Sheds for a thousand cattle were built, and he fed them with refuse from grain elevators. After a long unsuccessful battle to obtain permission to ship the remnant of his herds to Britain, Moreton sold for a song the thousand acres on which West Superior City now stands and so missed his second fortune. He was always just too early or too late.[1]

Eventually he resigned, passing the Company on to Horace Plunkett who described the saga as "an example of Moreton's brilliant imagination and even prophetic vision aborted by a fatal inability to face inconvenient facts". Lord Rosslyn, a Director, wrote: "Your only fault latterly has been you could not raise money fast enough."

This particular fault remained with him through life. Funds never caught pace with his schemes.

When asked if Frewen were rogue or fool, Lord Desborough, who had lost thousands in Wyoming, answered: "Worse than either. He is a genius."

[1] Streets and schools are named after Frewen to this day but the inhabitants of West Superior City do not know if he was a missionary or a lumber jack.

Ten millions of British capital had literally "gone West" and young Mr. Frewen, who had landed in America eight years before with £16,000, returned to his own country with an overdraft of £30,000. Unable to recognize defeat he wrote airily: "What had destroyed us was the magic growth of settlement and prosperity of the Great West—that and a bull-headed President."

No one could say Moreton was not a trier. No one could call him a satisfactory son-in-law either.

But the story had only just begun. Moreton's mania for changing the world over to Bi-metallism had already caused the Washington Senate to dub him "Silver Tongue". He had yet to earn the nickname of the century: "Mortal Ruin"!

46

AFTER the years of the Great Cattle Catastrophe, Clara Frewen had settled into Brede Place, a beautiful old grey stone house lying derelict on the outskirts of the Frewen estates in Sussex. Built in 1350 it had not been inhabited except by ghosts and gamekeepers for over two hundred years. The old beamed ceilings and walls, the winding oak staircases and vast fireplaces delighted her and she created one of the most interesting homes in England. A garden was laid out under her direction. Roses and yew hedges and sweet-smelling shrubs encircled the dreaming gables and (for she was not Mrs. Jerome's daughter for nothing) a procession of royalties and famous people came to plant trees for her.

There was no running water but servants hauled it in pails from a nearby well, and the earth-privies were emptied exactly as in Elizabethan times. Servants carried candles and arranged flowers and cooked huge meals in the brick-floored Tudor kitchen.

Clara loved this place, the only real home that Moreton ever gave her. She furnished the house with old oak and put high four-posters in the bedrooms. Occasionally a piece would be picked up locally which in the long ago had come from Brede Place. The villagers felt it good to see a Squire's lady in the big house even if the Squire seldom appeared. Here, amidst the flowering Sussex slopes, Clara found peace, and a family of three small children completed her happiness.

Occasionally Moreton came to stay, but not very often, for though ready to lecture the House of Commons and the Washington Senate on their currency needs, he proved singularly averse to paying his own servants' wages, preferring to keep them penniless "as part of the family". Strangely, they stayed on.

Leonard Jerome disapproved of these singular policies and refused to subsidize the Frewen home, but he gave Clara a London house in Aldford Street, and here she entertained Moreton's friends for him. Talk of high finance rang at her dinner-table. Randolph's brother, the Duke of Marlborough, a convinced Bi-metallist, and the economists Lord Courtney and Lord Wenlock, incessantly held forth in "the pretty mauve silk drawing room with the buffalo head on the wall". Clara did not understand one word of finance. She sometimes wondered if they did either.

Having lost every penny in Wyoming, Moreton now resolved to convert the entire world to a different currency standard. He describes his passion thus:

"When I was a little lad I had visited nearly every nest of our British birds, but that of Richardson's skua I had never seen. I heard that afar off, on an islet near Skibbereen there might be seen the nest of this little gull; I pined for the sight of it. I was not allowed to go, and I have never since seen it at its home. The void seemed to sterilize my childhood. I recall it all these years after as one of life's disappointments. There it is! and similarly I came toward early middle life to the conviction that there was but one problem that really mattered—the great problem of Exchange."

Money would prove as elusive as the Skua.

The self-appointed Herald of Bi-metallism, Tariffs, Federalism and Imperial Preference, Moreton darted around the world entertained by princes, listened to by chancellors and admired by sportsmen for his prowess with horse and gun. When creditors pressed for payment of his personal debts he rewarded them by counter-offensives written on notepaper headed "House of Lords", "The Bank of England", or "The White House". He wished it to be understood that

"if I am at Washington I am there for no other purpose: if I turn up in Calcutta, in Hyderabad or Lahore, or Sydney or Ottawa or distant Auckland, it is to learn the currency needs of those far-flung communities and to see whether some welding heat can be generated here and there, such as may close that frightful fracture in the exchanges between eight hundred millions of silver using peoples and the five hundred millions who finance themselves with gold."

Excellent. But the fissure in his own bank account might have been closed first. No hints from his father-in-law dampened Moreton and he relates blithely an incident in the Lobby of the House of Commons when Bright the famous Free Trader passed by.

Lord Courtney to whom he was speaking, clutched at Bright and said, "Do you know anything about this Currency problem?"

"No," said the other icily, staring at Moreton, "but I am credibly informed there are people who do."

Moreton could not be nonplussed:

"Had I tried to explain to him that there could be no Free Trade without fixed exchanges he would have said from sheer ignorance like Gladstone, that 'Bi-metallism is Protection in disguise'."

It was the experts' ignorance which galled Moreton. He was ready to forgive the bewilderment of simply sporting friends such as a master of foxhounds who came up in Mount Street asking: "Frewen, what is all this about Bi-metallism? I read your speech in *The Times* today. Desborough tells me you can explain it in a few words." Moreton would good-naturedly take the arm of such a fellow and, leading him into one of the smart London clubs, deliver a harangue over lunch or dinner. "Thank you very much, Frewen, I feel I've learnt something today," the ordinary Englishman would say, and go off more puzzled than ever. My father said: "Uncle Moreton had a first-class mind untroubled by second thoughts. . . . He passed so quickly from the truths of political economy to the pitfalls of fortune hunting that it was difficult to know whether he was trying to enrich himself or the whole white world."

A sporting trip to Egypt led to the discovery that the Nizam of Hyderabad was suffering a leakage of £10,000 a year from his coffers. Moreton met the Nizam's exiled Prime Minister Sir Salar Jung in Cairo, and speedily converted him to all his theories, political and financial. As the heat grew insupportable, Sir Salar proposed a pleasure trip through the Balkans and they moved off to Athens and Constantinople with a suite of turbaned retainers. The Dardanelles crisis was rising. Moreton 'felt the pulse of the Turk' and decided that it was time the European powers took over Byzantium from the infidel

> "to become the winter resort for half the tired millionaires of the working world, with their steam yachts and private railway cars. Consider its amenities: the countless isles of Greece . . . the sweep of the blue Aegean . . . the great sporting solitudes of the Black Sea littoral", etc. etc.

The Sultan treated Salar Jung with consideration and sent his chief naval aide-de-camp to act as a guide to sight-seeing. "Sir Salar was more or less unmarried and proposed to me to discover for him a Turkish lady who would return to Hyderabad." Moreton spent hours in a Harem trying to buy a wife, but the lady proved too expensive.

The party moved off to Vienna, Berlin and Paris and Moreton's views on the means of stabilizing every country he passed through deeply impressed Sir Salar. Arriving in England, they found that Clara had taken a large house for Goodwood Races. Moreton cheered up her house party with his Indians. "Amuse them," he ordered. So Randolph's brother Marlborough brought his coach and Count Charles Kinsky (the handsome Austrian who rode his own horse Zoedone to victory in the Grand National of 1883 and who remained a lasting admirer of the Jerome sisters) brought an entire Hungarian Band.

Sir Salar was enchanted. Then, forgetting the decree of exile, he obeyed Moreton's orders and started back to India. Moreton cajoled the party along, promising Salar that he would not be executed on arrival. (He knew he could invoke the help of a sporting friend, Lord William Beresford, who was secretary to the Viceroy.)

"I daresay my curiosity to study the great Silver Problem in its home in the Orient was the determining cause, but also I had become attracted by the idea that I should watch the machine of government working in the leading Native State. What a contrast to all I had left behind west of the Missouri River!"

Clara stayed alone in England while Moreton "straightened out the finances of Hyderabad". He lived in Sir Salar's untidy palace, in quarters of "rather tawdry Oriental splendour, but opening out upon a palmcourt with fountains". Sport was produced for Mr. Frewen, and he enjoyed the races which the great nobles attended in bejewelled Durbar costumes. The Nizam seemed to form a high opinion of him, and Moreton's busy mind started on various new plans. "When I left I was full of a great irrigation project which would have utilized some fifteen million acres of the wonderfully rich sugar-cane lands." He had also discovered an extraordinary series of frauds in the official yellow books and these he presented to a Select Committee of the House of Commons.

Clara's wedding present from her father, the necklace of diamonds, had been sold "because of pressing urgency". (When Leonard discovered this he angrily cut Moreton out of his will.) Now the Nizam offered a tiara of brilliants for Mrs. Frewen but for some reason Moreton refused it. Instead Clara was asked to present the ladies of Hyderabad at Court. Queen Victoria mistaking her for a Vice-Reine kissed her, and to her amazement received a kiss back! Poor Clara, blushing with confusion and trying to marshal her Indians who did not understand a word of English, saw the Prince of Wales shaking with laughter and realized she had made a unique breach of etiquette. Vice-Reines receive kisses. Only other Queens kiss back.

Having 'fixed' Hyderabad, Moreton's next venture was a Gold Crushing Machine, designed to extract gold from all the mine-heaps of the world.

Currency investigations had shown there was not enough gold in the world. He proposed to increase it.

A model machine was set up on Clara's dining-table. The Prince of Wales, Lord Randolph Churchill and Mr. Leonard Jerome admired it dubiously while London society eagerly invested thousands of pounds. Moreton, deciding to "skip Africa and India for the first experiment", acquired a share of Broken Hill Mine and sent the invention to Australia. But the machine only worked in miniature. When put into actual practice the ore crushed the crusher! Had Moreton but kept his share of Broken Hill he would still have been a rich man, but he let it slip through his hands like Superior City and, selling all, hurried off after a new hare.

A series of schemes followed and Frewen's long articles on how the Empire should be run appeared in the *Daily Telegraph*. When Moreton was in India a shy youth had committed to his care the MS. of *Plain Tales from the Hills*, which Moreton pressed on various publishers in vain. The *Daily Telegraph* returned the stories as "not up to the paper's standard". Kipling's fame broke soon after, and Moreton used the *Telegraph's* letter to tease them into publishing his own views.

After a plan to bring Siberian timber to England by a North-west passage open three weeks in the year, came one to collect bats' guano from caves in Texas (this ended when samples killed his friends' gardenias). He obtained an option on trams in Denver but let it slip while on a hunting adventure. Leonard Jerome watched with misgivings which slowly turned into amazement and anger. He lost trust in his son-in-law long before London society did. Winning new capital with his smile Moreton launched one splendid crash after another. Before the investors ever recovered from their surprise he was asking them for more money for a fresh venture. An American senator asked him to find an English firm to handle *Pacific Railway Stock* (in which lay real wealth), but he took it to Sir Ernest Cassel who "did not think much of American railways". Then came a non-poisonous disinfectant, made from specially treated sea water. Moreton insisted on pouring it on fish at dinner parties "to stop putrefaction", which annoyed hostesses. His friend Rhodes entered into a long entertaining correspondence from Africa on the subject, but because society did not like its smell Moreton had to relinquish his hold on this new venture.

During all these years Clara struggled to make a lovely setting for her family at Brede and to entertain with brilliance in London. Leonard helped her, for she was a gentle flower ill-suited to such a husband, but a programme of Frewen calamities lay ahead, which not even Leonard's imagination could have encompassed. The Ashcroft Sulphides, with nearly a million of capital, seemed about to reap a fortune when Moreton's option in America proved to be not "entirely correct in its legal form". The company was thrown overboard. Moreton immediately tried to float a new one with a fresh three-quarters of a million "to enable Stead the economist to edit his own newspaper". But in Stead's words: "I defy the Archangel Gabriel himself to do a smart Dialogue upon Bi-metallism." Moreton never ceased to work behind the scenes for his Silver Plan both in England and America and his persistent lobbying on both sides of the Atlantic did result in Penny Postage between the two countries. Leaving Clara with her faithful unpaid servants he explored the resources of the whole world. Prince Rupert, a Pacific port, "the short cut to China and Japan", nearly brought another fortune. So did the pine and cedar of Kenya. "Fifty years to exhaust this forest," cabled Moreton, but his friends were exhausted too. "He believed that, with the best friends as with the best horses, he could get anywhere." But not if you ride them stone dead.

"Being thought rich is the next best thing to being rich," said Moreton. His father-in-law did not agree but what could he do with this "thwarted Elizabethan", who "worked like a typist, lived like a dreamer, travelled like a King"?

"He left babies on other people's doorsteps," said Dr. Jameson.

But in the welter of his gigantic, disastrous schemes it is hard to measure exactly the slightly larger-than-life figure of Mr. Moreton Frewen.

47

IN OCTOBER 1884 Leonie married Lieutenant John Leslie of the Grenadier Guards in Grace Church. The event caused considerable excitement in the brittle little social world of New York City, for the youngest Miss Jerome had dallied with several Americans, and Leonard fervently hoped that at least one of his daughters would settle in his own land.

For several years Freddie Gebhard, described as "an amusing fellow who could perfectly render imitations of a cock crowing" and again as "the most fascinating of playboys", had tagged at her heels. Despite his riches, which impressed other mamas, Mrs. Jerome refused to admit he would make a desirable son-in-law, but Leonard liked him. They spent a few weeks together at Saratoga, where Leonard and Freddie enjoyed the fabulous casino called 'Canfield's Club House'. Once Freddie Gebhard won $10,000 there. He 'joshed' Canfield late at night: "Don't worry, Dick. I'll come over for breakfast in the morning and you can get even." Everyone liked Freddie, but Leonie announced, "If I hear Freddie crow like a rooster again, I shall go mad."

So that was that. Freddie bounced off on the rebound with Lily Langtry to whom Moreton introduced him "to stop any grizzling over Leonie".

His youngest daughter had maddened Mr. Jerome by leading on Charlie Fitzwilliam, one of the eight sons of Earl Fitzwilliam of Wentworth in England. Several letters survive and tell a most uncomfortable story. "Darling Kismet," starts one sent on an October day in 1880 when Leonie was returning to America.

> "One line just as you start to wish you happiness and comfort, cheer yourself darling with this assurance I am thinking of you with the tenderest truest and most devoted affections it is possible for any man to have for a woman. Darling Leonie, etc. etc. etc."

On the following New Year's Day when his father, rich cross old Lord Fitzwilliam, master of four packs of hounds and acres of Yorkshire coal mines, has threatened to cut his allowance, Charlie writes a lugubrious seven pages:

"Oh my darling will you let this new year bring us both true joy and happiness? Do but let me come to you, etc. etc. etc., let the very troubles we have endured only endear us so much the more one to another. You have wanted to please your Father, your Mother, yourself and me all at the same time. I do wish most sincerely I had come out, for you say that if we had married you would have been happier than you now are. I know you care for me darling. Why should we both be so miserable. You say you thought you could have married Freddie but now you find it impossible, that you would only spoil his bright young life. How can I get reconciled to things as they are. Oh my darling, etc. etc. Be my Kismet again (I would do my best to endear myself to your people) and I think I could make your Father feel he had not trusted his daughter's happiness to one who was altogether unworthy of her. We might travel about for a year or so. Go to China, Japan and India if you liked, till my father could get me some good appointment. In the meantime I might help Moreton with his affairs so as to be near you and your people. Of course we should never be very well off but we should have enough to get along with. My darling Kismet do tell me from your heart does your happiness depend upon me? or is there anything about me you don't like. Are you afraid you might not be happy as my wife? I am only too anxious to please you if I knew how. You say you cannot marry Freddy and unless you have some good reason against me what will you do Leonie? I always told you I did not in the least mind your temper etc. Anxious to satisfy your parents you have sacrificed your own interests to theirs, but you cannot make a marriage your heart revolts against. . . .

> Ever yr Kismet,
> Charlie."

Leonard had been exceedingly annoyed by Lord Fitzwilliam's attitude, and Moreton certainly did not need a helper of this calibre in Wyoming. A last sad letter ends the tale:

"I am writing with Randolph's consent. I had a talk with him this morning and he is so strongly of opinion that it would be detrimental to your interests that I should see you, that I fear I must, God knows how unwillingly, accede to his wishes. . . . You won't judge me too harshly, but rather by what you know than by what others may say now that I am down in my luck. I am to start for India on Thursday week, without a friend or acquaintance. . . ."

Exit Charlie Fitzwilliam, but Freddie Gebhard did not succeed in taking his place. The winner proved a good stayer. The only son of Sir John Leslie of Glaslough in Monaghan, and Lady Constance Leslie, a frail Victorian beauty with a will of iron, Leonie's favourite beau had sneaked across the Atlantic to push his suit out of view of the family. But 'Pink Jack' as they called him had seen active service in the Egyptian Campaign of 1882 and distinguished himself under fire, which was more than Freddie or Charlie had done. Leonie could not resist the glamour of a soldier.

Her wedding album contains comments from the papers of the day:

"Social circles have been stirred to their utmost depths by the announcement of the engagement of Miss Leonie Jerome to Mr. John Leslie a lieutenant in the Grenadier Guards. Mr. Leslie is a handsome young Englishman, owning a fine estate, and although not yet bearing a title, yet belonging to one of the oldest families in the kingdom. . . . His income amounts to about £30,000 a year, or $150,000, and with this he will be able to provide every luxury for his fair bride . . . [indeed one might hope so]. Mr. Frank Griswold acted as best man. . . . The bride was more than beautiful, she was regal—and glittering. [Jack had snatched what diamonds he dared from the family coffers before leaving Ireland]. . . . Mr. Jerome escorted his daughter and gave her away, and you may be sure he did it with grace, mingled with regret, for Leonard Jerome is a man of dignity, heart and feeling, hard man of the world as he is supposed to be. It may please the *Post's* lady readers to know what the bride wore. She did not wear a wreath of roses, but she wore a bridal veil of point lace held with pearls, diamonds and orange blossom. Her dress was of white brocade draped with lace. The corsage was cut low Pompadour style and decorated with a diamond star on either side. . . . The guests included the Astors, Lorillards, the Jays, Baron Frederick Blanc, William Travers, Ward McAllister, Mrs. August Belmont and Mr. James Gordon Bennett. So you see that the Commodore, in spite of his love for yachting, polo and other unholy things, has finally got into good society. Mr. Bennett spends a great deal of money in a lavish, showy, self-indulgent way, but he can't begin to use up his income!"

The same nosey-parker of the *Post* continued:

"It will be remembered that the bride's sister married Lord Randolph Churchill, a brother of the Duke of Marlborough, but an abler and a better man than the Duke who is badness personified."

Well really!

The happy couple walked out of church to the strains of the 'Grenadier Guards', and sailed away to England. No easy life awaited that unsuspecting "bride with large brown eyes and a lovely smile".

The Leslies were sore displeased. What was New York society? And why did Mr. Jerome drive a 'cart' in Fifth Avenue? These and suchlike questions were relayed to Mrs. Jerome who took them all as insults and rushed for her smelling-salts. Leonard thought the reference to his four-in-hand comic. The papers were full of his new black coach with red wheels and in the last Parade much praise arose when the crowd saw "Mr. Jerome was tooling a very handsome cross team of grays and bays". But he was truly worried because there was no fortune left to settle on his youngest and he was too tired to make one for her. His great health had begun to fail.

A description of him at this time comes from a New Yorker's pen:

"Every afternoon a tall, large, bony figure walks slowly into the Union Club; proceeds directly to the billiard room; is warmly welcomed by the two or three persons who are knocking the balls about while awaiting the newcomer, and begins at once a game of pool. The large, tall, bony figure is attired in a loose-fitting, old-fashioned black frock coat, a white waistcoat and grey trousers. The face is bronzed by exposure to the weather; the grey eyes are large but heavy-lidded; the hair is iron grey and closely cropped; a long drooping moustache conceals the mouth and adds to the semi-military appearance of Leonard Jerome. . . . Once he dominated Wall Street as Jay Gould does now; but his was merry despotism, and he was loved where Jay Gould would be hated."

Occasionally he stepped once more into the limelight, such as when he protested against fraudulent voters going to the polls in Ohio and Indiana, or when he defended the betting system at Jerome Park, but in the main he lived quietly, immersed in sporting and musical interests. For many years his name as a sportsman lingered on and "poor humanity in New York was overwhelmed with collars, cuffs, neckties, everything in short pertaining to dress all named after Mr. Jerome", but he himself cared only for private life.

With August Belmont he was regarded as a doyen of the Academy of Music where the best opera was heard until the opening of the Metropolitan in 1883. The old Academy had but eighteen boxes and the new capitalists such as J. P. Morgan, the Vanderbilts, Rockefeller, Jay Gould and William Whitney were kept out. "The social value of a box at the Academy was inestimable; its economic value could only be gauged by the number of millionaires who, wishing to possess a box, were denied that privilege." When August Belmont, chairman of the Academy, heard that the Vanderbilts were heading a crusade to construct a new vast opera house where they could have all the boxes they wanted, he offered to add twenty-six to the Academy, but the war between 'old aristocracy' and 'new millionaires' was on. The Metropolitan Opera had a tremendous inauguration. According to *The Dramatic Mirror*, "The tiers of boxes looked like cages in a menagerie of Monopolists." Two years later the old Academy closed down and Mr. Belmont and Mr. Jerome had to seek their musical entertainment among the 'upstarts'.

When Mrs. Jerome followed her three daughters to England, Leonard shut up his house in Madison Square and moved to the Brunswick Hotel on Fifth Avenue which was considered "headquarters of the aristocratic horsey set". The annual spring and autumn parades of the Coaching Club assembled here, and the elect would return afterwards to celebrate. Now that his family had left him entirely alone, it was something to have the company of fellow sportsmen.

Leonie's husband resumed his military career. In those days soldiering in the regiments of Her Majesty's Guards consisted chiefly of horse sports. Officers were supposed to hunt regularly with a view to training their eye when chasing enemy cross-country, they also rode steeple-chases to show how they could lead a charge and polo was becoming a fashionable super-expensive game. Occasionally Lieutenant Leslie went to camp or led his troop out on manœuvres. England in the 'eighties demanded little of an eldest son. Life had to be made sweet for him with gun and rod. Horses and yachts were his due. Since Lord Grey's Reform Bill of 1832 had taken the power of government out of the hands of the agrarian aristocracy a curious atrophy had set in. Sense of responsibility seemed to be replaced by mere sense of snobbism. Moreton Frewen's unbiased pen describes the "vast numbers of rich, well-dressed, idle people who constituted the society of the day".

John Leslie's father had been a Member of Parliament until defeated by Parnell's secretary, Tim Healy. Then he withdrew from Irish politics for ever, and did not expect his son to take up the cudgels. A charming fellow with blue eyes, pink cheeks and fair hair, Leonie's husband belonged to a 'caste' and had been brought up according to the caste system. Educated at Eton and entered into the Guards, he was not really expected to do very much except enjoy himself, marry a nice girl chosen by his parents, and eventually inherit large Irish estates.

In the eyes of New York society, Leonie had made a smart match with a nice-looking Grenadier, with a huge romantic place somewhere in the background, he was rich and the son of a baronet—whatever that might be. No guess could have been made at the responsibilities attendant on marrying an elder son of landed gentry, in Ireland. The Jerome girls had been educated to be ambassadresses, princesses or patrons of art. The management of thousands of acres of farmland, forest and bog in a country where the peasantry were approaching revolution had been left out of the curriculum.

48

SIR JOHN and Lady Constance retreated to Ireland and did not receive their daughter-in-law on her arrival in London. She was merely sent to tea to be 'vetted' by Miss Julia and Miss Emily Leslie, two maiden aunts who lived together in Bourdon House, off Berkeley Square (preferring luxurious spinsterhood if they could not, like their sister Christina Marchioness of Waterford, marry into the upper strata of derelict peers). Julia reported severely on her hair-do, complaining that she had no fringe. But this ominous verdict was counteracted by kindly, music-loving Emily who discovered Leonie's knowledge of composition. The Leslies unbent sufficiently to send a summons to the young couple to spend Christmas at Glaslough. They travelled across the Irish Sea and arrived one rough winter's night in the big stone hall hung with antlers and decaying armour. Little Olive Leslie, Jack's fifteen-year-old sister, ran down the stairs and stopped dead at the "lovely lady in the Hall. Leonie was standing there alone looking very slim in a tight-fitting grey dress with a big bunch of violets pinned to the neck. She looked more elegant than anyone I had ever seen".

The week's visit passed quietly. Lady Constance could find nothing to criticize in her new daughter-in-law except that she "would overload the Christmas Tree".

By January 1st Leonie was back in London picking up threads with which to weave a life of her own. She started a diary but it only records the most trivial details. Pink Jack was absent-minded. He missed parades and having arranged to take his wife out to lunch, forgot, and left her standing on the doorstep! Such incidents loomed large in her first months of marriage. However he takes her to the theatre with Jennie and the Duc de Morny. They see Mrs. Langtry in *Princess George*, "such a fiasco, can't act and is badly made up, red hands. Freddie Gebhard with the mother. Looked ashamed of her, rather disgraceful". Visits to the Leslie aunts continue, "Emily off to a prayer meeting. Julia foul," interspersed with musical evenings with Mrs. Ronalds, Lady de Clifford, and Consuelo (Duchess of Manchester). On February 5th "Lady Blanche Hozier[1] comes in with news

[1] Later to become mother-in-law of Winston S. Churchill.

of the fall of Khartoum, consternation! Lady de C., Jennie and I drive to the Tower and lunch with Jack who is on guard and inspect the damages made by dynamite by an admirer of General Gordon." Then comes a "vile letter from Jack's mother—makes me blue—feel so wretched".

Unfortunately Leonard remained in New York. If only the fathers-in-law could have met, the strain would have ended, for horses and Italian opera were the great interests of both gentlemen and Leonard would have put an end to Lady Constance's nonsense.

In February the Leslies returned to town and on the 14th Jack is asked after coming off guard to bring his bride to Stratford House to be re-inspected in a London setting. "Dreadfully out of spirits," writes poor Leonie. "After lunch Lady C. receives us. Children all in the next room. Very formal and stiff. Then they come in, we sit in a row and discuss the war. I talk to the governess, etc. So dull and tiresome."

Lady Constance had "an awful temper". As a young bride she had always "jumped on to the window-sill in Berkeley Square and threatened she would dash herself down if not yielded to in every dispute".

Stratford House[1] was a nobly proportioned Georgian edifice, with splendid drawing-rooms and no sanitation. The Irish staff including footmen and stable-boys, who were brought over from County Monaghan, each spring invariably got 'sore throats' and diphtheria which they attributed to the treacherous London climate. No one dreamed of inspecting the un-drained cess-pit which terminated underneath the kitchen floor. From the upper storeys of this white temple the Leslies enjoyed the grandiose side of each London season.

Whenever summoned there Leonie arrived trembling with nervous indignation but she determined to show no emotion and to put the Leslies in their place. Soon Sir John who had known Chopin, Rossini and Mendelssohn appreciated her touch on his piano—that Broadwood Grand on which the great Anton Rubinstein also came to play. Lady Constance thawed slightly. It seemed exceeding strange that a 'Colonial' with that questionable Second Empire and barbaric New York as a background, should play so much better than her own daughters who, despite much scale-practice with their old governess, could hardly differentiate one tune from another.

Eventually Jack and his wife were invited to stay at Stratford House (and here in a fine bedroom of supreme discomfort two of Leonie's sons were born). The Leslies, with great wealth behind them, were determined to imprint on the young couple that they were very very poor, certainly too poor for Leonie to have a carriage "unless Mr. Jerome gives her one".

[1] Later Derby House, now Hutchinson House.

1889

Mrs. Leonard Jerome with her daughters and grandchildren

L. to R. sitting: Clara Frewen with Oswald, Shane Leslie, Mrs. Jerome with Clare Frewen, John Churchill, Hugh Frewen, little Norman Leslie on lap of Leonie.

Back Row standing: Jennie Churchill with Winston

Brede Place

For a time the vivacious and hitherto spoilt American bride recoiled in amazement from so grim a welcome. Then she proceeded to write cheerful letters to her father describing Lady Constance's efforts to entertain writers and musicians in the midst of a dull frumpy Victorian society. "The dear kind fat Duchess of Teck and her dear sweet thoughtful daughter Mary"[1] often visited Stratford House, which, straitlaced and formal as it may have seemed to a young lady reared in Paris, did present a curious artistic oasis for royalty.

Old John Leslie, the most talented of the Victorian dilettante, held occasional exhibitions of his own work and collected old masters with discrimination. When he took Leonie to see Whistler's pictures she noted, "We liked them, everyone else says 'clever but a fraud'."

Sir John, who could already speak of three reigns and would see five, treated her with kindness from the start for his sixty-five years made it hard for him to remember anything for long, even the fact that an American daughter-in-law must be "severely trained to English ways". Born in 1822 (a little later than Leonard), he had grown up against a very different setting. Hardship seems to have been accepted naturally by all that generation. The journey from Glaslough to Harrow School took one week in those days, and the Leslie boys were sent on top of a coach without overcoats! When still very small John Leslie had been taken to see his cousin, the great Duke of Wellington, and never forgot that "he gave me no tip". He had seen George IV, and Talleyrand, and had talked to Sir Walter Scott. At Harrow he learned to write Latin verses with Drury, who had taught Lord Byron, and at Oxford he ragged Ruskin.

After playing cricket for Oxford against Cambridge, he went on the Grand Tour, meeting Rossini, and Mrs. Browning, and George Sand. As a young officer of small means, he rode his best hunter in the Grand Military Steeplechase. Unattended and unbacked "he won as an outsider by beautiful riding". In the same year he painted a picture which was hung in the Royal Academy.

Then he became a Member of Parliament and, inheriting the Glaslough estates, drifted into an artistic dream for the rest of his life. Holman Hunt, Millais, Landseer and Watts became his friends. He let them paint his lovely wife, and it was to Lady Constance that Watts wrote a delicate letter explaining that he had married Ellen Terry—to save her from the stage! Dickens and Thackeray were often seen in the Leslie drawing-room and Thackeray (who had pilloried Lady Constance's relative Lord Hertford as the Marquis of Steyne in *Vanity Fair*) had been due to dine the night before he died. He sent Constance a note:

[1] Later Queen Mary.

"I have only this minute crawled down to my sofa and no one can be more sorry than

> Yours very faithfully,
> W. M. Thackeray."

And never lifted pen again.

A few months before Leonie's first child was born Lady Constance presented her daughter-in-law to Queen Victoria. The "Drawing Room" which took place in the afternoon does not sound very stimulating.

> "Sit in carriage long time. Go in. Stand an hour. Queen still there. Kiss her hand. Princess shakes hands. Curtsey to the rest. Prince shakes my hand and congratulates."

During the remainder of the spring Leonie found herself sitting through the quiet afternoons with her hands folded, listening to the old man's reminiscences. One of his brothers, Charles, had accompanied Lord Harting-ton through the lines of both armies during the American Civil War. Another brother, Tom, occasionally called at Stratford House and himself related the episodes which led to the Charge of Balaclava. He had been on Lord Raglan's staff when told to gallop off with the order which ran, "Lord Raglan wishes the cavalry to advance rapidly to the front, and try to prevent the enemy carrying away the guns." But a senior officer, Captain Nolan, asked for the honour of transmitting this message and snatched the paper from Tom's hand. On receiving the order, Lord Lucan asked Nolan if Lord Raglan meant the Russian guns at the end of the valley, or the more possible objective of some Turkish guns. Without any authority, Nolan pointed to the Russian trap and asked if he were afraid. Lucan passed on the incorrect order to his brother-in-law Lord Cardigan, a duelling rake, who instantly led the famous charge. Nolan galloped off, perhaps to check on his mistake, but he was saved a court-martial. As the Brigade thundered into the jaws of death, a headless horseman fell across their tracks. It was Captain Nolan whose hot-headed answer had been their doom. Meanwhile Tom Leslie, who might have carried the order without impetuously presuming it alluded to Russian guns, had collapsed with a bullet in his leg. Lord Raglan had it picked out and dispatched with a note of praise to Tom's mother whom he admired. "Wait until you get to Glaslough," old Sir John would tell Leonie, "then I must show it to you with all the letters and things that will be yours some day."

But Lady Constance was quicker at "letters and things" than her old husband. A true Victorian, she went through every box and diary, snipping out with scissors that which she considered "improper", leaving in many cases a mere filigree of paper to tease posterity. Happily she missed the trunk of 18th century letters concerning the outcome of a game of hide and seek played on the top storey in the 1730's. Sir John's great grandfather aged sixteen and the young daughter of an Irish Earl had hidden in the linen press and not been found for two hours. A baby girl resulted and was brought up as a spoiled pet by her mother's family and eventually became the ancestress of a particularly brilliant line of statesmen.

The months Leonie spent in London were easier than those which had to be devoted to amusing her mother-in-law in an Irish country home. Lady Constance had, in 1876, made her husband dynamite the old square Castle Leslie, and build in its stead an immense rambling Victorian edifice. By happy chance he had imbibed sufficient taste during Italian travels to design the interior proportions, and to vault ceilings and paint frescoes pleasingly. An entire marble fountain was transported from Florence, Michael Angelo's cloister of Santa Maria degli Angeli in Rome was reproduced "to lead to the library and billiard room" and a Della Robbia fireplace, as well as the contents of a Venetian palazzo, arrived in what must have been the giantesque crates of the 'seventies.

Amidst the accumulated possessions of three centuries, Leonie would sit down at the drawing-room piano, stare out at the lake with its grey melancholy, its brooding magic of an untouched world, and attempt to keep up her practising. Sir John bought her a superb piano and begged her to play Mendelssohn while he looked out at the mists, but her mother-in-law would not allow the necessary grind. When a few bars needed constant repetition, Lady Constance bringing her embroidery and settling into a chair nearby inevitably purred, "Now dear, play me that pretty piece you *do* know."

Leonie, by nature a perfectionist, would weep with exasperation.

Misunderstandings constantly arose. Only "the sisters", four blue-eyed, auburn-haired Leslie girls, worshipped 'Jacksy's choice'. Two were married,[1] the younger ones Mary and Olive had been educated amidst the Irish woods by 'Bobby', a dear decrepit old governess, and although they cared for music were unable to pick out the simplest tune. The peasants knew and loved the Miss Leslies and so did the stable boys, and the horses and innumerable spoiled dogs, but Leonie thought it "extraordinary" to bring girls up amidst this remote forest land before launching in London society. On the first occasion Olive drove her out in a dog-cart they allowed a groom to turn it and having supped a little poteen he upset it into a bog cutting. "Are you dead, Jamie?" called Miss Olive's tremulous girlish voice. The answer came slowly: "I am not. I'm just spaachless." While the girls introduced Leonie

[1] Lady Hope and Lady Bagot.

to their friends the cottagers, she talked to them of the elements of harmony. They proved tone deaf but something of her own flair for repartee grew in them. She had that gift much rarer than wit, of being able to make others witty.

Mrs. Jerome visited Glaslough and the mothers-in-law eyed each other like two formidable hens. The big walled demesne, with its grey lake and great dripping trees, struck Mrs. Jerome as "bleak and sad" and the Góthic lodge gates as "outlandish". As for the huge new house with its senseless wings of museum corridor which old Sir John on a step-ladder was covering with Italian style frescoes it delighted her not at all. She merely wondered if his paint-brush could compete with the decorations of green mould creeping over every unused room.

"It was different in the Tuileries . . ." she remarked rather too often. Lady Constance cut short her derision: "Louis Napoleon used to hang around London hoping to be invited for a meal anywhere. He often stayed at Came, our home in Dorset, and we thought him *so* dull and *such* a poor sportsman, penniless too, but this did not prevent him trying to bribe me with barley sugar because he wanted to marry my eldest sister Lady Fortescue. Our father was on Cathcart's staff at Waterloo and had a very poor opinion of *all* Bonapartes. He refused Louis Napoleon point blank!"

Lady Constance insinuated that her sister had done far better as a real English Countess than married to "that sort of Emperor". Although herself scorning the Irish squirearchy it was unbearable to see Mrs. Jerome unimpressed by Leslies and full of the vulgar glories of the Second Empire.

Lady Constance never possessed a pair of walking shoes. When in a huff she would drive off in her carriage through the lonely countryside distributing cold pudding to the grateful peasantry. She found it a sore trial that she, the sister of an English earl, should be reduced to the hierarchy of Irish baronets. The grandeur of her London life never left her mind. On these long dismal drives through bogs of purple heather and low-lying woods of beech she yearned to get back to civilization. Inwardly she began to thank heaven for Leonie's company but she kept her words hard. "How long seem the days here," she wrote to her sister, those days which began with the sun rising over the lake and the clatter of housemaids laying and lighting fires in the forty-odd fireplaces of the house. Lady Constance pretended to like the country because (like white-painted bedroom furniture) that had become 'the thing' but inwardly she longed for the time to embark for England. Then horses would be sent ahead with thin Weir the coachman, and fat Charles, a twenty-stone footman who had to accustom the animals to the glories of the Hyde Park Church Parade, a terrifying change after desolate Ulster bogs. The white-haired butler Sammy and footmen wearing the canary-and-olive Leslie livery followed. After them travelled the cook and her minions, the stillroom maid, a host of domestics under a head housekeeper, and the parrot. Last of all would come the governess, the unmarried daughters and her ladyship with personal attendants all inclined to weep and faint at the drama of the journey.

Lady Constance's mother, Minnie Seymour, had been the adored adopted daughter of Mrs. Fitzherbert, first wife of George IV.[1] The child was presumed to be the King's daughter by the dead Lady Horatio Seymour, who in her will left Minnie to Mrs. Fitzherbert. As Prince Regent, he had made a great pet of the little girl. Her letters addressed to "dear Prinny" rest in the Windsor archives, but many of the personal presents, the jewellery, diamond-initial lockets and miniatures which George IV gave to Mrs. Fitzherbert had become the property of Minnie Seymour's daughters. Lady Constance wore them with reverence. Whatever the truth may have been the Prince Regent showed a strangely lasting and intense affection for "little Minnie" in contrast to his behaviour to Princess Charlotte.

With the merits of their children, the Second Empire and the Regency to disagree on, these long-drawn-out meals in the Castle Leslie dining-room, hung with family portraits, must have become insufferable. Happily dear old Sir John was growing deaf.

Lady Constance had devised an enormous centre-piece of flowers for her dinner-table. This she spoke of as 'un cache-mari'. "After thirty years of marriage," she said, "one simply cannot see the same face chewing every day."

Doubtless it was a relief when the time came to close down the Irish country home, and ship horses, carriages and servants to London for the Season. Leonie could then lead an independent existence and she became one of the most-sought-after young women in English society. She lost the Kaiser a race in Cowes Week by jamming a lavatory porthole open but he forgave her (and the Prince of Wales was of course delighted). Somewhat naturally she found invitations to travel on royal yachts proved far more alluring than long unwanted 'rests' in the depths of Ireland.

Among the stories she used to tell against herself was one concerning the summer after Clara's wedding.

Leonard had written her that a great friend was coming to London and that she must be particularly nice to him. At a large dinner of Jennie's she found herself sitting next to a charming gentleman whom she vaguely remembered

[1] She refused the title of duchess as savouring of a royal courtesan, but her servants wore the royal livery. After the death of George IV the new king gave her leave to wear widow's weeds, but the Duke of Wellington induced her to burn all the papers in her possession except the certificate of marriage and a few notes.

in Papa's racing set. She held forth on what he ought to do and see in Europe with all the authority and assurance of her twenty-five years. "I explained the sports of England, the Tower of London, and Hampton Court and ended by telling him rather patronizingly all about the Derby. 'That will take place next week. You really ought to see it.' 'Yes,' said Mr. Lorillard humbly. 'I hope to. I won it last year.'"

LADY RANDOLPH CHURCHILL in Connaught Place, Mrs. Moreton Frewen in Aldford Street and Mrs. Jack Leslie in various small houses adjacent to Stratford Place; these were the three most brilliant and original young hostesses of London in the eighties. They entertained 'on a shoe-string', making their own charm and wit substitute for the grandeur and pomaded footmen they could not afford. Leonard found his daughters grown into ladies of high repute in intellectual and musical circles; during his brief visits he only wished they had more time to spare for 'poor dear papa!' Their children delighted him, despite the strange English upbringing which made them so different to the go-getting little boys of his own recollection. How far off was that scene of early western New York, the scene into which he had been born where every youth breathed the clear air of an untouched land, and planned to create a pattern of his own. English children found a world ready-made; they were informed of their setting, and expected to conform. They heard much of the importance of gentle-manly birth but not of Leonard Jerome's definition: "The character of a gentleman I consider within the capacity of all—at least it requires no extra-ordinary intellect. A due regard for the feelings of others is in my judgment its foundation. . . ."

The education of Jennie's eldest son during this period when Grandfather Jerome can have been but a vague benevolent figure appearing annually from across the Atlantic has been described in detail. He begins at the time when his father was in full ascendency:

"I was first threatened with school when I was seven years old. At the time I was what grown-up people in their offhand way called 'a trouble-some boy'. Although much that I had heard about school had made a disagreeable impression on my mind, an impression thoroughly borne out by actual experience, I thought it would be fun to go away and live with so many other boys, and that we should have great adventures. Also I was told that 'school days were the happiest in one's life'. All the boys enjoyed it. Some of my cousins had been quite sorry—I was told—to come home for the holidays. Cross-examined, the cousins did not confirm this; they only grinned."[1]

He described the dark November afternoon when Jennie took him to his preparatory school, and as the sounds of the beautiful Lady Randolph's carriage died away, a small sad boy was led to an empty class-room and handed a Latin grammar.

"Behold me then on a gloomy evening, with an aching heart, seated in front of the declension of *mensa*.

What on earth did it mean? It seemed absolute rigmarole to me. However, there was one thing I could always do; I could learn by heart.

In due course the master returned.

" 'Have you learned it?' he said. 'I think I can *say* it, sir,' I replied, and I gabbled it off.

He seemed so satisfied with this that I was emboldened to ask a question.

" 'What does it mean, sir?'

" 'It means what it says. *Mensa*, a table.'

" 'Then why does *mensa* also mean O Table,' I enquired, 'and what does O Table mean?'

" '*Mensa*, O Table, is the vocative case,' he replied. 'You would use that in speaking to a table.'

" 'But I never do,' I blurted out in honest amazement.

Such was my first introduction to the classics from which, I have been told, many of our cleverest men have derived so much solace and profit."

He entered Harrow after submitting a Latin paper adorned solely by a blot and smudges. Evidently the Headmaster, reckoning he could entice better efforts later from the son of the brilliant Lord Randolph, did not wish to turn him down. Winston was placed in the lowest division of the bottom Form, a situation which he later regarded as advantageous, for instead of struggling with Latin he was taught English.

"We were considered such dunces that we could learn only English. As I remained in the Third Fourth three times as long as anyone else, I had three times as much of it. I learned it thoroughly. Thus I got into my bones the essential structure of the ordinary British sentence which is a noble thing."

[1] *My Early Life*, by Winston S. Churchill.

Blenheim Palace

Castle Leslie

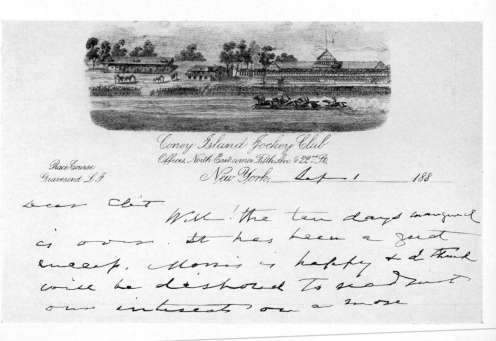

Coney Island Jockey Club,

1890

GOVERNORS:

J. HARRY ALEXANDRE,	JAMES R. KEENE,
JAMES GORDON BENNETT,	LAWRENCE KIP,
J. H. BRADFORD,	J. G. K. LAWRENCE,
GEN. D. BUTTERFIELD,	R. C. LIVINGSTON,
A. J. CASSATT,	J. A. LOWERY,
ROBERT CENTER,	L. L. LORILLARD,
J. O. DONNER,	P. LORILLARD, JR,
C. FELLOWES,	A. NEWBOLD MORRIS,
F G GRISWOLD,	H. I. NICHOLAS,
JOHN G. HECKSCHER,	W. L. SCOTT,
H. B. HOLLINS,	F. AUG. SCHERMERHORN,
LEONARD W. JEROME,	GEORGE PEABODY WETMORE,

WILLIAM K. VANDERBILT,

President:
LEONARD W. JEROME.

Vice-Presidents:
C. FELLOWES. WM. K. VANDERBILT.

Treasurer:
J. H. BRADFORD.

Secretary:
J. G. K. LAWRENCE.

Executive Committee:

THE PRESIDENT, THE VICE-PRESIDENTS, } *Ex-Officio.*
THE TREASURER, THE SECRETARY,
GEN. D. BUTTERFIELD, R. C. LIVINGSTON,
LAWRENCE KIP.

Clerk of the Course: *Clerk of the Scales:* *Starter:*
F. A. LOVECRAFT. SAMUEL E. RORK. J. F. CALDWELL.

Offices: 5th Ave., cor. 22d St., New York.
Race Course: Sheepshead Bay, L. I.

Frontispiece of Leonard Jerome's last racing book

Leonard's last letter to his wife, September 1890

The masters became maddened by the selectivity of this boy with his naughty blue eyes and rather pugnacious little face who remained impervious to chastisement and closed his mind against learning all that bored him. At intervals he showed a remarkable memory, reciting over a thousand lines of Macaulay's *Lays of Ancient Rome* which happened to appeal to him, but generally he lowered shutters around his brain as if to protect it against the accumulation of useless knowledge.

"In retrospect my school years form the only barren and unhappy period of my life. Actually, no doubt, they were buoyed up by the laughter and high spirits of youth. But I would far rather have been apprenticed as a bricklayer's mate, or run errands as a messenger boy. It would have been real; it would have been natural; it would have taught me more; and I should have done it much better."[1]

This was the verdict of one who mingled ducal and pioneer blood in his veins, and who, from the beginning, felt the futility of wasting time. Young Master Churchill could not and would not see the trees for the wood. He refused to pick up twigs he did not want. No punishment altered this resolve.

He also differed from others in his readiness to show emotion and by his moral bravery. A letter to his mother from Harrow reads: "I am getting on in drawing and like it very much. I am going to begin shading in sepia. Everest came down yesterday." His beloved old Nurse had arrived in a poke bonnet and Winston walked her round the school and kissed her good-bye at the station. No other boy would have dared to reveal this simple loyalty and affection for a nurse. The story went like wildfire around the school, arousing jeers among the more conventional and less courageous, but Churchill showed a curious toughness in withstanding the criticism.

The adored 'Tante Leonie' often looked after Winston if his parents were abroad. She found her lonely snub-nosed freckled little nephew full of fun and unselfconscious: "he doesn't mind people calling him 'copper-top'." In 1887, when Winston was thirteen years old, he begged a favour and Lady Constance, who always had time to do a good turn, wrote to her friend Rider Haggard:

"The little boy Winston came here yesterday morning, beseeching me to take him to see you before he returns to school at the end of the month. I don't wish to bore so busy a man as yourself, but will you,

[1] *My Early Life*, by Winston S. Churchill.

when you have time, please tell me, shall I bring him on Wednesday next, when Mrs. Haggard said she would be at home? Or do you prefer settling to come here some afternoon when I could have the boy to meet you? He is really a very interesting being, though temporily *uppish* from the restraining parental hand being in Russia."

Mr. Haggard was kind and gave Winston *Allan Quatermain*. Winston wrote to thank him. "I like *A.Q* better than *King Solomon's Mines*; it is more amusing. I hope you will write a good many more books."

In London 'Tante Leonie' tried to give Winston a good time—too good a time according to his grandmother, the Duchess of Marlborough, who, in a letter deeply bordered with black and weighted with black coronets, writes thus from Blenheim:

"Dec. 27, 1887.

My dear Leonie,

    I must say I am very much disappointed at Winston's not being allowed to come here for a few days. I had made every arrangement to take great care of him knowing he is susceptible to colds, and I do not think there could have been as much danger as there is in going to Pantomimes in London. Besides I feel it's all an excuse of that horrid old Everest to prevent my having him and his being happy with his cousins without her.

    I feel that Randolph and Jennie would not have objected to me seeing a little of him as really I hardly ever see him, and must say I am very much vexed. He is not fit to go to Harrow if he is not fit for a visit here. The house is quite warm. But it cannot be helped. I have heard nothing from R. and Jennie, but the newspapers are full of them. I hope you are well and enjoying a happy Xmas. With much love.

Yours
F. Marlborough."

Jennie and Randolph had gone to Russia leaving their fourteen-year-old son and his old nurse in Leonie's charge. He was madly happy in their company. Cozy old Everest and the gay understanding young aunt may have spoilt him but he needed a little spoiling. His father's cold indifference frosted the boy's eager approaches, and Winston has clearly described his feelings for his mother: "She shone for me like the Evening Star. I loved her dearly but at a distance. My nurse was my confidante."[1] While Winston

---

[1] Winston used to visit Everest in her old age and confessed that this friendship led him to realize the plight of many who were not like her pensioned in retirement. He then pressed for Old Age Pensions.

thoroughly enjoyed himself in the company of his 'favourites' his parents visited St. Petersburg and Moscow, sleighed, tobogganed and skated, and were received in audience by the Tsar. Jennie found the Russian aristocracy lived in "over-heated apartments far worse than American ones", and while the women struck her as beautifully educated this seemed pointless as they took no part in guiding their men in politics or any other career. The memories she carried away were of snow-covered plains, a gracious Tsarina, wonderful jewels and Tzigane music. The memory she left (one which long survived the dispersal of the Russian court), was of "the most beautiful black-haired woman ever seen, who danced light as a moth on skates".

In England the newspapers boiled and bubbled, *The Times* in particular warning the Tsar that Lord Randolph, "the most versatile and volatile" of English politicians, should not be accepted as having official status.

"Meanwhile the object of this merry chatter was enjoying himself. When the word has gone forth that a visitor is to be well received, he need not trouble about details. Everything moves *sur les roulettes*; railway officials and Custom House officers are transformed into attentive servants—often a considerable transformation."[1]

Unaware, or uncaring, of editorial comment at home, Randolph drove "in bright sun and bitter cold to the Winter Palace, and after long delays, relieved by cups of tea, in interminable corridors adorned by wonderfully dressed servants with *panaches* of red and orange ostrich feathers, he was conducted to the Emperor's apartment." Their talk, which lasted nearly an hour, concerned the possibility of maintaining peace between their respective countries.

On the following day Lord and Lady Randolph were commanded to a party at Gatschina. The marked consideration shown to the English visitor increased the gossip—good-humoured and spiteful alike at home. And in St. Petersburg the whole of society devoted itself to amusing the distinguished couple; Randolph wrote his mother:

"I am sure in England it would bore me dreadfully to go to all these dinners and parties and things, but here it amuses me. I wonder why it is. . . . You must not believe a word the newspapers say. I was most careful and guarded in all my communications, and confined myself to general beaming upon everyone. Lord Salisbury may or may not be angry, but I am certain that my going to Russia has had a good effect and can, at any rate, do no harm."

[1] *Lord Randolph Churchill*, by Winston S. Churchill.

On arriving back in England they found *The Times* devoting three columns to speculations on the possible import of Randolph's visit to Russia. It seemed as if this dynamic and controversial figure, whose every excursion conjured up excitement, could not fail to return soon to power, but Jennie wrote to her sister Leonie, and there is sadness in her assessment of the facts:

> "2 Connaught Place
> W.

Dearest Snippy,
>   I confess I have been a brute not to have written, but what with letters to R. and the Duchess besides others, and my painting and music, I haven't a moment. I shall be *so* glad to see you dear—but I do not think that I shall be over until the 6th or 7th of March as I want to go to the Drawing Room here on the 3rd on account of the Queen [being offended by Randolph's resignation]. The Duchess writes that you are considered the 'belle of Dublin!' You must not be low dear. I shall soon be over and intend staying the whole month. I feel rather in the dumps myself to-day. I dined last night with the Salisburys where they had a dance afterwards. I had a long talk with Ld. S. after dinner but I did not get much out of him. He was very shy and nervous and I had the greatest difficulty to get him to speak of Randolph. It is too long to repeat but I rather had the impression that they could never come together again. Don't repeat this, of course it is impossible to say what may happen in the House. As Arthur Balfour said—their difficulties haven't commenced yet and when they do—they may have to go to Randolph. But Snippy I feel very sick at heart sometimes. It was such a splendid position to throw away. In the bottom of my heart I sometimes think that his head was quite turned at that moment and that he thought he cd do *anything*. However 'it is an ill wind that blows *no* good' and R. has been so much easier and nicer since that I ought not to regret the crisis. He writes most affectionately and very often and I hope all will be righted when he returns. . . .

> Yr loving
> Jennie."

If, sensing the failing powers of Randolph, Jennie felt her heart ache, she continued to keep up a brave front. The most interesting people of the day, ambassadors, statesmen, writers and artists, flocked to her house. From Mrs. Ronalds she learnt how to launch struggling musicians. One day a young pianist came to her from Poland. He carried a letter of introduction from a mutual friend and after a cup of tea, during which she noticed he seemed very nervous, Jennie said: "Come on, let's try a Beethoven duet together."

"You're too good," she laughed at the end. "You leave me breathless. I shan't play with you any more."

During the next days she gathered all the people she knew in London who were capable of judging an artist fairly. The young man received an appreciation which enabled him to approach his first concert in the St. James's Hall with confidence. The place was only half full. Jennie placed herself in a seat in front of the critics and listened to their comments: "There's not much in this fellow," said one. "He would be all right," said the other, "if he would leave Chopin alone, which he plays against all traditions."

She could not resist speaking loudly to the friend beside her:

"Stephen Heller who was Chopin's pupil taught *me* and *he* said that Chopin himself never played his works twice in the same way."

A year later the pianist returned to London. This time his audience stormed the stage to kiss his hand. When he came to tea with Jennie he took both her hands in his. "Come on," Paderewski cajoled, "let us try that duet again. I shall not feel so shy this time."

50

BETWEEN the old Duke of Marlborough and Mr. Jerome there had never been many words, but Randolph's brother, the Bi-metallist eighth duke, joined the wide circle of admiring younger men who surrounded Leonard. He also became one of Moreton Frewen's cronies and they scraped up several 'marvellous ideas' together. Two days after Lord Randolph's resignation, in 1886, Marlborough expounded his views gloomily:

> "My dear Moreton,
>   Randolph's resignation is a fearful blow to the agricultural and currency interest. . . ."

Righting of the monetary systems of the world held more allure to both men than the improvement of conditions within their personal orbits. Moreton's glib pen pronounced judgment on his associate thus:

> "I have known also one or two quite first-class minds whose achievements have been nil. Take George, eighth duke of Marlborough, an almost incomparable mind; indeed in receptivity, range and versatility, hardly to be matched. . . . But to play the whole great game there must be the really master mind. . . ."

Despite a certain receptivity and range this unfortunate duke seems in the 'whole great game' to have failed as patently as Mr. Frewen. After his wife, Lady Blandford, divorced him, Marlborough turned to chemistry on the grand scale and set up a laboratory on the top floor of Blenheim where he devoted himself to experiments in electricity and metallurgy. When the Frewen ore-crusher failed to extract gold from boulders, he could more subtly try to convert it from other minerals. He also made tentative efforts, under Leonard's supervision, to discover happiness with a new wife from the millionaire set of New York city. But even in this operation success remained elusive. For the eighth duke no alchemy was able to transform the dross of life.

The environments into which Leonard's daughters stepped after marriage produced a curious assortment of characters. Moreton Frewen's friends constituted half the British sporting aristocracy, and he brought them to Clara's house to mingle with European royalties, 'intellectuals' and musicians, whose company Moreton did not always relish. Sir Arthur Sullivan (of Gilbert and Sullivan) once scribbled her a note while arranging a dinner for H.R.H. the Duke of York. "I want another lady without a man badly. Will you come to my rescue and I will give Moreton any satisfaction he desires afterwards, either pistols, swords or Utah shares!"

Leonard regarded Moreton as less amusing every year. Now that Leonie had won her battle with the Leslies the most genial of the British in-laws proved to be old Sir John whose fund of anecdote covered all the years during which Jerome had known only the turbulence of early America. Sir John had been a member of the hallowed Marylebone Cricket Club since 1841 and had seen his first Derby in 1839. "In his youth prize-fighting was the national sport and the 'champion of England' was, after the Archbishop of Canterbury, unofficially the second person in the realm." To Mr. Jerome he could give an eye-witness's account of the famous fight between Sayers and Heenan which had raised such feeling between England and America. "Sayers faced his rival like a polo-pony against a dray horse, and though his right arm was soon put out of action fought thirty rounds with his left until Heenan's face was a red mash."

Sayers' backers broke the ring rather than lose their money, and the fight was declared a draw. This was the last time that deputations from the House of Lords and House of Commons attended a prize-fight and it was the gory, if glorious, end of the old English boxing without gloves.

A curious 'at home' was given by Lord Caledon in the late eighties to which Jack Leslie took his bride and her father. The Caledon estate walls met those of Glaslough in Ireland, so the families were well acquainted and Leonie's four sons ran wild in the Ulster woods alongside the four sons of Lord Caledon.[1] Apart from being a good neighbour, the noble earl was also a sportsman of repute; he had trailed alone across Wyoming, lived as a blood brother with Blackfoot Indians, shot bears with Moreton, and brought a buffalo back to his deer park.

After many years of travel it dawned on his lordship that the time had arrived when it became incumbent on him to make some effort to entertain London society. His grand house in Carlton House Terrace overlooking the Horse Guards Parade was opened forthwith and stocked up with servants raw from the bogs according to the wont of those who owned Irish estates.

[1] At present, the Earl of Caledon, Field-Marshal Earl Alexander of Tunis, Hon. Herbrand Alexander, Hon. Sigismund Alexander.

Invitations went out for what Leonie and her husband assumed to be a soirée dedicated to some art. They arrived in a gilded drawing-room to be received by the Countess of Caledon looking somewhat dazed beneath her tiara. "Sports have been arranged upstairs," she said. A bevy of gentlemen escorted ladies in jewelled evening dresses up the magnificent staircase to the ballroom where, beside a roped ring, Lord Caledon was greeting guests and supervising referees at the same time.

"I will never forget entering that room," Leonie used to say, "for the name of the boxer being called out was Billy Blood! A terrific fight then took place which made the chandeliers swing and I can remember the tremor which went through the men as someone shouted: 'He's drawn the claret!' and a scarlet stream shot from the nose of aptly-named Billy. The gentlemen may have enjoyed it but not the wives, who stood with faces growing longer and more horrified at every round. 'Claret' proved the last straw and most ladies cleared off, clutching their silken trains. Refreshments were served in the next room to those who could bring themselves to swallow and our dear Irish neighbour all charm and affability (though rather a shy man) beamed on his friends saying, 'I thought it would be nice to have something a little different.'"

When Leonard returned to America after a month spent almost entirely in the proximity of Leonie and Jack he wrote her a tactful letter. In the fashionable worlds of New York and Paris only the worldly endowments of Lieutenant Leslie were emphasized, he was good-looking, he was rich and some sort of title would come his way. Lucky young man! Probably conceited, thought the envious. Leonard's vision was more acute. The pink cheeks which reddened so easily, the blue boyish eyes and old-fashioned courtesy of 'Jacksy' hid a painful shyness, which was in no way being dispelled by his irrepressible scintillating wife. Leonie was at that time impetuous and so full of vitality and *joie de vivre* that she had not time to notice the effect on a husband consistently forced to take second place. Society proved heartless. Leonie 'made parties go'. She was inundated with invitations which added almost as an afterthought, "and bring Jack too". He felt himself tagging at her heels, merely tolerated, while the exuberant young lady he had married became the star of every gathering.

Only Mr. Jerome noticed his discomfort. Because Jennie had married the most brilliant parliamentarian of the century a like situation had not been able to arise, and Moreton was of course a steam-roller in his own right. But Leonard realized that Jerome verve often needed curbing. How to accomplish this task?

The letter he wrote her was not very long and she kept it all her life, taking it out to read over whenever she might have thoughtlessly dominated an evening. She showed it to me once. I can only remember the last sentence:

"Do not forget that you have married a very amiable and gallant gentleman who will never *show* when his feelings are hurt but who will be unable to forget the slights of society, when it is made apparent that you are more wanted than him. It will rankle in the future. A man may say nothing but he will never be able to forget. . . ."

These timely words helped an uneven match to culminate in long years of happiness. Many of Leonard's letters of 1888 survive. There is also a sarcastic note from Lady Constance to the Duchess of Marlborough (who had always assured her that since taking up politics Jennie had made a "very good wife") to say: "Old Mr. Jerome starts on Saturday for America to make a new fortune for Clara and Leonie." Obviously she rejoiced in the discovery that, despite Leonard's reputation, he could offer but meagre financial help to his daughters.

In actual fact, he had abandoned efforts to earn big money on the market. Having settled all he possessed on his girls, he simply kept an eye on his racehorses and lived contentedly in a room of the Brunswick Hotel where the Coaching Club met annually and he saw sporting friends. (Conveniently the hotel had been forced to reduce its rates after a Bowery gangster had wrecked its social standing by bringing an after-sleighing party for supper into the unsuspecting restaurant). During the spring and summer of 1888 Jerome was struggling to transfer his original Jockey Club to a new racecourse financed by rich John Morris, for since 1887 the city of New York had threatened to extend an aqueduct and reservoir over Jerome Park.

"To give up Jerome Park, to see the American Jockey Club decay, was a bitter blow to this man of energy and brains. It was like seeing a loved child shrivel and die. . . . Mr. Jerome determined to build before he died a new home for the Association founded in his prime. Months passed before he succeeded in raising a dollar. Carry him back twenty-five years and he could have millions for the asking: now he could interest no one in his plans. It was the joke of the day to ask him if he had yet found the 400 dollars with which to build the new track. He bore the taunts with resignation and went about his business. On a certain day, when the question was put to him for the hundredth time he responded with the light of vindication burning in his eyes 'No, I have not found the 400 but I have found 40 millions.'

He had met John A. Morris who was ready to use his fortune building a new Course, 'the Million Dollar track'. Once again Leonard burned with enthusiasm and the public's interest flared anew in racing."[1]

On April 4th he wrote Clara (who remained on patrol in London):

"Coney Island Jockey Club.
We are getting on nicely. We have 292 acres, all the land we want except ten acres in one corner which we will have in a day or two. The work of surveying and laying out the track has commenced. Morris is in high spirits. . . .

I dined last night with Kitty [his niece, Mrs. Mott, daughter of Lawrence and Sister Carrie]. 'Awfully small dinner of 16!' Lord Walter Campbell on her right and the celebrated orator—a lawyer Fergerson on her left *between Kitty and her mother!* Judge what a charming time he must have had entertaining Carrie! Kitty of course devoted herself wholly to the Lord. Kitty was fairly dazzling with her diamonds. Her dress was *very* low while her mother had a shawl pinned tightly round her neck. I looked at Carrie many times while the lawyer was trying to entertain her. She never smiled once or even opened her lips as far as I could see."

Red Indian blood can sometimes lend more dignity than charm! Mrs. Lawrence Jerome would have been extremely annoyed however had anyone ever remarked on her resemblance to a meditating Iroquois.

Another letter from Leonard to his wife reads:

"Washington D.C.
You must not worry about my health. I am at the present writing in perfect condition and if I get ill I promise to let you know at once. They tell you its a shame that you let me come off here alone, that you ought to come out and take care of me. What nonsense! They simply don't know what they are talking about. Alone! Why I am in the midst of a host of friends and relatives who would fly to me instantly if I were ill. As to your coming out you would make a great expense, bore yourself and do me no good. And I don't see why, if I am comfortable, you should take a step that is sure to make me otherwise. When in town I have a small room in the rear of the Brunswick sixth story where I sleep and dress. It gives square to the sun and is warm enough without a fire. I am as comfortable in it as if I had the whole house. I spend my time mostly at the Jockey Club and its office. At the office horse-talk and

[1] New York *Tribune*.

business, at the Club meals, library, whist, billiards, talk with friends. When it gets a little warmer I shall be off racing, yachting, visiting and knocking about generally. If you had any go in you like either of the girls and could mount your horse and keep up, we might knock about together and enjoy it. But you haven't a bit of taste that way and never had. And you couldn't stand that sort of life now even if you liked it once upon a time!

And you say you should be here in duty bound *to take care of me!* What stuff! I don't want to be taken care of and what's more I *won't* be, not by anybody. I gave Eugenc [a Jerome nephew] to understand that. The first day his wife pounced on me as if I were a newly arrived poodle and fairly smothered me. She ordered a huge wardrobe into my little room. I ordered it out and told her I preferred to unpack myself as if I put away things myself I knew where to find them. Of course in being together we could indulge in our habitual confidential talks and they are very pleasant and this is about all the good that would result from your coming out. I shall make up for that by writing you very fully. . . .

Randolph is doing magnificent work. Every move he makes strengthens his record. I hope we shall have good news of Moreton soon. Hope you are not pinching too closely. No necessity of it. Love to all."

Perhaps she felt a twinge at her husband's words. There had been a time when she longed for the capacity to show that mixture of helplessness and audacity which Leonard desired in women. But the plump lady encased in whalebone and stiff silk and rustling jet who had installed herself in London as a guardian of her daughters knew it was now too late for regret. "If you had any go in you like either of the girls and could mount your horse and keep up . . ." Once the words would have hurt. Now she could smile philosophically and admit the truth. She had never been able to keep up with Leonard. It was not in her to ride plunging horses, or hit high notes or 'knock about'. Now it would be best to remember only that far romantic past in Rochester. With a wistful sigh, Mrs. Jerome took up her quill and agreed: she had never had "a bit of taste that way".

51

DESPITE his disappearing means Leonard remained on terms of easy friendship with the old millionaire set. The Commodore's eldest son William Henry Vanderbilt had inherited ninety million dollars, built himself an immense brownstone morgue and lived less merrily than Leonard in that "small sunny room needing no fire". Leonard did not wish for a "clutter of possessions". Sense of achievement sufficed. The most generous of men, he could literally cut himself off without a penny and not care. In his time he had hurled money around and said: "Never give in a small way. Always give, if you give at all, in a big way; I mean from the heart, not worrying about it." Perhaps owing to an austere youth he had kept his health right through the peak of his career, so that in maturity he could spend with a zest which few possessed. Now he would have been happy with a tent.

In May 1888 Clara received a letter from Leonard, who was always amused by the Duke of Marlborough's matrimonial affairs:

"Vannie has written a nice little book on Western New York and dedicated it in some flattering terms to me. It is a most interesting story of the last 100 years. The Duke has gone off this morning with Lawrence and a party to the Adirondacks trout fishing, to be gone a week. I rather think he will marry the Hammersley. [Mrs. Louis Hammersley, a widow famous for having the walls and ceiling of the *salon* behind her opera box entirely covered by festoons of orchids.] Don't you fear any responsibility on my part. Mrs. H. is quite capable of deciding for herself. Besides I have never laid eyes on the lady but once. At the same time I hope the marriage will come off as there is no doubt she has lots of tin. [She had just changed her name to Lily from Lilian because the latter rhymed with million and she did not like verse.]

My papers with Morris are ready. It is a wonderful piece of good luck. My friend furnishes all the money, gives me complete control and half the profits for ever. We will have our 200 men at work on Tuesday.

I get few papers with Randolph's speeches. One at Preston, of which the cable gives a synopsis, shows he got the Govt. on the hip. We needn't worry about him. [Only Jennie did.] He knows what he is about.

I see Labouchere is doing the Eastern business in the House for Moreton. It *must* be settled in favour of the Nizam. The swindle is so plain."

Moreton's efforts to improve the finances of Hyderabad had impressed Leonard more than other ventures but when the time came to claim "one year of leakage" Frewen's assassination looked the more likely reward.

On May 22nd Leonard wrote:

"I think we are to have a good year with plenty of glory heaped upon Morris. He is modest but he can't help that. He has just made a present to the Club of the Club House i.e. we are not to pay interest on that, about $250,000. The new members are coming in at the rate of about twenty a day. At this rate we will have 3,000 members by May 30. Dr. Ash will *scarify* my knee to-morrow and every three days till further notice, object: counter irritation. I have been improving daily since I landed. Don't want a valet. Shouldn't know what to do with him.

I made two gold pieces yesterday. Don't think I can do better than send them to Leonie. In fact I hereby dedicate all such findings in the future to her. She must spend them as she likes *without accounting to Mama*!

Last Sat. I went down to Willie K. Vanderbilt's with the Coaching Club, a very delightful party. We had perfect weather coming and going. When I tell you I rode 54 miles each way over a good deal of bad road and felt no inconvenience whatever then or thereafter you will conclude that a certain supposed ailment of a fundamental and fatal nature has existence only in the brain of Dr. Pratt. We are racing daily at Jerome Park and working with many men and teams at the 'new Jerome Park' (that is what Morris insists on calling the new course). We are also preparing for Sheepshead which opens Thursday next. I am in perfect accord with my Morris Committee. We have been looking for an office to-day. Will pay out $5,000 to labour to-morrow. It is now two to one that I run over the last of July for a short visit, say ten days in England. I hate winter visits. The weather is always horrible.

The Duke I see frequently. I think he will marry the Hammersley though he does not confide in me any more. Lawrence is all right again but he has had a loud warning.

Union Club (Later)

Well Blandford is married! I went with him to the Mayor's office in the City Hall at one o'clock to-day and witnessed the ceremony. The bride was looking very well and all passed off quietly. I took charge of his cable to the Duchess, also sent one of my own to Jennie. I dine with them at Delmonico's this evening: a dinner given by Mr. and Mrs. Clews to the Duke and his bride. I shall go down to the *Aurania* in the morning to see them off. They had great difficulty in arranging the religious marriage. The clergy refused, he being a divorced man.[1] However they found a parson of the Methodist persuasion who consented to perform the service. An hour ago it was all done. I am pretty certain now to come out by the *Umbria* July 21 returning about August 21. My health is all right but I must have my annual ocean trip."

'Dear dear Mama' may have stood gallantly by her progeny and tried to help them face their difficulties but even so they occasionally found her 'trying'. When Leonie returned from a trip with the Princess of Wales who told her with artless sincerity, "We never seemed to know how to enjoy life until you showed us," she described the rest of the party and their mannerisms to Mrs. Jerome. In the recital she used the phrase "it was the pot calling the kettle black". Mama froze. "Leonie, how can you use such *coarse* expressions!"

"How else should I say it?"

"At least you might use the word casserole instead of pot!"

This incident amused all the daughters, who hurried off to bask in royal circles where they were never scolded and their *bons mots* fell like manna from heaven through the dull air.

Jennie's worries, mostly of a political nature concerning Randolph's growing rift with Lord and Lady Salisbury, were poured forth to Leonard, who clung pathetically to her letters for he was sure his son-in-law would make a come-back. Now that Randolph was out of office he had become keener about the turf and bought a number of racehorses. The star of his stable was a great-hearted little mare by Trappist out of Festive which he bought for £300. Jennie had been reading Renan's *L'Abbesse de Jouarre* and gave her this name which turned into a popular 'Abscess on the Jaw'. In 1888 she won the Oaks at 20 to 1, and Leonard wrote jubilantly from his Jockey Club:

"We had a great success these last two days and weather superb. I have Jennie's cable! A splendid victory the Abbesse! I am anxious to hear if they had anything on her. A little at 100 to 20 would have been nice. Even letters this morning seem exciting. It would be grand if that African

[1] The Duke's first marriage to Lady Blandford, the daughter of the Duke of Abercorn, had been dissolved of her own petition in 1883, just before he succeeded.

venture turns out what they expect. Give me early news. [Randolph planned exploring and mining in undeveloped South Africa.] I have a trap stationed at Fordham which meets me every morning and I drive back after the races. Everything at Sheepshead progressing beautifully."

All through this spring his daughters wrote him of their various fortunes, Leonie from Naples, where Jack yearned to 'take up painting' (alas, for he had no talent), Clara from Brede Place, where she was living alone while Moreton engaged in one of his world tours, and Jennie from various country houses. At a party at the Viceregal Lodge, Dublin, where she went for Punchestown Races, Jennie wrote all the family to buy things for her in whatever country they were. After listing the guests—people then considered so smart, now forgotten—she asks for a nice set of toilet table combs from Leonie, whose friends (the Abercorns, Leinsters, Ormondes and Londonderrys) all ask after her, from Clara table-mats to be ready for her return and from Papa advice on how to bet! She had just won £26 at the races and thought it should be more. She ends:

"To-night there is going to be a dinner of 70 at Dublin Castle—the investiture of Lord Ormonde afterwards and then St. Patrick's Ball. I am going to wear my white satin with pearls and feathers."

Leonard sighed, and yet he loved her for the exuberant pleasure she could obtain from dressing up. She was so like him thirty years before; his generosity and extravagance and drive were all part of her nature. But Jennie was a woman, she had not his male ability to earn what she was going to spend.

Leonie used to describe Jennie's remedy for "the dumps", an affliction to which all Victorian ladies were prone whenever thwarted. "Come on, let's cheer ourselves up at Worth's!" she would exclaim, taking her younger sister by the arm. Sweeping into the shop she then proceeded to order one gown after another without asking the price. Months later when the bills arrived she gasped with amazement and horror. How was it possible that she owed so much? These trips to Monsieur Worth were regarded very solemnly by Leonie, who received a far smaller allowance than Jennie and hoped that in time she might inherit the models chosen. The Leslies with £25,000 a year considered themselves far too poor to help Jack's wife, who had not been 'brought up to be practical and got in a dreadful tangle when she tried to scrimp'. Carriageless, dressed in her sister's cast-offs and harassed by monetary troubles generally, poor Leonie appealed to Papa, but she touched him at a bad moment. He had nothing to spare and wrote back:

"Madison Club.

I think you must give up your Newport excursion. It would be very charming but unavoidably expensive. It is the first time I ever refused any of you girls anything on the ground of expense. I must really know how some things are going to turn out before spending any more than we can reasonably help.

What an ass Freddie is making of himself. You made a lucky escape.

Your photograph in your court dress is capital. Bridget made a great ado saying 'it must be a wedding dress'."

Freddie Gebhard was scandalizing America by his open love-affair with Lily Langtry. When she went on tour the newspapers reported to the nation that "wealthy bachelor socialite Gebhard" accompanied her publicly, showering her with flowers and jewels. When 'the Lily' returned to New York he provided her with a luxurious residence in West 23rd Street where the 'fast set' attended her glamorous parties. Freddie escorted her to Delmonico's, he drove her through Central Park and he openly paid homage at private parties. It never occurred to Mrs. Langtry to try to hide her royal associations. She carried herself with the haughty air of *Maîtresse du Roi*, a post new to Americans, who did not know if she should be 'cut' or curtseyed to. Moreton, who had started the whole trouble by introducing Gebhard to his former lady friend, wrote coarsely that he himself had found it "quite impossible to compete with Prince Rudolph much less the Prince of Wales, but I had the joy of seeing her riding my horse when out exercising with H.R.H. Anyway lilies can be dreadfully boring when not planted in a bed!"

Mr. Jerome may have censured young Gebhard for his indiscretion and certainly he rejoiced that his daughter had not married that charming gambling playboy, but he was not himself averse to "looking after Moreton's poor beautiful friend". A single letter in Mrs. Langtry's handwriting falls from the Jerome papers. Dated only "Wednesday" it reads:

"Dear Mr. Jerome,

How kind you have been. I should indeed like to drive again in your carriage. Would you please call for me at 3 in the aft on Friday if it is quite convenient.

Yours sincerely,
Lily Langtry."

He probably found it very convenient indeed. Gentlemen usually did.

On June 15th Leonard wrote his sons-in-law some advice he had learnt at Canfield's:

"I have been yachting and fishing the last three days with Morris. To-morrow we start for Bar Harbour in the *Cora*, stopping a day or two at Newport. The yacht is a beauty and we have it all to ourselves. I have missed some of Randolph's speeches. The club's mail has failed several numbers, however, the Secretary is writing for the missing ones. I don't think there is any chance of R. going back into the Cabinet at present, but he is growing stronger every move he makes and when there does come a change he will be counted in to a certainty.

How much did Jack lose? There is no system but mine that can ever beat the Bank. A small amount, loss limited each day—always the same amount and when in luck *press* it as I did that last day. Win all you can, keep on till you think your luck is changed. But it's hard for Jack or Moreton to follow that system rigidly. I couldn't have done it myself twenty or thirty years ago."

In late July, Leonard sailed on the *Umbria* and by September 1st he was back in New York. The city and its modes of life altered with surprising swiftness and many of his old friends were dying off. Rough old Commodore Vanderbilt had gone to his grave leaving behind a dynasty of nervy patrons of art to build themselves palaces in various European modes, to argue precedence in and out of dining-rooms and to marry a variety of titles.

In 1887 William Travers, Leonard's great friend, had died in Bermuda after a last gay letter ending: "The waiters get the change and the hotel gets the rest." Now Lawrence suddenly cracked. He and James Gordon Bennett had been known for their frolics together in America and France for many years. During the last decade their pranks on the Paris-Bordeaux express had baffled countless travellers. Even in late middle age they feverishly 'created jollity' by impersonating escaping madmen, hysterical jilted lovers, etc. Their jokes, which became steadily rowdier and more uncouth, appealed to their epoch. Bennett kept his own four-in-hand coach at Pau and one day when Lawrence complained about wild driving he shoved his friend inside to be 'quiet and safe'. Bennett then galloped his horses off at speed. When they came to the formidable Morlaas hill the horses ran away. While Bennett tugged at the wheelers' reins, his secretary, clinging on for dear life, was ordered to take the leaders. At last the coach rattled to a standstill and Lawrence stepped out white in the face to remonstrate. Then he saw Bennett pouring with sweat and shaking. "Whose joke was it anyway?" he asked. The secretary collapsed. "Not mine."

Bennett's final prank (presumably while on an excursion outside of that 'good society' mentioned by the *Post*) was to take over a certain establishment in Paris, go to bed covered with bandages and set all the girls nursing him. At three in the morning the same long-suffering secretary was sent by brougham to wake Lawrence saying Mr. Bennett had suffered a fearful accident. Lawrence arrived post-haste and knelt beside the swathed figure before he looked around at the twenty strange nurses. A burst of laughter and magnums of champagne followed. Happily Lawrence's wife, Aunt Kate, did not hear of this episode. A strict teetotaller, she had already snubbed Leonard at a dinner party when he defended the drinking of wine. He quoted the Miracle of Cana, at which she snorted: "In that case our Lord showed poor judgment." After which there really was nothing more to be said.

Lawrence's first stroke had laid him out after a fishing party in Maine. The Duke of Marlborough, a departing guest, received at the station an urgent telegram to return. "Another of Larry's jokes," he said and continued his journey.

A few months later Larry finally collapsed. New York headlines read: "Lawrence Jerome Dying: the Prince of Good Fellows Slowly gives up the Fight." "The merriest spirit in all the world goes when Lawrence Jerome crosses the dark river."

Leonard mourned deeply for his favourite brother.

At about this time Clara Jerome developed a most unlikely friendship with a Frenchman named Monsieur Eiffel who was busy on a 'construction of amazement' for the forthcoming *Grande Exhibition*. He delighted her *salon* with little engineering sketches and took her to the top of his celebrated Tower. There he signed a picture of it saying that she was the first woman in the world to have been so high. It was *the* adventure of her old age!

In 1888 Leonard planned to meet his wife and daughters in Paris for Christmas, and offered to pay everyone's expenses.

"The scheme strikes me as very sensible, very possible and very jolly. Clara should take her children by all means. I have proposed to let Jerome Park for ten years—think I will get it. The three courses will then work in perfect harmony, Jerome P., Sheepshead and the New Course. We will make Jerome P. the *Auteuil* of New York not altogether steeple-chasing but principally. It is admirably adapted to steeplechasing and too cramped for modern flat-racing. The New Course will open May 30. Jennie and Randolph have promised to come over for the occasion. You may be sure it will be a great event. Travers made a great hit in the Trial of Emerson . . . spoke for over an hour: compliments on all sides."

Travers Jerome carried exactly the same mixture of blood as Leonard's three daughters. He was half-Hall, half-Jerome. What would the uncompromising Puritan Catherine and roistering, light-hearted, uncontrollable Lawrence produce? Leonard watched this nephew with admiration and with astonishment. Travers was tough. That might have been expected in a Jerome, but he showed a streak of iron completely lacking in his father's make-up. Prank-playing Lawrence only wished to make the world laugh. His son wished to make it honest!

"And by heaven he nearly succeeded!" commented a fellow lawyer. Within a year of Lawrence's death Travers was well launched on his career as New York's famous Attorney Reformer. He fought corruption, he fought graft, he fought Tammany Hall. Travers' upbringing had been Puritan, his zeal was that of the Inquisition. In the most spectacular of legal careers Travers organized many an *auto da fé*, and the press revelled in his exposures. He hounded the racketeers of New York city and flayed the owners of vice-haunts not because they were naughty but because they bribed the police. Travers disliked hypocrisy. He wanted all the spades called spades and the Bosses of Tammany Hall called something else. "Everybody is talkin' these days about Tammany Hall growin' rich on graft," said State Senator Plunkitt, "but nobody thinks of drawin' the distinction between honest graft and dishonest graft." Certainly not Mr. Travers Jerome.

The slick guys must have hated him. Even Uncle Leonard was less uncompromising on one point. Among the extraordinary characters of New York was Richard Canfield who ran exclusive gambling casinos. Only millionaires were allowed into his 'palace' on 44th Street, stakes were higher than anywhere in the world and Canfield always kept $500,000 in cash to hand to pay off house losses. Patrons were sometimes entertained in his office but never invited to the top floor where in his private apartment Canfield led a quiet gentlemanly life, assembling rare books and interesting pictures. He was a collector in the real sense. Unlike his friend J. P. Morgan who only bought up the museum-stamped masterpieces of Europe, Canfield studied the work of living artists and was almost unique among rich New Yorkers in showing discrimination. One cannot quite say that Canfield 'discovered' Whistler, but at a time when Leonie's friends, the 'cultivated aristocracy' of London, could only decipher Whistler's genius as 'clever but a fraud', Mr. Canfield of 44th Street was building up a collection of his best paintings. Canfield was proud to make a friend of James McNeill Whistler, who painted a portrait of him ironically styled 'His Reverence'. It now hangs in the Cincinnati Museum. Leonard had first met Canfield at Saratoga where he operated the Club House. That was in the days when Freddie Gebhard was courting Leonie and at the same time trying to learn how to act as a man of the world from watching her Papa. Leonard had never been a very big gambler but it amused him to guide rich youngsters. When Jerome first came to New York a millionaire meant a man who owned a million dollars. Now the title was only bestowed on those who passed the ten-million mark. Fortunes were getting vaster and more complicated with great trusts consolidating them. Leonard had stepped right out of the category of wealth; horses were his only luxury, but his friends were the richest men of America. Jerome advised Freddie on how to play, and how to comport himself at the Club House. Soon he had found Canfield's views on art more stimulating than the endless gossip of the playboy world. "Such passion for the rare and beautiful gives one a feeling that the man is alive, much more so than most of his clients."

Now that his fortunes were gone Leonard never stepped inside a New York casino but he visited that top storey which the gambling Vanderbilts and Whitneys never saw. To the tall curious Mr. Canfield Leonard admitted that he "could not help liking Gebhard despite all the fuss". Freddie had really made himself into a national figure, he represented the adolescent male infatuated out of his wits, which is so dear an ideal to the average housewife.

"It is a pity," remarked Mr. Canfield, "when those who want to be gentlemen don't know how."

Canfield bluntly described his own conversion to bibliomania. At the age of thirty he had been imprisoned for six months and thus obtained time to read and study. ". . . I do not care a rap about what other people think of me. I never did. . . . So long as I know I am honest with myself, I am satisfied," he stated. Most New Yorkers agreed with this code of ethics. Only Travers Jerome continuously called the arty Prince of Gambling a "common felon".

Neither Leonard's wife nor daughters took much interest in their cousin's clean-up of New York City. They were immersed in their own battles and triumphs. In the autumn Leonard wrote:

"I presume you are by this time installed in Paris. It seems to me a very sensible move. Paris is cold and wet in the winter but a thousand times better than London. I have written to your mother to go over, and Clara also. Why not? Don't try to live together. You have done it several times heretofore and successfully but it is not good policy. Something might occur in which you couldn't agree and then it would become disagreeable. Jennie and Randolph might come also? By the way, will you have my friend 'John Randolph of Roanoke'[1] and his tub with you? A very great additional inducement for me to come over if you do. I am myself entirely out of the way of gossip being immersed day and night in my racing schemes. Tell me how you propose to live, how to amuse

[1] Leonie's three-year-old son, now Sir Shane Leslie.

288

yourselves in Paris. It is the place of all others for young people capable of enjoying the world's pleasures without running to excess. £100 bill enclosed."

The grand-children splashing in their bath-tubs grew ever more dear to Leonard now that he felt the sands were slipping fast. These Christmas plans did not materialize but Leonie produced this story: "John Leslie spent a dreary evening at a ball where Count Charles Kinsky introduced a 'dull little mouse of a girl from Vienna' to him. Unable to find her other partners Pink Jack remained tied to her all evening and reproached Kinsky for planting him with a wallflower. He did not expect to hear the lady's name again, but in January 1889 shy dumpy Marie Vetsera was found murdered beside the body of Crown Prince Rudolph. Lieutenant Leslie then wished that he had noticed more of the charms of the 'little mouse'."

Another story which made him chuckle was this: Jack Leslie had made friends with a most charming Mrs. K——. When walking together at Sandown Races they met the Prince of Wales and "dear Jacksy introduced his fair companion. The Prince immediately asked her to accompany him and his face lit up with such a smile that Jacksy knew he would not see her again for a long time!"

Mrs. K—— proved to be one of the most important influences in the Prince's life; in fact her name is still well known on the Continent where the Latins take an inordinate interest in royal romance. Leonie often visited her in Italy and once had the joy of standing beside her in the Piazza San Marco when an Italian guide passed by and called his party to a halt. "Do you see the gentleman walking over there?" he asked breathlessly. His band of sightseers stared at the distant figure of Mrs. K——'s elderly husband walking across the square.

"That," hissed the guide, "is the lover of Queen Victoria!"

52

"If only Moreton could have let the Silver question rest, he was promised material friendships, interests, and position. It definitely excluded him from the House of Commons. . . . While regarded abroad as a very prop of Empire, he was often without visible means of support. But there was an unconquerable element in him which kept him afloat."

Spectators of his struggles proved less buoyant. Mrs. Jerome, appalled and exhausted by her son-in-law's letters and schemes, which Rudyard Kipling described as 'apocalyptical', retreated to the seaside near Hastings where she hoped the air might revive her while she made personal economies 'for honour's sake'. "As long as a member of my family owes money anywhere I shall not have a fire in my room." And there she sat with hands folded staring into the unused grate of a cold lodging house. Leonard was shocked when he heard of this stoicism but Moreton merely laughed. Corresponding with viceroys, presidents, ambassadors, ministers and senators throughout the world he remained unimpressed by 'icy martyrdom'. Clara groaned, "Mama won't have a fire while we owe *anything*," but Moreton had an easy way with creditors. "He carried them with his debts into his next scheme and repaid losses in the past by fairer hopes ahead."

Leonard had entertained hopes when his son-in-law led the Hyderabad delegation to the House of Commons but even here Moreton's position remained delicate, "for while he was undermining the schemes of others he was advancing some of his own."

Undaunted by failures to persuade successive Prime Ministers to engage in a fight for a Bi-metallic Union of England and America he would eventually pass into the wilderness.

Meanwhile his gentle blue-eyed wife continued to entertain in Aldford Street. Poets, cabinet ministers and royalty hobnobbed in her mauve drawing-room. Philippe d'Orléans and Count d'Esterhazy had been her admirers for a long time, now Mr. Jerome heard extraordinary rumours. Clara, not content with the troubles of her husband was taking on fresh ones, which savoured uncomfortably of dynamite. The exiled King Milan of

Serbia appeared on her doorstep each day laden with grievances and bunches of flowers. Moreton took him off (with a strapping Balkan foster-brother) to shoot at a few country house parties and then himself departed on one of his celebrated tours. Milan continued to call daily at Aldford Street and the sight of a well-known Balkan king weighed down with gardenias caused comment in Mayfair.

Mama Jerome had always cherished a weakness for European royalties, but King Milan proved the exception. Like *Punch* of the time she could but hope that "His Majesty did nothing consonant with the character of a plotter" and "conclude that the visit was in every way an innocent one, and that London is the better and not the worse for it". Leonard's letters studiously avoid any reference to the subject which must have been uppermost in his wife's mind. Apart from news concerning his own horses and the successes of the three Racecourses he ran at Gravesend, Westchester and Sheepshead, he mentions only a pleasant week on the Vanderbilt farm and in September writes from the Union Club:

"Dear Clit,
        I took a little trip last week, Saratoga three days, and Williams-town two days, where I stayed with Eugene. Fine weather, quite refreshing, good appetite, leg about the same.
        Eugene drove me over to see your father's house. It is a fine old English country house. Do you remember the house where we stopped when we drove down to Rockaway in a buggy some *several* years ago? Just such another house, wide hall running through the centre with a number of rooms on both sides. . . ."

Clara thought often of the early days of their married life. How simple everything then seemed! What a clutter of complications and distresses her daughters had collected with their English commitments—yet she herself had willed it.

Determined to expiate for all the family follies and extravagances she let another draught blow in. But despite Mrs. Jerome's refrigeration the facts remained rather warm.

Some of Clara Frewen's journals of the 'eighties still exist, page after page mentions the weather, the dresses she wore, and whom she found 'civil':

"Dined at Ldy Blanche Hozier, Consuelo [Manchester], Ldy Lonsdale, Lord Hood very cheery. Leonie came in late, wore my blue—Leo and I walked down Piccadilly to buy a boutonnière. Ld. Dunraven to lunch. Mrs. Ronalds came in after. Moreton dined on guard. Leo and I dined alone and she practised while I read. . . . Blanche Hozier, Fanny Roche, and Wharncliffe and Leo dined with us. Sat about talking while Leo played. The Hozier nurse dear Bessie is leaving baby Clementine to look after Leo's boy. How lucky. Moreton so cross about my remark on the mistletoe. . . . Drove about all day shopping. Duke of Manchester to dine, Moreton very tired after Board Meeting. . . . Saw baby washed. Kings X Station at 1. No Moreton. Had to go all alone to Bretton. Big party. Dressed for the ball. White tulle and satin. Drove 7 miles."

On she travels through the country homes of England to "go for a little walk, write a letter before tea, meet kind Mrs. B . . .", etc. Occasionally there is mention of the "famous pictures" and the "beautiful beds", but no descriptions emerge. She is usually without her spouse. It sounds a deadly round, creeping from swan-feeding to reading of newspapers to gold tea-gowns for tea and other dresses for dinner. But whenever there is a ball she writes "danced like mad all evening" and lists the more pleasing partners. Moreton only appears as not turning up when expected, failing to write a promised letter or as "very cross". In London she practises the piano for three hours and sees baby washed daily, politicians and lords and ladies come to dine, and things go wrong with the brougham. She dines at Randolph's house: "Sir H. Wolff, Arthur Balfour, Lord Falmouth. Very dull considering so many clever men together." A daily walk with Leonie in the Park often ends with lunch at Jennie's, where Winston flits in the background like a little ghost. "Randolph not much interested in children but thought Baby sweet. Winston came in to say goodbye as the poor little fellow had to go back to school." Arthur Balfour takes her to the opera "which finishes just as we get there". Lady Blanche Hozier (whose baby daughter Clementine would some day marry "poor little Winston") appears on almost every page, so does Lord Grey (Moreton's truest political friend) and Mrs. Ronalds with her new harpists and violoncellists. Sundays always mean "the Park after Church". "Saw lots of pals under the trees but I wanted a man for luncheon so went to the Row." That was apparently the place to find one. Lists of grand names at parties end with "horrid sweet champagne, thought 11 o'clock would never come". The entries become fewer during Moreton's travels: "No news from Moreton to-day but a telegram he hopes for results. . . . M. writes from Montreal. . . . Good news from India . . . feel very blue." Then the pages are blank. Only a box of carefully tied letters show that she thought sufficiently of King Milan to keep his compliments.

Serbia suffered from two rival royal families, the Obrenovics and Karageorgevics who at intervals, and by means of intrigue or assassination, replaced each other on the throne. King Milan (Obrenovic) was at this time 'Ex' in name rather than function, for although he had rid himself of certain troubles by abdicating in favour of his son Alexander, he continued to exercise considerable influence in his native country. Basing himself chiefly in Paris and Vienna he pulled strings at a safe distance while his wife Queen Natalie from whom he was separated chased him with her "tiresome Memoranda". She influenced her son King Alexander, turning him against his father, which Milan bitterly resented and when he met Clara Frewen in London and fell in love with her he made no secret of his wild hope that it might be possible to become free to marry again. What his intentions were concerning Moreton we do not know. Clara fluttered and sat safe on her mauve brocade sofa, keeping the tea-table between herself and dangerous propositions. King Milan was an enormous man with round, black eyes and what she described as "overpowering ways". The only one of his gifts which has survived is an exquisite little tortoiseshell music-box with a tiny golden bird which pops out of the lid and delicately trills a tune. King Milan's surname meant 'bird' and no more fascinating souvenir of himself could have been devised.

The twenty-odd envelopes addressed to Mrs. Frewen, 18 Aldford Street, are all embossed with different regal designs of brilliant colour. Large gold crowns supported by Serbian eagles and the name Milan in red and blue stand entwined with the Obrenovic motto, *Tempus et meum jus*. For an exile he kept a splendid assortment of notepaper. The correspondence begins with a menu card signed by Paul Metternich, and then Milan who in his favourite joking way inscribed his name "1,000y" (mille-an), after which he writes *"non pas adieu mais au revoir."* Then come an assortment of crowned calling-cards in different colours: *"Chère Mme Frewen. Je me permets de mettre a vos pieds ces quelques gardenias sachant que c'est votre fleur favourite. Votre biene reconnaissant Milan."* Others ask affectionately after her daughter *la petite Clare* ending, *"Je vous baise les mains et suis votre dévoué Milan."* A series of undated notes on different coloured notepapers asking when he can come and see her to discuss ominous news from Paris make us long to know what was really going on. Clara must have acted on his behalf in London for Milan ceases to be 'devoted' and becomes instead 'grateful'. All the letters are in French and full of puns:

> *"Chère Mme Frewen. Dans le jardin de la vie pour parler le langage imagé d'un Oriental—ces quelques lilas et muguets* peuvent être *douces et avoir un parfum, tout comme vous, Madame, vous êtes bonne et aimable. Ils son blancs et innocents tout comme mon langage est plus qu'innocent—même muet—*in the language of green flowering Albion, they seem like you, Madame, to appear innocent of a slow plot to obtain a professor for an ignorant savage.

Look at his face. See how he blushes because he is ignorant. Throw one pitying look on this little bunch of mysterious violets. See how shy they are. Just so the savage will soon have to hide his face if he cannot say more than 'to learn or not to learn that is the question'. *Dois-je mettre au bas de cette page mon nom d'oiseau ou dire que je suis un*

Ass."

This balderdash followed a suggestion that Milan should take English lessons. Most of his letters liken himself to a 'bird of passage' and mention an accompanying gift, special bonbons from Paris, foreign cigarettes, a box at Drury Lane, the book they had discussed the day before and torrents of various flowers all 'deposed at her feet', with fine words. Several notes beg Clara to see him to talk over "the matter of great importance" and ask rather pathetically if "Lady Churchill" could help. Every morning regularly a box of her favourite gardenias arrived on the doorstep of Number 18.

Invited to lunch to meet a famous beauty he writes coyly to say that like the swallows he only admires the "beauty of nature and smile of spring", a lesson which apparently Clara has taught him. "Belonging to the race of birds, how could you wish me to be otherwise?" In November 1890 he is writing "*Chère et charmante amie*" and begging for her advice. He is deeply unhappy and grateful for her friendship. "An exile feels kindness more profoundly than others and all the more so as in this country I am not only unknown, but have all against me."

Moreton reappeared and after expressing annoyance at the boxes of gardenias proceeded to ask Milan to his club (where the poor King could not find the way in), and then to induce the *Pall Mall Gazette* to publish a political letter for His Majesty. Not knowing the customary formalities in England Milan asks Clara for advice concerning an audience with Queen Victoria "at the risk of displeasing". The card with next day's gardenias reads: "*Chère et charmante amie*. I understand. Of course you are right. . . . Milan."

Clara had told him there was no hope.

When the King departs for Belgrade he writes pages of thanks for Clara's advice and help. He expects to return to Paris for the spring:

"I don't expect to stay with my son more than two or three weeks and then to come back to Paris for *la belle Saison*. . . . I would like to follow Lord Randolph to Africa but because of my son I will have to stay in Europe, without being able to make any definite plans. *Dans le* 'struggle for life' *ma part est dure*. How I envy those who are free. My aim in this journey is to regain my liberty. Will I succeed? I don't know. But as it is my existence is odious. What shall I say to you concerning

"I have your letter and am amused at the number of your hopes. Fortunately I can satisfy you at once on most of them. I am not 'safe and comfortable at the Brunswick Hotel' but I am all that at the Lenox. Sitting room, bedroom and bathroom—3 windows facing south. So much for hope No. 1. No. 2 you hope I am 'feeling better'. All right, I am. You hope my 'affairs don't bother me'. *They don't*.

I have paid an ugly bill of taxes this morning of $4,586 and have plenty of money in the bank. I am delighted to hear Randolph won such a lot of money, also that Moreton's prospects are so encouraging and last, though not least, that you are recovering from your illness.

The *Sun* made a statement two days before I arrived that I was dangerously ill in London and would never see New York again! It has been contradicted since."

On May 15th he wrote:

"My knee is better. I walk without pain only soon get tired. Travers has just made a great hit by the conduct of a case and an hour's speech in Court as Assistant District Attorney. He fought a great Tammany leader on a brutal assault and got him convicted and sentenced to one year's imprisonment and $500 fine.

I have no use whatever for a servant. He would only be a nuisance. When one has been in the habit of putting on one's own shoes and stockings for 60 or 70 years it would become rather awkward to have another do it. Randolph has come out of the Temperance affair very nicely. I hope to live to see the day when he will be the great leader in that richest of all rich fields *Free Trade*."

All through the summer Leonard attended to his racing fixtures. A red leather programme for the thirteen-day September meeting of the Coney Island Jockey Club at Sheepshead Bay lies on my table. The production is lavish. Every owner and trainer had one of these leather-bound programmes with his own name engraved in gold letters on the cover. Unlike a modern race card this booklet was not meant to be thrown away, but to grace a gentleman's reference library when the events it enumerates were over. Out of the hundred issued in the sunshine of that 1890 meeting, probably only this one has survived and that because Leonie's handwriting has pencilled in "Dear Papa's last racing book".

The conditions of entry vary, the races are large and go up to seven a day and the stakes compared very favourably with those in England at the same period.

Paris. Nothing to interest you because I lead the life of a savage, seeing no one. Public life is absorbed by two things, the Empress Frederick whose visit to Versailles and especially to Saint Cloud which is still in ruins, has produced an acute emotion and the sitting of the Chamber yesterday. They voted for the complete suppression of Pari-Mutuel, betting, book makers etc. Many people think that it bodes the end of racing in France."

A later letter from Vienna reads:

"*Chère amie*,

Returning to Vienna from Moravia I went to the country for a week to friends and found your little letter from Paris—which I have definitely left—to carry my penants to Vienna and follow more closely, for Serbia's sake, the intrigues political and private of my horrible spouse. It is a constant battle. Paris suited me personally. I departed leaving many friends but the government looked at me sideways and openly protected through the French Minister in Belgrade the intrigues of Queen Natalie, who having played such a fatal role during my reign is now concentrated on the ruination of her son, who lets himself be led and cannot see that her acts and gestures have but one end, which is her own immeasurable ambition."[1]

One more letter remains. Sent by hand to Clara at the Hotel Vendôme in Paris, it carries a gold embossed M over an inch long, surmounted by the royal crown. "*Ma chère amie*," he begins, but Clara, considering discretion the better part of sentimentality, has unfortunately cut out the comments we would most like to read.

Leonard thought that Moreton created sufficient havoc without taking on Balkan stewpots as well. When he came to London and found his daughter "very blue" because Queen Victoria insisted on treating Balkan monarchs as if they were walking bombshells, "unwise to receive in audience", Leonard finally expostulated, "Why couldn't she have married a normal American and lived in my country!"

[1] Queen Natalie's intrigues ended in bloodstained tragedy. Milan's last public act was to write a letter to his son King Alexander forbidding him to marry Draga, one of Queen Natalie's Ladies-in-Waiting. His son disobeyed and later evoked great unpopularity by refusing to go to his father's funeral when Milan died in Vienna. In 1904 King Alexander and Queen Draga were murdered in horrible circumstances and Peter Karageorgevic took the throne, riding from his coronation on his predecessor's white horse and using the Sixth Regiment, which had torn Queen Draga to pieces, to supply sentries at his palace. The *Daily Mail* remarked ominously that he began to resemble Alexander I who walked "preceded by assassins of his grandfather, surrounded by those of his father and followed by his own".

——◆—— 53 ◆——

Leonard Jerome accepted stoutly the role of Phoenix. His daughters never realized they were devouring him. Letters to his wife throughout the summer of 1889 are obviously intended to restore her spirits:

"April 6th. It has come off warm at last and there is comfort in visiting my ranches. I go out to the New Course on Sheepshead Bay and to Jerome Park about every other day. I mean to make young Morris give me a horse to drive. He might give me half a dozen and never miss them. I don't suppose they know into twenty or thirty horses how many they have. The enclosed cheque of course for Leonie. . . ."

"April 26th. I dined with Morris yesterday and then drove over the Course. He is pleased with the whole thing and showed no signs of weakening though he had already paid $700,000. I shall send you the girls' money next week and £8 for the Epsom trainer."

Mrs. Jerome worried because Winston had not inherited his mother's sublime beauty. He rather resembled a naughty little sandy-haired bulldog and seemed "backward except for complicated games with toy soldiers". It appeared "very difficult to tell what goes on in his mind". School reports were not complimentary; Jennie thought that the Army might offer a solution some day. "Let him be," advised Leonard. "Boys get good at what they find they shine at."

But there was precious little shining at this stage. The spurt took place quite suddenly some eight years later. Then Steevens, most brilliant of war correspondents, would be writing of a junior subaltern:

"He is what he is by breeding. He is the eldest son of Lord Randolph Churchill, and his mother is American. Lord Randolph was not so precocious as he was popularly supposed to be, but they begin early in America. From his father Winston derives the hereditary aptitude for

296

affairs, the grand style of entering upon them, which are not the les hereditary in British noble families because they skip nine generation out of ten."

From his mother's side, thought Steevens, came the shrewdness, keen-ness, personal ambition and sense of humour.

Leonard, interested as he had always been in breeding, refused to worry over his snub-nosed grandson. With that father and that mother—well, in a horse he would have seemed a likely winner. And what could you do with a stubborn colt but keep the reins light?

In July 1889, the new course, Morris Park, was opened. It was Leonard's last venture. Foreseeing the doom of Jerome Park he had perhaps been wise to make one huge effort to hold public interest. "A gorgeous Marquee was erected on the lawn but this did not replace the shaded slope at Jerome Park. The Gala Opening day brought out only six coaches whereas any day on the old course there were never fewer than twelve." The *Tribune* wrote:

"The outstanding feature of the Morris Park course is its immensity. The enclosure seems to have no bounds, the stables may be measured by miles. The betting ring would hold all the book makers in the U.S. and the Grand Stand looks big enough to seat all the race-going communities combined."

Towards the end of the year the press lamented the possibility of the American Jockey Club disappearing if it proved unable to sustain itself in the vastness of Morris Park. "How strange the whole thing seems. The man who gave Jerome Park to the public is the man who has done most to take it away. Is this honourable and honoured institution to die?"

Leonard fought on, determined that his Jockey Club should remain in the hands of honourable sporting gentlemen and not be run by 'tykes'. He expressed himself strongly to a friend: "I tell you, sir, these men stop at nothing. They are capable of all kinds of peculiar work. They play to win. The public must pay and they see that it does. Really it seems a great pity that racing associations should do business to enrich these fellows." The just and the unjust combined to defeat his high aims. It was as though his Puritan ancestors had risen from the grave in judgment. Sister Catherine made one of her horrid obtuse remarks: "The Jeromes seem to have so much sense of honour and hardly any sense of sin."

Now he knew well there could not be much time left to tie up the loose ends of material arrangements but he never let anyone know he was dying. After returning from England in May 1890 he wrote his wife:

Leonard Jerome's name appears as President of the Jockey Club (C. Fellowes and William K. Vanderbilt were Vice-Presidents) and also as the owner of three horses. He could no longer afford 'fashionably bred stuff', but his name remained at the top of the racing world, and among friends his charm, his kindness and his fire would never be forgotten. They said a man with such drive could never grow old.

In December, having played every card in efforts to perpetuate the strength and honesty of American racing associations, he left New York for the last time. There was little enough to close down, he merely paid a hotel bill and embarked with a couple of trunks, still hotly refusing to be bothered with a valet. Only four horses in training remained as commitments in the American continent. On arriving in England he scolded his wife severely for her icy moral vigil. He remarked "that isn't the way to make other people do things" and taking a house in London, he ordered fires to be lit in *all* the grates.

The daughters were horrified to see dear Papa grown tired and worn. His chaff could not reassure them and for the first time they realized how incessantly they relied on him, writing continuously to ask him to do something, burdening him with their troubles because his shoulders had always seemed so broad. Now they were overcome with remorse at not having gone to America more often. Leonard's nephew Eugene Jerome wrote apologetically to Clara Frewen:

> "I can understand how much you regret that one of you did not come over to him. But he would *not* consent to change his surroundings . . . it was his wish to remain at the Hotel Brunswick and we *had* to submit. . . . Had Uncle Leonard permitted me to do so I certainly shd have cabled you to come. When he sailed Henry Jerome went on board with him, and did all to make him comfortable. He would not listen to my getting a servant for him during the trip and had I been in a position I should have accompanied him . . . none of his family here were inattentive to his true condition. On the contrary he was a constant source of anxiety. . . . During the past ten years he has taken the place of a father gaining my affection as a man and dear friend. He wanted to save you anxiety and I could not—against his wishes send you word. . . . Uncle Isaac died on Monday. . . . Uncle Tom and your father are all that are now left of the nine brothers."

Once or twice Leonard dined out, in Jennie's house where Randolph still collected the most brilliant political brains in London, at Aldford Street where King Milan talked Balkan politics, and in Leonie's new house where she was arranging lectures to familiarize society with the *Ring das Niebelungen* which had been produced some years previously in New York but was still considered too "queer and discordant" for a London audience. A well-known German exponent of Wagner lectured and his lady attendant sang the motifs. Leonard delighted in the Professor's efforts to keep the story of Siegfried *comme il faut* for the young ladies present.

"Dee ladees mus not mind dis bad business of Sigmund und Siedlinde; it is *Schrecklich*, but it is only zee lofs of zee gods, vich do not count. . . . Und here we have zee lofe motif illustrated by 'triolets' or 'triplets' as you say in English. . . ."

But Leonard's outings were limited. The bleak London fogs descended and his lungs hurt. His daughters hardly left him, seeking to atone, rather late, for having taken so much. "If you make yourself into a rock," said Leonie later, "people *will* climb up and hang there." Of the three girls—now mature women—Leonie seemed to have solved her problems most happily. After the birth of her second son Norman at Stratford House, old Sir John had written her:

"Well done My dear Leonie. Well done! Another son and punctual to the moment. These dear boys with God's blessing will be delightful companions and fight the battle of Life side by side. I was but 14 months younger than my elder brother who from the first confided in me so that I knew everything he thought of and was in all his pursuits a companion at school, at College and afterwards in the World, and no one knows the grief it was to me to lose him and have to take his place. Therefore these two remind me of former days and their destiny appears very similar. Little Jack [Shane] aged 14 months has made great progress and when he trots on his little feet with his little red shoes I see you in all his motions—and I may say that I never knew anybody bear their burden so gaily and trip about so actively as you did without all those necessities to Fine Ladies in interesting situations which one is accustomed to observe. But you are entitled to a rest from your labours. I should recommend a pause, and if these dear children had been girls not boys I should have given the admonition to Jack but according to my theory it is under the circumstances to you that I think this sage Counsel ought to be addressed.

Much luck to you,
Yr. affectionate father-in-law,
John Leslie."

Jacksy had always teased his wife because she 'trotted about indoors' and to his surprise Leonie answered: "That's my Indian blood only don't let Mama know I told you—nor your mother either!" Lady Constance was gradually relenting. After many years of stringent remarks she turned into a delightful old grandmother. Alas she would live to see that second grandson Norman killed in the first month of the 1914 war; but the elder, grown from his little red shoes, showed her several volumes of verse before she died. At ninety Lady Constance's wit remained acute. Her last words, having been asked, "How do you feel today?" were "Pretty poorly I'm afraid . . ." and then with a faint smile, "and not very pretty."

To Jennie, who had tea with him almost every day, Leonard spoke encouragingly of Randolph's future, of that 'come-back' he must surely make. She did not argue but the sadness never left her eyes. Her husband was as ill as her father. Within five years he would be dead.

Of Clara, blue-eyed, affectionate, and still surprised by life's vagaries he spoke most lovingly to the other sisters. She needed protection and soon he would not be there to give it. King Milan proceeded with admirable tact to send rare old brandy for Leonard instead of gardenias. "*Quelques bouteilles de vieux cognac que j'ai procuré de Paris pour votre cher malade*" read his cards throughout January.

Moreton, blustering around the clubs, could hardly object to kindnesses for which he himself had no time.

And then in late February Leonard's cough grew worse. Clara insisted he must be moved from fog to the sea air of Brighton. He wondered briefly if it would not have been better to die in America, independently as he had lived, but it meant so much to see those he loved—even if they did fuss and hand him Bibles. The March winds blew hard and sea spray lashed the boarding-house windows. It was a drab place in which to say farewell but Leonard had always been at heart a traveller untrammelled by possessions. He felt that America belonged to him and he to her. Such as he was, she had made him, giving her vitality to his blood, her wide horizons to his mind. They would take him back to New York for burial. The 'odds and ends' he left were in order.

Now the cough racked him and his heart beat an uneven measure. Clara's eyes widened with anxiety and his three daughters hovered like frantic angels around the big brass bed. Their faces grew carved into lines of despair as they realized the impossibility of preventing that fiery spirit from quitting them. Their orbits had revolved around his all through the years. "Don't go yet," whispered Leonie. But he was slipping into the shadows, out of their ken. Again his eyes turned towards the screen which hid an occasional grand-child and his hand found strength to wave at a small peeking face. He was finished. The future lay with them.

Little Clara came, his six-year-old grand-daughter, and Mrs. Jerome's hands could be seen tying her blue shoulder ribbons—her adventures in life as sculptor and explorer could by no stretch of the imagination have been compassed by any man in the 'nineties, but the poems of Leonie's first son would some day echo the quality of a life that Leonard understood. The tempo of his own pulse throbbed in *Fleet Street*:

> I never see the newsboys run
>   Amid the whirling street,
>   With swift untiring feet,
> To cry the latest venture done,
> But I expect one day to hear
>   Them cry the crack of doom
>   And risings from the tomb,
> With great Archangel Michael near;
> And see them running from the Fleet
>   As messengers of God,
>   With Heaven's tidings shod
> About their brave unwearied feet.

Jennie's eldest was at Harrow. Red-headed, blue-eyed, freckled and 'difficult', he still showed no outstanding characteristic save a determination which grown-ups seldom appreciate in the young. Winston Leonard Spencer Churchill. What would he come to? Where would his road lead?

The firelight glowed suddenly strong and flickered into unreal shapes, momentary as breaking waves. As Leonard's thought travelled through time the Atlantic swung into his mind, the ocean he had crossed under storm canvas, the ocean which had divided him from his young. Now he must lay down his torch in this fog-wrapped island. Who of the grand-children might lift it again? His own impetus in living gave him presentiment but the form of the future's violence remained beyond vision's range. A battleship of strange pattern tearing through the ocean to bring an English War Leader to confer with America's President—around them long-snouted guns and 'planes and deep-dived death. . . . Too strange a jigsaw. . . . He could not grasp the pieces.

Leonard died quietly just before a wintry dawn lit the sky.

BIBLIOGRAPHY

Dr. Blake McKelvey. *Rochester the Waterpower City*

Henry Clews. *Twenty-eight Years in Wall Street* (1886)

Frank Griswold. *Clipper Ships and Yachts* (1927)

Frank Griswold. *Afterthoughts* (privately printed)

Stephen Fiske. *Offhand Portraits of Prominent New Yorkers* (1884)

John Motley. *Correspondence*, Vol. II, ed. Curtiss (1888)

Minnie Hauk. *Memoirs of a Singer* (1925)

Reminiscences of Lady Randolph Churchill (1908)

Moreton Frewen. *Melton Mowbray* (1924)

Alfred Loomis. *Ocean Racing*

Winston S. Churchill. *My Early Life*

Winston S. Churchill. *Lord Randolph Churchill*

Lord Rosebery. *Lord Randolph Churchill*

Viscount D'Abernon. *An Ambassador of Peace*

J. R. Hale. *Famous Sea Fights*

Shane Leslie. *Sublime Failures*

Shane Leslie. *End of a Chapter*

Seymour Leslie. *Glaslough in Oriel*

Wayne Andrews. *The Vanderbilt Legend*

Duke of Portland. *Men, Women and Things*

Cleveland Amoury. *The Last Resorts*

Dr. J. Brown. *Brownstone Fronts and Saratoga Trunks*

Stewart Holbrook. *The Age of the Moguls*

Virginia Cowles. *Winston Churchill*

Churchill, by his Contemporaries

Lloyd Morris. *Incredible New York*

INDEX

Anita Leslie has also written

TRAIN TO NOWHERE

Her adventures as an ambulance driver on four fronts

. . . what renders her book exceptional is her modesty, her observation, and her gift of writing . . . with all its grime, its suffering, its tragedy, this book leaves one with a sense of elation; it is a fine thing that there should be people in the world who can endure such things and write about them with such impersonal integrity.

THE DAILY TELEGRAPH

Books on the maquis have been numerous in this country, but the advance of the French Regular Army, seen with this fragmentary close vividness, is a less familiar theme. And with the growing intensity of experience Miss Leslie's gift for writing matures from the clever and callous to, at its best, a terse, keen reticence and the summing of deadly situations in a line or two.

THE TIMES

Few war books, men's or women's, have its calm youthful candour, its forthright acceptance of the whole duty of war-service.

THE OBSERVER

. . . she describes in a brisk and light-hearted fashion her arduous life behind the fighting zone, mainly in Egypt and the Middle East. She shows a pleasant sense of humour, and especially diverting is her account of an interlude spent on the staff of an English newspaper edited, with a Marx Brothers technique, by Arabs for the British troops.

SUNDAY TIMES

and

LOVE IN A NUTSHELL

Her happy cruise in the Caribbean with husband and baby

Nevertheless, it is all wonderful fun, as Miss Leslie would have us believe, and even to a landlubber the beauty and the excitement are clear.

THE SPHERE, Vernon Fane

. . . an uncommonly good narrative of a small boat cruise in West Indian waters. . . . All this is enchantingly described in language always witty and often wise.

THE FIELD